THE AUTHOR

Colin MacInnes was born in London in 1914. His mother, the formidable Angela Mackail, granddaughter of Burne-Jones, cousin of Kipling and Stanley Baldwin, later became famous as the novelist Angela Thirkell. His father was the singer James Campbell McInnes. Both Colin and his elder brother Graham, afterwards a writer and distinguished diplomat, had a stormy childhood: their parents' marriage foundered and in 1919 they set sail for Australia with Angela's new husband, George Thirkell. They settled in Melbourne and the boys did not see their natural father again for fifteen years. Both attended Scotch College, and at the age of sixteen Colin won a scholarship to Melbourne University, but went instead to work for the Imperial Continental Gas Association in Belgium. In 1936 he enrolled at the Chelsea Polytechnic to study art, continuing at the progressive Euston Road School; but with the outbreak of war he joined the Intelligence Corps, and saw active service in the wake of the Normandy Landings.

He wrote about his war experiences in *To the Victors the Spoils* (1950). This was followed two years later by *June in Her Spring*, the first of his Australian novels – *All Day Saturday* (1966) is the other; both are published by The Hogarth Press. His other books include the famous 'London' trio – *City of Spades* (1957), *Absolute Beginners* (1959) and *Mr Love and Justice* (1960) – and non-fiction such as *England, Half English* (1961). Throughout these years he was a controversial figure on the artistic and social scenes: as art critic for the *Observer*, one of the first participants in the BBC radio series 'The Critics', and as a commentator on black affairs, politics, music, literature, art and sexuality for, amongst others, *Encounter*, the *New Left Review*, and the *Spectator*; he was also a founding contributor to *New Society*. Colin MacInnes died in Hythe, Kent, in 1976 and was buried at sea off Folkestone.

ENGLAND, HALF ENGLISH

Colin MacInnes

New Foreword by
Paul Weller

THE HOGARTH PRESS
LONDON

For Charles Causley

Published in 1986 by
The Hogarth Press
Chatto & Windus Ltd
40 William IV Street, London WC2N 4DF

First published in Great Britain by MacGibbon & Kee Ltd 1961
Copyright © The Colin MacInnes Estate 1961
Foreword copyright © Paul Weller 1986

British Library Cataloguing in Publication Data

MacInnes, Colin
England, half english
I. Title
823'.914[F]   PR6063.A239

ISBN 0 7012 0597 0

Printed in Great Britain by
Cox & Wyman Ltd
Reading, Berkshire

FOREWORD

England, Half English is a fine collection of snapshots taken by Colin MacInnes. Out of focus and distorted (and no doubt the camera does sometimes lie) but nevertheless entertaining and an album for posterity.

London of the Fifties – not so much swinging as vibrating – with youths dressed to the nines in coffee bars decked out in rubber plants and steam.

Jazz wafting down Soho side-streets, the new edition of black faces warming these grey and austere shores, and the new-found independence of a group of people called – thereafter – Teenagers!

Mobility, optimism, affluence and a sense of the *new*. Sounds like a fairy-tale – or was it only a film?

Paul Weller, London 1985

COLIN MacINNES
AND
ENGLAND, HALF ENGLISH

In the Fifties and Sixties . . .

I don't want to judge or to pretend to any special knowledge but to be a witness to the society of my own age, so that those who do me the pleasure of reading what I have written may make their *own* judgements and draw their own conclusions. – Colin MacInnes, television interview.

[1958–60] were productive [years] for MacInnes. He not only composed two of his three most memorable novels – *Absolute Beginners* and *Mr Love and Justice* – during this period; he also wrote the majority of the essays collected in *England, Half English* . . .
Among the 'key' essays published in the first half of 1960 were 'The Other Man' (an offshoot of *Mr Love and Justice*, outlining his attitude to the ponce), 'The Englishness of Dr Pevsner', 'Hamlet and the Ghetto' (a defence of Bernard Kops's play), and a self-confessedly Orwellian analysis of cartoons by Giles, Appleby and Osbert Lancaster in 'The *Express* Families'. His enthusiastic essays on the writings of Anthony Carson ('The Game of Truth') and Ada Leverson ('The Heart of a Legend') came later. What MacInnes says of Pevsner, in his tribute to this 'thoroughly inside outsider' – that his 'natural instinct is to praise' – is also true of the author of these essays. Colin's generosity of spirit, so blocked in life, pours out in his critical writings. In this respect he matches his own estimation of Orwell, whose 'critical imagination', he reckons, 'was as superb as his "creative" imagination was defective . . .' – Tony Gould, *Inside Outsider: The Life and Times of Colin MacInnes*, 1983.

To read *England, Half English* is to be reminded how few writers there are nowadays who are prepared even to attempt what should be the writer's first task; simply to tell us how we live . . . who will bother to look at the way we walk and dress and take our holidays, who will listen to the music that erupts from our loudspeakers, who will try patiently and assiduously to see if he can learn anything from the crowds, you and I among them, who swarm on the pavement outside his window. – Dan Jacobson, *New Statesman*, 1961.

Until quite recently I believed (consequent upon reading *City of Spades*, but not the blurb) that Mr Colin MacInnes was a black man. Indeed I not only believed it; I told other people as much . . . The trouble is that having read *England, Half English* I am rather more than half-inclined to believe that I was right all the time. At least, if Mr MacInnes is not black, then he must be green. Or he has two heads, or three legs, or a cyclops eye, or telepathic powers . . . At any rate, he is different from us. What sets Mr MacInnes apart is the fact that in him we have one of the most penetrating, sensible, balanced, yet deeply passionate observers of England to check in for centuries . . . He is not merely a reporter, a chronicler; he is an analyst, and one of extraordinary range and power, of warmth and sympathy as well as understanding, but quite without any hypocrisy and quite without any mercy for the shoddy, the inadequate and the cold. – Bernard Levin, *Spectator*, 1961.

He wants people to *see* . . . But his vision extends beyond London and England; and the star piece of the collection is his essay on Nigeria (discovered via London, though), which rescues the travel-writer's art from the magazine degradation into which it has fallen. Here all Mr MacInnes's gifts are displayed, and all his personality. He is shrewd, analytic, at times amused, always tender. Most important, he is capable of delight, and capable of transmitting this delight. This is a rare ability . . . Mr MacInnes is important to half-English England, and she is lucky in him. – V. S. Naipaul, *Listener*, 1961.

The only writer he is at all comparable with is Orwell. Both had sharp eyes for an England that most people neglected or didn't even realise was there . . . MacInnes was a passionate man whose passion could find no lasting outlet in his personal life but flowed instead into his writing and his espousal of whole bits of London and its flotsam and jetsam. What was his personal tragedy is our gain . . . Let's hope *England, Half English* [will be reprinted] as the modern classic it deserves to be. – Sasha Moorsom, *Listener*, 1983.

He was, in short, the first Pop anthropologist, the first post-war style sub-culture essayist: he created the trade. – Peter York, *Harper's & Queen*, 1983.

A homosexual, insomniac, beer-junkie, with a typewriter and trunk to live out of and a weekly account at the local café, mooching around the French pub and Muriel's drinking club in Soho, consorting with jazz musicians, young Nigerians, dealers and hustlers; he was scarcely going to write about adultery in Hampstead. – Don Macpherson, *The Sunday Times Magazine*, 1983.

After the war he became the *Observer*'s art critic, living first in Soho, then in the new Bohemia of Notting Hill ('Napoli' in his novels), moving in on one friend after another . . . covering the waterfront for the BBC and the intellectual periodicals. He wrote about Tommy Steele for *New Left Review*, the Notting Hill race riots for *Encounter*, his own drug bust for *New Society*. Latterly he wrote for *Oz* and *Gay News*. He defended the Boy Scouts and called for the return of the Elgin marbles to Greece . . . A chronicler of exotic cultures he fell into the anthropologist's error, investing a culture with character and falling in love with this rather than an individual. He paid the price, living and dying a loner, wrecked on the coast of Bohemia. Belonging nowhere, in no single country and in no one's heart, by his own wish he was buried at sea. – John Ryle, *The Sunday Times*, 1983.

Absolute Beginners was after all the teenage declaration of independence, and many of the essays were the very first anthropological studies of what was then an undiscovered tribe – MacInnes's own rejection of conventional behaviour allowed him to empathise with all those who were outsiders, to recognise the vitality of those sub-cultures that live by their own lights . . . It was a privilege to have known him. However much we may have dreaded finding that tall, good-looking, casually elegant, sardonic figure on the doorstep determined to take up as much of our time as *he* chose and probably insult us at the end of it, we all learnt a lot from him. Those teenagers could learn a lot too. – George Melly, *Observer*, 1983.

And in his own words . . .

As for the boys and girls, the dear young absolute beginners, I sometimes feel that if only they *knew* this fact, this very simple fact, namely how powerful they really are, then they could rise up overnight and enslave the old tax-payers, the whole damn lot of them – toupees and falsies and rejuvenators and all – even though they number millions and sit in the seats of strength. And I guess it was the fact that only little Wizard realised this, and not all the other two million teenagers they say exist throughout our country, that makes him so sour, like a general with lazy troops he can't lead into battle . . . – Colin MacInnes, *Absolute Beginners*, 1959.

CONTENTS

Nothing is altered in the texts of these pieces as they were first published, except that most editorial or printers' improvements to the original writing have been deleted. New footnotes to the essays, added for this collection, are preceded by the word *Later*.

I am grateful to the editors of *The Twentieth Century*, *Encounter*, *New Left Review*, *Saltire Review* and *Cahiers des Saisons* who first commissioned these studies, and to the director of the Whitechapel Art Gallery who invited me to write the catalogue introduction.

YOUNG ENGLAND, HALF ENGLISH

The Pied Piper from Bermondsey

WHEN THE tabs part you see the 'Steelmen', his band of four musicians, cavorting in a wild, archaic 'ragtime' manner—pianist playing standing, saxophonist on his knees. In the centre, before the mike, is a gold-haired Robin Goodfellow dressed in sky-blue jeans and a neon-hued shirting who jumps, skips, doubles up and wriggles as he sings. At certain ritual gestures—a dig with the foot, a violent mop shake of the head—the teenagers massed from stalls to gallery utter a collective shriek of ecstasy. Tommy has *sent* them: their idol has given bliss for gold.

Today, youth has money, and teenagers have become a power. In their struggle to impose their wills upon the adult world, young men and women have always been blessed with energy but never, until now, with wealth. After handing a pound or two over to Mum, they are left with more 'spending money' than most of their elders, crushed by adult obligations. They are a social group whose tastes are studied with respect—particularly by the entertainment industry. No teenager is without his radiogram and collection of pop discs that have won a current place in the top twenty of the Hit Parade. A sale of a million copies of a pop is not unknown in England (in America, it can be five times as many)—in which event the recording company presents the performer with a 'golden disc' (it is, in fact, gold-plated).

Almost all the best-sellers are recordings made by singers. Until quite recently, the vast majority of pop discs bought by English teenagers were sung by American singers, and written by American lyric-writers and composers. This meant that

English boys and girls identified themselves, imaginatively, with a completely alien world—the world of a double dream. Today, while most pop successes are still American, the names of British singers are found increasingly in the weekly list of the top twenty: and among them, consistently, that of Tommy Steele.

★

Earlier this year, when Tommy was not yet twenty-one, a film about his life appeared, called *The Tommy Steele Story*. This picture, which I believe to be enormously revealing of contemporary English folk-ways, was, so far as I could check, entirely ignored by serious film critics. It told, with embellishments but accurately enough, the Cinderella story of Tommy's rise, in less than a year, from the total obscurity of the Old Kent Road to the status of a national teenage idol.

Briefly, his story is this. He was born Tommy Hicks, worked as a merchant seaman, studied the guitar, and then, at the height of the rock'n'roll craze, he played and sang as an amateur in coffee bars and jazz clubs. He was 'discovered' by an extremely able team of business managers and agents, and within a matter of months he had recorded with Decca and made TV, Variety, and cabaret appearances, culminating in his memorable conquest of the hallowed cellarage of the Café de Paris. Since then there have been the film, a Continental tour, offers for an American musical,[1] a full-scale BBC television tribute, and another film about his life is in the making.

Tommy's detractors attribute this prodigious success to a gimmick ('The English Elvis Presley') and to astute promotion. I cannot agree with this, and think it is the coincidence of a really remarkable talent with a particular state of mind among English teenagers that explains it.

First, the talent. The most striking feature of Tommy's

[1]*Later:* The musical was a myth. I fell for the ingenious habit of John Kennedy, Tommy's 'personal manager', of unloading phoney publicity items—together with authentic 'inside' information—on candid journalists.

performance is that it is both animally sensual and innocent, pure. He is Pan, he is Puck, he is every nice young girl's boy, every kid's favourite elder brother, every mother's cherished adolescent son.[1] His charmingly ugly, melancholy, cheeky countenance, and his elfin body with its gesticulations like an electric eel, are irresistibly engaging. Even in the film which, by any serious standards, is a dreadfully bad one, his charm, verve, and abundant *joie de vivre* continually rescue scenes of otherwise total banality.

And what of the kids? I've spoken with some of Tommy's teenage fans, who send him 2,000 letters a week (150 containing proposals of marriage), and wear autographed 'Tommy Steele' garments for both sexes. When they talk of Tommy, a look suffuses their earnest faces that I can only describe as one of rapture. They love him: it's as simple as that; and his fan mail reveals that children and, significantly, Mums, adore him too. When I saw his film I sat next to one such Mum and child, and there was no mistaking the cooing maternal note of joy, or the delighted infant cry of 'Tom-mee!' whenever he appeared upon the screen.

*

But I think there may be something more: the fact that Tommy Steele is English; and that many teenagers have hoped for, and now found, a troubadour with whom they can identify themselves more fully than they ever could with Elvis or with Johnnie Ray.

The pop song of the past decade is an American invention, and its greatest practitioners have undoubtedly been Americans. Although these songs are despised by educated persons (who never hear them) and, even more so, by lovers of serious jazz music (who, with pain, occasionally do), there is no denying that pop songs have a certain artistic quality which resides, almost exclusively, in the art of the individual singers. The tunes and lyrics in themselves are often of meagre quality—

[1]*Later:* This phrase was quoted extensively (and sometimes ironically) when the 'serious' Press at last got on to Tommy.

although manufactured with extreme competence—and the emotions they evoke are almost invariably synthetic: that is, they are songs about the idea of life, but rarely about life itself. Yet when projected from the larynx of a compulsive pop singer, they acquire an obsessive power to hold the mind and feelings, even if at the most superficial levels.

Why has the American pop song so dominated the English market—whereas, in the countries of Continental Europe, the native ballads have continued to flourish vigorously beside the imported transatlantic pop? Simply, I think, because we speak the same language, more or less, as the Americans. Until some forty years ago, the English song about English life resounded boisterously in the Music Halls. Since then, new American musical idioms, potently diffused by the cinema, radio, the gramophone and now TV, have swamped our own ditties with the help, above all, of the shared language of the lyrics.

The most admired singers in this style, very naturally, have been Americans; and the recent change has come about because English singers have mastered the American idiom so completely that an artist like Lonnie Donegan, for instance, is as big a success in America as he is here. Even the skiffle singers—a thoroughly English phenomenon—use mostly transatlantic ballads. The battle for a place among the top twenty has been won by British singers at the cost of splitting their personalities and becoming bi-lingual: speaking American at the recording session, and English in the pub round the corner afterwards.

This strange ambivalence is very apparent in Tommy's art. In his film or when, on the stage, he speaks to his admirers between the songs, his voice takes on the flat, wise, dryly comical tones of purest Bermondsey. When he sings, the words (where intelligible) are intoned in the shrill international American-style drone. With this odd duality, his teenage fans seem quite at ease: they prefer him to be one of them in his unbuttoned moments, but expect him to sing in a near foreign tongue: rather as a congregation might wish the sermon to be delivered in the vernacular, and the plainsong chanted in mysterious Latin.

★

Now that the singers are finding an English place for themselves on the golden disc, will the English lyric writers and composers try to do so too? In other words, will they begin to write songs in an English idiom, about English life, that the performers can sing as Englishmen not only in body, but in voice as well? Can teenagers, in short, take songs about *themselves*?

There are signs of this occurring, though as yet but faint. From the skiffle cellars there come rumours of ballads no longer about American jails, gals, and railroads, but about English ones (for we, after all, have these things too). On the pop level, Tommy's very gifted music and lyric team of Lionel Bart and Michael Pratt (and of himself as well) has certainly composed some numbers—*Butterfingers*, for example, or *Cannibal Pot*—that do possess a certain English essence of sentiment and wit. Perhaps one day Tommy will sing songs as English as his speaking accent, or his grin. If this should happen, we will hear once again, for the first time since the decline of the Music Halls, songs that tell us of our own world.

I must confess I don't think this very likely, though, since the commercial forces behind the American pop are so tremendous, and the talent of their artists so compelling; and, at all events, it's certain that if English pop songs, as well as singers, do appear, they'll be profoundly influenced by America. It's a question of measure, though: of an influence not becoming, as it has done in the pop world, an eclipse. Song, after all, is the simplest, most instinctive way by which a people expresses its own ideas about itself; and if a people—like the English—sings about another people—the Americans—then this may be a sign that it is ceasing to be a people in any real sense at all. Perhaps this is happening: perhaps it has to. Yet who, ten years ago, could have foreseen the sensational rise of professional jazz artistry in Britain? Or, two years ago, the eruption of amateur performers in the skiffle cellars, ungluing their ears from the juke-box to pick up and play themselves the washboard and guitar? Who, for that matter, could have predicted Tommy Steele? Who knows? Tommy may be the first English pop artist to sing English songs.[1]

Encounter, December 1957

THE TITLE of this piece was the consequence of 'group-think' between the then joint editor of *Encounter*, Irving Kristol, and myself. I'd come up with something dreadful like 'Top Pop Idol', and Irving would have none of this. Fixing me with his bland, sharp, kindly eye, he told me the essence of group-think was for two (or more) minds to probe for the chief themes of any article, imagine names for them, and then to fire phrases at each other until both hit the target simultaneously with the telling, essential verbal blend.

Irving Kristol is the best editor I've ever worked for, or could hope to. Entirely open to unusual, even weird ideas, he would almost instantly decide if he liked them—and as instantly if he didn't; and having decided, back the piece unreservedly even giving, if he liked the writing, 'star' treatment to a writer little known. He loved England, I think, but was wonderfully unimpressed by any of those English 'things' that are supposed to impress Americans. Confident in the value of his own

[1]*Later:* When I wrote this piece, I hadn't yet met its hero: who turned out to be as attractive a human person as he is a performer. Tommy in private is withdrawn, self-possessed, rather grave and even sad, though by no means glum or solemn. In conversation he is sagacious, shrewd, and respectful to his elders only—and rightly —to the degree he estimates they may know more than he does. His personal responsibility as a 'teenage idol' he takes most seriously: 'It's scaring—very scaring,' he said to me. When one pauses to think what the 'top English teenage singer' of the 1950s might have turned out to be (and what some later mannerist nightingales have been), one can be grateful that fate—and John Kennedy's instinct for a double winner—gave us so honest and healthy a young man as Tommy Steele.

Jewish-New York-American culture, he generously appreciated the reality he saw in that of any European: but to convince him, it did have to be real.

There were three Irvings: the editor, brisk and imaginative; the sociable Irving, affable, considerate and slightly diffident; and Irving the writer: in whose work a quite unpredictable personality emerges—more pensive and urbane than his lighter conversation might have suggested. When he left for America in October 1958 he took with him much English gratitude and affection.

*

My good fortune in meeting Irving Kristol at *Encounter*, was matched by that I had in knowing John Weightman when he became editor, until nearly the end of 1955, of *The Twentieth Century*. I had met him on radio quiz programmes of the French service of the BBC, at which he had long-sufferingly presided over mixed 'teams' of voluble Latins and of English handicapped by defective syntax and native taciturnity.

The reason I speak of a double good fortune is that there are very few publications in England (of any description) whose editors can immediately grasp the value (or even the meaning) of an unusual theme, or of an unorthodox approach to it. To take as an instance the case of the new young English pop singers, like Tommy Steele. Anyone could see that their 'case' might be the pretext for a picturesque, or camped-up, or satirical description: but very few that the whole phenomenon of teenage singing 'idols', and of the transference, after 1956, of teenage favour from young Americans to young Englishmen, had a deeper social significance. This fact—now, I suppose, evident to all—I flogged in vain around Grub street until *The Twentieth Century*, like *Encounter*, saw what I was getting at. For the most usual practice of editors is to invite you to write on a 'new' theme of this nature only when you have already written on it at length elsewhere—even, it may be, extensively in a book. By this time, of course, you are yourself as bored with the subject as all lively spirits have become. When you tell editors this, they are surprised: and needless to say, fail to ask you what fresh theme you might now be obsessed by.

To this depressing rule, *Encounter* and *The Twentieth Century* have been most happy exceptions. And both magazines possess another great attraction to their writers—that they have a power of penetration quite disproportionate to their (relatively low) circulations. A piece in either monthly is likely to be read by many of the minds one most hopes to speak to; while those printed in organs of much higher circulation—and certainly of far more lavish remuneration—disappear, after publication, into limbo, unremembered.

★

Soon after I started writing for *The Twentieth Century*, John Weightman relegated himself to the chairmanship of its editorial board, and the new editor was Bernard Wall. It is he who has kindly steered past any obstacles unknown to me some of the odder pieces I have written for the magazine. No more agreeable—nor, to myself, disconcerting—editor could be imagined than he is. From editors I prefer a strong reaction (unless, of course, one totally unfavourable) as, however exhausting this may be to one and all, it does enable the writer to sharpen his conception against another mind professionally involved. But Bernard, though he sometimes says no, when he does say yes, says nothing more.

I cannot leave the subject of *The Twentieth Century* and of *Encounter* without praising two key female figures of their very different establishments. At *Encounter* there is its assistant editor Margot Walmsley who sits in a cubby-hole adjacent to the twin editorial offices, and from it radiates an extra-ordinarily pleasant atmosphere of good-nature and efficiency. I have never seen Margot other than unruffled, apparently more delighted to see you than any other creature in creation, and unfailingly obliging in a hundred kind and tactful ways; yet when it comes to practicalities (as the horrors of proof-correction), though the smile still hovers pleasantly, this paragon turns out to be ruthlessly, though always amiably, professional.

As for Eirene Skilbeck, her opposite number, as it were, at *The Twentieth Century*, a more helpful, positive and optimistic colleague one could not find. Herself the grand-daughter of James Knowles who founded the monthly in 1877, Eirene, born thus to the purple, has a hereditary instinct to preserve the journal's quality and essence. And this she achieves, as managing editor, by a firm, even severe attention to production details, and by a generous open-mindedness to ideas not necessarily of her own culture and generation.[1]

★

The essay that follows is the first I wrote for Bernard Wall. It is also the first thing of my own, I think, which really 'penetrated' in the sense I have described. It is of course monstrous to try to analyse the social relations of three races in 3,500 words: though the ground certainly needed breaking open, and perhaps to try to say too much in too little was the only possible way to begin. My present hindsight on the piece, I have printed after it.

A SHORT GUIDE FOR JUMBLES
(*to the Life of their Coloured Brethren in England*)

What is a Jumble?

You are, and I, if we are white. The word's a corruption of 'John Bull', and is used by West Africans of Englishmen in a spirit of tolerant disdain.

Do Africans not like us, then?

Not very much, because our outstanding characteristics of

---

[1] While this is in proof (March 1961), the sad news comes that *The Twentieth Century*, as an independent monthly, may be no more.

reliability and calm don't touch them, and we lack the spontaneity and sociability they prize.

Then why do they come here? And all those West Indians?

The world has broken suddenly into Africa and the Caribbean, and Africans and West Indians are determined to break out into the world. Locked in the heat of a cinema at Ibadan or Kingston, watching a gleaming newsreel of Europe or America, they find it intolerable to be confined—cut off from the modern centres of creation, wealth and power.

But are there not economic motives for their coming?

Yes, particularly with West Indians, who know their islands can never support their bursting populations. So young Africans will go on coming here to spend their *Wanderjahre*, and West Indians, increasingly, to settle.

'To settle.' Is this coloured influx to be permanent?

Unless our immigration laws should alter when the status of each coloured colony changes, the influx will be permanent indeed. A coloured population—and this means a growing half-caste population—is now a stable element in British social life. This will afford splendid opportunities for practising their preaching to those who attack the colour bar in other countries. Or more probably, it will not; as most of us here seem blindly to believe that coloured immigration is a temporary phenomenon.

But is there a colour bar in England?

I've not yet met an African or West Indian who thinks there isn't. The colour of the English bar, they say, is grey. Few of us love them, few of us hate them, but almost everybody wishes they weren't here and shows it by that correct, aloof indifference of which only the English know the secret.

How can this attitude be overcome?

Coloured people think it never will be, until the African and West Indian colonies achieve political independence. A coloured trade commissioner with a million pounds to spend in England, would change more hearts in a day than hosts of Negro-loving propagandists have failed to do in years.

But meanwhile, personal contacts, surely, are important. How does one talk to Africans and West Indians?

The gambits to avoid are those that are cheerily condescending, or prompted by guilt-ridden tact. Instances of the first, used frequently, and always thoroughly inhibiting to amiable intercourse, are:

> 'You won't mind my asking, but why do you people come to this country?' (Unspoken answer: 'Why did your people come to mine and, anyway, why the hell shouldn't I?')
>
> 'I do envy you fellows your wonderful teeth.' ('Well, I don't envy you your yellow fangs and, as it happens, most of my back ones are gold.')
>
> 'Don't you miss the hot weather over here?' (They're *very* tired of that one.)

Fatal examples of the supposedly ingratiating approach:

> 'I think conditions in the Union are a scandal.' ('Then go and tell Mr Strijdom that.')
>
> 'You'll find there's a certain amount of prejudice here, but some of us are just as worried about it as you.' ('Look after your own worries, man, and leave me to handle mine.')
>
> 'I like coloured people, myself.' (This last one wins the Malan Prize outright, and is absolutely guaranteed to shut up any coloured stranger like a clam.)

A coloured man can tell, in five seconds dead, whether a white man likes him or not. If the white man *says* he does, he is instantly—and usually quite rightly—mistrusted.[1]

What it comes to, then, is that it's simply a matter of being affable and polite?

'Courteous' is a better term, since 'polite' has a certain hint

[1] Among the many injustices of the world, is this one: that coloured people aren't much interested in what your political-social views about them happen to be, but only in your personal behaviour. In Englishmen, they prefer Marc Antony to Brutus, even though Antony may read the *Daily Mail*, and Brutus the *Manchester Guardian*.

of brief frigidity. All coloured people (American Negroes as well as Africans or West Indians) attach tremendous importance to good manners—however uninhibited, violent, or even villainous they themselves may be. The secret of courtesy is, of course, respect—and as this is impossible to simulate, one doesn't stand much chance with coloured men and women unless one happens to feel it.

The other golden rule—and probably, for most of us, a much more difficult one to follow—is always to be patient. Brusque, matter-of-fact, 'hullo-good-bye' behaviour that would be quite acceptable to a fellow Englishman can give offence to a people with a sense of time more spendthrift than our own.

So coloured people have better manners than ourselves?

Well, we have none, have we, even by European standards. The reason for this critical distinction between us is probably that African and West Indian children are brought up much more strictly in respect to manners than our own kids—who, though of course delightful, are utterly uncouth.

This courtesy—dignified and quite unservile—is one of the most attractive qualities of coloured people. Though they can be casual, quarrelsome and even treacherous, it is extremely rare to find them rude.

And what other special virtues do they possess?

What most differentiates an African from an Englishman is that our chief ambition is to put our lives into a savings bank, while he as firmly believes that every day is there to be enjoyed.

Thus if, for instance, the spirit moves you to call up Afolabi in the small hours of the night, and awake him to suggest driving to Manchester to hear Ade play his bongos in the new band at Moss Side, Afolabi will regard this proposition as eminently reasonable.

This eager buoyancy does not prevent coloured people from falling into deep troughs of sudden gloom, but their melancholy is rarely morbid, and never lasting. Of course, this wonderful instinct for the pursuit and capture of joy goes with a certain fecklessness. They aren't *responsible* in the way so many Englishmen are; but then, so many Englishmen are little else.

And have they no other grave defects?

Certainly. Coloured people, particularly Africans, seem extraordinarily suspicious by nature, even of one another; and their beaming smiles can turn easily to sombre glares of jealousy. When Ade goes up in the world, Afolabi tries to pull him down, even though he likes him, and will not profit personally by his fall. If Hamlet is our emblematic character, Othello is as certainly their own.[1]

Does all this apply equally to Africans and West Indians?

Africans and West Indians (understandably, when one considers their varied histories) are as different as Canadians and Australians, if not more so, though I think they have in common all the basic virtues and peculiarities suggested hitherto.

The chief difference between them is that Africans 'belong' more profoundly to Africa than West Indians do to their Caribbean islands. Speaking their own private tongues, rooted in the life of their own tribes, they feel sustained, amid the alien corn of Whitechapel and the Harrow Road, by the reassuring memory of ancestral gods. The boy slouching down Cable street with his pockets full of pawn-tickets, to sign on at 'the Labour' (he will, almost certainly, be late), hears from afar a chorus of loud, comforting voices arising from a solid tribal past.

But West Indians are wanderers, cut off by centuries and distance from the countries of their origin, and ready to move on again from their stepping-stones strung out across the sea. It is this that accounts for the greater poise, air of assurance, and self-sufficiency of the Africans. The chip—when it exists —sits lightly on their shoulders; on those of the anxious West Indians it weighs heavily.

[1]*Later:* I am positive Shakespeare talked with coloured men in Deptford, or elsewhere. His penetration of African psychology seems otherwise merely miraculous.

This also explains (as well as their English mother tongue, and the greater antiquity of their colonies) the more 'British' outlook of West Indians. If one is not quite sure what one is— Negro, Caribbean, or American—one is all the more ready to be 'British'. Africans have no such doubts; for them, the oblong blue passport is no more than a temporary convenience.

How does one distinguish between the two?

At first it may be difficult to tell on sight, though Africans can usually be recognized by their more loping, prowling, jungle-creeping style of movement, and their greater air of inwardness, of secrecy. The voice is, of course, an immediate give-away: West Indians speak a kind of falsetto, transatlantic Welsh—lilting, accelerated and urgent, and often richly interlarded with obscene and vivid local oaths. Africans talk English as if from the belly, and easily relapse into their rumbling, voluble, staccato dialects.[1]

The two don't usually mix much (cf again, Australians and Canadians—who's ever seen *them* together?), though certain clubs, bars and night-spots are common ground. To the white man, however, they will, if necessary, present a fairly solid front.[2]

In their dealings with the natives, the Africans—paradoxically—are more forthcoming, if encouraged to be so, because of their greater self-assurance: they have little fear, as have West Indians, of being patronized. But basically, they are in fact more inaccessible, because of their blithe indifference to any opinion white people may have about them.

'Indifferent.' But surely they're not 'indifferent' to our women?

An article of faith among racialists is that every coloured man is longing to embrace a white woman. It is somewhat disconcerting to discover that there seems much truth in this

[1]*Later:* In fact not dialects at all but—however innumerable—true languages.

[2]American Negroes, too, seem cautious in their attitude to Africans. I once asked a GI to an African club where, taking one penetrating stare at the direct descendants of his ancestors, he said, 'Collins, get me out of here.'

(though it certainly does not mean that white girls are in any greater danger of rape than they may have been before the coloured influx).

In England, of course, conditions are such that one cannot really judge, since coloured men vastly outnumber coloured women. If Africans and West Indians are to have a sex life of any kind (and one can hardly imagine them without one), most of their girls must necessarily be white.[1]

On the other hand, an actual preference for white girls does, in many cases, certainly exist. Afolabi, for example, who has married a white girl (a very nice one, but manifestly his social inferior, as is so often the case in local mixed marriages), says that nothing would induce him ever to marry one of his own race. This doesn't seem to be due so much to an attraction of opposites, or even a desire to integrate himself more comfortably into the world of the white majority,[2] as to the holy terror that Africans, especially, seem to have of the bossiness, the 'demanding' nature of coloured women and, even more, of their women's families. In fact, a prime motive for Afolabi's departure from his homeland was to escape not only the relations of the numerous brides that were proposed to him, but equally to elude the tender clutches of his own loving kith and kin. In England, he says, you can live your own life, however miserably; in Africa, the family gobble you up.

Incidentally, when a coloured man does marry a white girl, he doesn't think he's marrying 'above himself' at all. On the contrary, there's no doubt whatever in his mind as to who's being done a favour.

But what of these tales of coloured men corrupting our young girls?

It's true that the coloured races have contributed—along with the Maltese, Cypriots and, outstandingly, our good selves

[1]*Later:* This—as so many other social factors that gave substance to the article—has now altered greatly since it was first printed. The new coloured immigration of the late 1950s was that of the West Indian women—by now firmly and domestically dug in with a great many of their own men; who nevertheless still outnumber them considerably.

[2]*Later:* Racial revenge may also occasionally be a motive.

—their quota of pimps, ponces, weed-pedlars and all-round hustlers to the English city undergrowths; but also true that the activities of these doubly black sheep, when detected, pursued and punished, enjoy, from the Sunday press, a generous publicity withheld from the deeds of the less exciting native entrepreneurs.

A peculiarity about any coloured 'bad boys' one may encounter is that, unlike those of a European race, they often seem delightful personalities.[1] Yet, if this be believed, it will not impress at all the sterner English moralist: rather, the contrary; it will, in fact, convince him that the coloured races have no moral sense at all; that if they can be charming sinners, then the devil has marked them for his own.

This theme of different moral conceptions among different races—which is one of immense fascination, and the cause of infinite misunderstandings on the political and social planes—is too vast for this slight, superficial essay.[2] Suffice it to say that if coloured men and women seem, to our eyes, more happily amoral, we should perhaps remember that the Christian conceptions are still incredibly novel to them (in Uganda, for instance, not a soul had heard of Christianity less than 100 years ago), and also that their spiritual ties, which do undoubtedly exist, are very different from our own. They have, for example, sacred tribal loyalties of a kind quite unknown to us. It is not for nothing that, on a serious occasion, an African will swear not by a god but 'on my mother's life'; although—as when we solemnly swear upon our sacred book—the great oath may often precede as great a perjury.

Yes, but those hemp-pedlars: what of them?

Of those who smoke hemp, perhaps this may be said. In the

[1] I stood bail once for an African who had the misfortune to be charged with living on the immoral earnings of his wife. This pair appeared to be a devoted couple, and the chagrin of the wife, when he was at last convicted, seemed due as much to genuine woe as to the disadvantage of losing, temporarily, an efficient professional associate.

[2] *Later:* So much so that I should perhaps not have touched on this theme at all; in this paragraph, I get badly out of my depth.

countries they all come from, hemp is readily available and smoking it, though illegal, is thought a venial offence. Many coloured boys make its acquaintance at the same age as that at which our own experiment with tobacco; and just as French mothers sometimes still their babies' cries with nips of wine, so may an infant African be calmed by a soothing maternal puff.[1] One should also remember that in Mahometan countries (and millions of Africans are Mahometans) the Islamic ban on alcohol is strictly enforced, so that hemp becomes something of a substitute.

Arrived here in England, those who are used to smoking hemp find it hard to shake the habit off; the more so as the legal forms of intoxication here are both more expensive and often more inconvenient to obtain. For the price of a double whisky, an *aficionado* can, apparently, enjoy a stimulus equivalent to that of half a bottle, and do so at any time he wishes outside the restricted liquor licensing hours.

Coloured addicts, incidentally, make the same sort of distinction between those who 'charge' (smoke hemp) and those who 'pop' (inject heroin and so on), as we do between liquor boozers and those who take any drugs; and for a man who 'pops', they feel the same horror and pity as we do for a person who takes drugs of any kind. Believing that hemp is not habit-forming, they can't see what all the fuss is about and regard its prohibition with the same annoyance (and the same determination to evade the law) as would an English alcoholic the ban on spirits in Bombay.

But how does one tell such reprobates from the rest?

As with ourselves, by learning to 'read' coloured faces, which takes some time since all their enigmatic countenances seem, at first, identical; just as, apparently (humiliating though the thought may be), our own various features do initially to them.

[1]*Later:* Africans who've read this have indignantly denied it. Many others have told me it is so. The explanation may be that the African bourgeoisie—just as with that in England—know far less than they imagine about how the majority of their countrymen do live.

If one achieves this, then the way is free to the most delightful acquaintances, for their sense of hospitality is almost Celtic in its intensity.[1] As soon as his door is opened, Afolabi will never 'turn you loose' until you've suffered the pangs of eating the last burning scraps of foo-foo, and drained to its dregs the ultimate bottle of VP wine: even when (as is so frequently the case) his West Indian landlord, Mr Hamilton Claude Mackenzie, is clamouring for arrears of rent, and the last shilling for the gas meter has been spent on bags of cashew nuts.

There is often, about these African and West Indian interiors, tremendous comfort and tremendous squalor. The well-appointed items are the bed, the food-cupboard and, until all else is gone, the cherished radiogram. The other bits of furniture may be decrepit and the wardrobe empty—even of the favourite suit of gaberdine sky-blue, and the shoes made of imitation snake, both now reposing in the hock-shop. But snapshots, pinned up everywhere upon the walls, will grin back bravely: Afolabi himself and friends, manifestly 'high', all teeth and eyeless, blinking in a night-club at the magnesium flare; Miss Lena Horne and Dr Nkrumah and Sugar Ray; and framed on the mantelpiece, a formal, votive group of Mum and Dad and solemn brothers and sisters far off in Abeokuta, or in Port of Spain.

Friends will drift in and out, talk, talk and talk, be given portions of what may remain; even the unwelcome are not snubbed, humiliated, but allowed, at least, their glorious half-hour. Somebody suggests an outing, and though these seem rarely planned beforehand, they always happen. Like the Pied Piper, Afolabi gathers up his band from basement rooms, from Indian restaurants, and from coloured cafés and public-houses all over town. The impression grows on the bemused, intoxicated Jumble of a sort of seething underground, a *maquis*

[1]May there not be a resemblance between the Celts and Africans? The clan—or tribal—instinct, the love of music, singing and dancing, the admiration for temperament more than merit, the excitability and moodiness, the easy bellicosity and as unpredictable despair, and, most of all, the hospitality which, once accorded, is arrogantly unconditional?

of coloured people organized to live at the rhythm of their own private instincts within, and apart from, the exterior solemnity of the huge white world.

But is it really possible for a white man, and a coloured, to be friends?

One hastens to say 'Yes'; but then, remembering the *distant* look that sometimes comes into the opaque brown eyes—that moment when they suddenly depart irrevocably within themselves far off towards a hidden, alien, secretive, quite untouchable horizon—one must ultimately, however reluctantly, answer, 'No.'

The Twentieth Century, March 1956

THE FIRST THING I want to say about this piece is that the years which have passed proved to me what I didn't then believe—that an African or a West Indian, and an Englishman, can be friends. A great deal, of course, is against this happening. Superficially—but horribly effectively—the colonial relationship of their countries stands guard against a developing intimacy. (Older readers will recall the same malevolent, inhibiting spectre that haunted their relationship with Indian friends.) Next, is another dreadful, attendant ghoul—the continuing presence of the whole world-wide 'colour' situation. Lastly—and ultimately the only real obstacle—there are the truly and formidable differences of social and psychic background. Even in, say, Anglo-American friendships, this factor may present a real difficulty: in Anglo-African or Caribbean, it is obviously greater; but given goodwill and fortune, it is surmountable.

My second comment is to apologize for using the odious word 'half-caste' to describe the *English* children of Africans or West Indians, and of our women. These boys and girls—

thousands of whom have now been born and bred among us—are, and feel themselves to be, as 'English' as any one is. They represent (together with the children of other immigrant groups of the 1940s and 1950s—chiefly Poles, Cypriots, Maltese and Pakistanis) the New English of the last half of our century: the modern infusion of that new blood which, according to our history-books, has perpetually re-created England in the past and is the very reason for her mongrel glory.

My third note is on my obsession with 'Indian hemp': partly morbid, but there's also this to be said. The 'problem', because of the barren acres of malignant rubbish written about it, needed opening up. And it remains disgraceful (and all too characteristic not so much of hypocrisy as of our profound national instinct for confident social moralising, and often cruel ensuing action, on a basis of utter ignorance) that in a country where, after the pubs close at 11 pm, the killer rate among tanked-up car drivers rises wickedly (without any danger of severe subsequent punishment), and where any obliging doctor or chemist will dole out happy pep pills to the kick-hungry English natives, young coloured boys are persecuted, and savagely sentenced, for using this non-habit-forming 'drug'.

*

In the next piece, about the three 'family' cartoons in the *Daily Express*, the debt to George Orwell will be evident. It was he who taught us to see how English popular art and writing could be made to reveal an England of which 'educated' persons, as well as those who made and enjoyed these pop art works, were all largely unaware. His triumph in this virgin sector was due as much to his sensibility as to his mind: he never, as aloof prying 'sociological' writers do, stood outside his crude endearing raw material: he liked the seaside postcards and boys' mags even as he dissected them. I think that Orwell's critical imagination was as superb as his 'creative' imagination was defective: the essays, by their penetration and astringent style, are timeless; the novels and later fantasies and fables seem to me bereft of grace, and laboured.

THE *EXPRESS* FAMILIES

THERE ARE three of them, of course: the Giles family, prosperous working-class; the Barry Appleby family, commercial petty-bourgeois; and the Osbert Lancaster family, displaced aristocratic. They've all appeared every day for years in cartoons in the *Daily Express*, and sometimes in the *Sunday Express* as well. First, just to refresh memories about them:

The Giles family

The only one of the trio to which its artist has given his own name. They are twelve in number (or by adoption—see below —thirteen), and there are *four* generations of them, namely:

Grandma (in fact, as will be seen, Great-Grandma). Though treated with no deference whatever by the family, she is clearly well-loved and not just tolerated. A survival from the distant Music Hall era, she embodies the robust virtues (and appalling nuisance-value) of the vanished, or vanishing, working-class matriarch.

Father (who is Grandma's son) and *Mother*. Father must be at least in his sixties, since it appears he served in World War I (as well as II). His dress and habits are resolutely proletarian (shirt-sleeves indoors, pints of truant wallop with the lads, bawdy flirtations and fundamental loyalty to the home), and in character he is entirely insensitive and endlessly patient, though liable to outbursts of exasperated rage. Mother, his wife (from whom, even more than from Grandma, the children would seem to inherit their pig-like faces), is the massive, imperturbable, competent linchpin of the household. If one word exactly describes her, it is 'Mum'.

This pair have five children—three adult, two still juveniles.

The older three are *George*, *Ann* and *Carol*. It is George who wears the meerschaum pipe and beret, apparently does no work at all, but instead (Giles's own words about him) 'reads everything, and that's about the lot for George'. George is, in fact, Giles's idea of a working-class highbrow. (In moments of stress Father turns to the whisky bottle, George to gin.) He is married to *Vera*, his (Giles's words again) 'intellectual wife', who wilts and faints and doses herself with aspirin. Ann is the mother of 'the twins' (see below), and one may search the cartoons in vain to discover who was these children's father. (A nice, very accurate, Giles touch: my own guess is a wartime GI.) Carol, who 'causes less trouble than the rest' (Giles again), personifies the nice, common, plain, placid, mildly sexy fag-dragging English girl.

The two younger children of Father and Mother are *Ernie* and *Bridget*, little devils both, and really closer in age to the 'Giles babies' of the fourth generation, whose youthful uncle and aunt they would thus appear to be. This fourth generation consists of *George junior* (the son of Vera and George—and how, one may wonder, did their skinny love produce so tough a child?), and of Ann's two (illegitimate) children, 'the twins', called *Laurence* and *Ralph* after Ann's favourite actors.

To this little lot we must add item thirteen, that diabolical nipper with his hair dangling like a prize puppy's over his eyes, who sticks around with the family, clicking his infant news-ghoul's camera, but whose exact blood relationship to the rest (if any) I have not been able to trace.

The Barry Appleby family

Only two here: *George* and *Gaye Gambol*, husband and wife—though their niece and nephew, *Miggy* and *Flivver* (cousins, apparently, and not brother and sister) pop up regularly in the cartoons. George and Gaye, in fact, are very resolutely childless: and when, for a while, a friend of Gaye's who went into hospital left her baby with Gaye to look after, great play was made with George's initial horror because, not knowing whose the baby was, he thought, for a fearful moment, it might be his wife's. George's (and even Gaye's) incompetence in baby-lore (George trying to 'change' the infant, for example) were also greatly emphasised.

The Osbert Lancaster family

These are, of course, the *Littlehamptons*: Earl and Countess of, or *Maudie* and *Willy*. Their two children, girl (older) and boy (their names?),[1] began as short-pant and skirt products, but made a sudden jump, a year or so ago, into adolescence— the only instance, I think, in all these three static sagas, of an admitted change of age. (And a very crafty and useful manoeuvre on the artist's part, because it then enabled him to satirise, from within, the 'teenage' and 'deb' phenomena.)

*

Before a more detailed analysis of these families is attempted, we may first ask ourselves what on earth all three of them are doing in the pages of the *Daily Express*? For while Giles's appeal would seem to be universal, and Barry Appleby has, as we shall see, an almost fanatical but, I think, restricted following, the behaviour of the Osbert Lancaster quartette is probably too 'sophisticated' for the greater bulk of the *Express*'s daily millions.

The first answer is that, ghastly though its whole 'ideology' may be (a mild adjective, but it will do), the *Express* is still, of all dailies, the one that casts its net widest and most efficiently to draw in contributors. The inspired recruitment of individuals like Low and Vicky to the sister *Evening Standard* is, of course, well known, and it's often forgotten that Giles himself was lured away from *Reynolds News* where he (perhaps more appropriately) began. Appleby was, I think, an *Express* 'discovery', but the enlistment of Lancaster for his strategically placed (front page) but minute ('pocket cartoon') daily drawing, was a master stroke. The fact is that for pure *visual* 'presentation', the *Express* remains unbeatable: and their team of cartoonists (among whom I'd also like to praise their sports artist, Roy

[1]*Later*: Jennifer and Torquil, it would seem.

Ullyett—though, for our present purposes, he and his sparrow scarcely constitute a 'family') is the best there is by far today in England. As for the *text* which, in its accidental accessory way, accompanies this galaxy of photographic and cartoonist talent in the *Express*, one can perhaps only say that its matter is so pre-digested and regurgitated, and its purely technical lay-out so unfailingly effective, that it constitutes a sort of visual appendage to the art work proper: and one of no intellectual content whatsoever.

The deeper answer as to why this particular trio has set up house in the pages of the paper will be found more fully, I think, when our exploration of the 'families' is completed: and it is, in brief, that however varied the three groups may be, they are all *fundamentally* (and despite, in some cases, surface 'criticisms' that are often apt and accurate) well satisfied with our society *as it is*; and, even more important, that each of these families turns out, on close examination, to be essentially *consumers* rather than *producers*: which is—one may judge I think quite fairly—exactly what the *Express* conceives its readership to be, and what it encourages it to be at a time when, more than at any in our history, our very survival depends on stepping up production (both material and intellectual) at the quickest possible speed.

★

Back then, for a moment, among the various bosoms of these three family circles. The first questions we may ask about them are, how rich are they, where does the money come from, and are they, in this respect, really characteristic of the three class groups they are supposed—more or less—to represent?

The Giles family, even by the new-working-class standards of the 1950s, is very well off indeed. Not only do they have all the home comforts and luxuries one might anticipate (and good luck to them!), but a car with caravan, a yacht, and holidays (all twelve of them!) abroad as well. Who earns all the money to pay for this? Not, one presumes, the five kids (though one wouldn't put it past them to be in on some juvenile racket), nor highbrowed George (as has been said), nor, surely, swooning Vera, nor even Mum who's perpetually busy round the house, nor Ann (likewise with 'the twins'), nor, certainly, that obstinate old artful dodger, Grandma. That leaves Carol, of course, who's probably an earner and, above all, Father. What Father exactly *does*, I've not been able to discover: I imagine he's by now the owner of a biggish business (garage? contracting? haulage?) and, if so, not in fact technically 'working-class' any more. One must visualise, at any rate, an annual income of *at least* about £3,000 (tax free—or fiddled). (This meant, by the way, that when Giles wanted to take a side-swipe at the *Express*'s own 'woman's page' for recommending wildly expensive items to its readers, he had to set his satirical vignette in another, unidentifiable, household.)

The case of the Appleby family is even more mysterious. We know George is a prosperous salesman (though not of what) which might mean, with expense account and bonuses (both frequently referred to in the cartoons), a maximum of around £2,500 a year *before* tax (about which George and Gaye are almost neurotically conscientious). With this, although childless (just as well!), he is able to support a chronically extravagant wife and his own extremely greedy self (both facts constantly emphasized), plus a home with all conceivable 'contemporary' luxuries ('model kitchen' for Gaye, telly, radiogram and portable, stereo, ciné-projector, motor-mower and so forth), plus a car (small, admittedly—and maybe 'on' the firm?), plus extensive gambling and frequent attendance at race-meetings (in a grey topper, which I just *don't* believe) both equestrian and speedway. Holidays, it is true, seem to be spent (judging by the décor) in England, though at 'posh' hotels, and there are frequent visits to equally 'posh' restaurants (*not*, presumably, on expense account since George goes alone with Gaye) and innumerable taxi rides in any crisis.

The Lancaster family presents no problem: it's quite clear they're 'living on capital' (of which, in spite of their lamentations about death duties—and about high costs in general—there would still seem to be quite a store), and Willy, no doubt (though I don't think this is said specifically—and indeed, would *any* city company take him on?), may have directorships. Their annual income—or rather, withdrawal—may be between £6,000 and £10,000 or more: it doesn't matter much which sum—just take your pick!

★

Economically speaking, then, I don't think it's unjust to describe the worlds of these three families as those of fantasy. What, now, of their social conceptions—their ideologies, one might say? Here we must distinguish, I think, two aspects of 'reality': the accuracy of the three artists' visions of what English people do think about themselves, and the truth, if any, of these conceptions.

The Giles world is often praised—and in some ways very rightly—for its realism. To consider him first, for a moment, as an *artist*, there is no one (and may I repeat, *no* one—no film director, no photographer, no painter) who has caught, as precisely and poetically as he has, and with such strength of wit, fantasy and sardonic-tender observation, the true aspect of the contemporary urban scene. (And—in his non-family cartoons —those of the nautical and agricultural scenes as well: to which, being himself a yachtsman and a farmer, he can give a salted and a dung-like stench of truth!) No one, better than he, has evoked the dreamy desolation of our cities, the nightmare jumble of gas-works, warehouses, by-passes, docks and overhead railways—the cobbled perspectives of crumbling Victorian terraces and the concrete austerities of the new 'garden' towns. None has seen more sharply than he the slums, the pubs, the derelict schools, the all-night 'caffs', the lock-up shops and alleys and backyards; and no one is better on our cities in rain, in fog or, especially, after dark. It is a real triumph of Giles's to be, as he is in this respect, an artist who, at a time when our culture is so dreadfully fragmented, can appeal at once to persons of every class and of every degree and kind of 'education'.

One must also give Giles top marks for certain features of

his social—and human—observation. The 'Giles baby' is an obvious example: 'Fred's just heard the first cuckoo—and GOT it' epitomises his vision of the shameless, amoral, tirelessly energetic little Gengis Khans we all now (thanks greatly to him) recognise the dear little things to be. The care for the aged, as he depicts it—the automatic acceptance of their tedious presence—is equally true to traditional working-class social morality; though this instinct may be waning, so that soon these 'old folk' may be joining those of the petty-bourgeoisie and middle classes in the single back rooms and 'homes' into which our society—proud of its superior civilisation—banishes them as no 'primitive' African family would ever do. Among tough, horny-handed types in general he's hard to fault: though here an unpleasant aspect of his art emerges, which is his frantic adulation of the powerful—and chiefly of coppers (an adoration shared, one must admit, by most of his country-men, though by no one else in their senses in the western world), of cigar-sucking Rocky Marciano-type GIs (no wonder they're such fans of his at the bases!) and, in fact, of any 'practical' man who's hefty, domineering, and a potential bully. (He's tiresomely fond, too, of paying not very oblique compliments to Prince Philip and Prince Charles—though the Queen herself is less, and much more tangentially, referred to.) He is excellent, also, on favourite butts of quite amiable satire—especially schoolmasters, doctors and nurses, guardsmen, railwaymen, and their lugubrious places of occupation. Somewhat surprisingly, he's sympathetic (artistically speaking), too, when drawing whores, and he cracks down beautifully on minor hypocrisies (for instance, on that of a noted transatlantic evangelist about London park life), or on idiocies (like that of the magistrate who told us recently that, in law, we have no right to *stand*, without moving, in any street).

But when we come to consider Giles's social outlook in general, we soon find there are wild inaccuracies of contempor-ary detail, and that fundamentally he turns out to be an archaic romantic—wedged, psychologically, in much the same vanished and now idealised world as that of the Crazy Gang: or, at any rate, in a world that has never progressed essentially beyond the Attlee or 'Welfare' era of the 1940s. Types he fails completely to get right—and doesn't even try to—are his be-spatted, tea-swilling bureaucrats, baby-kissing politicians, lords soaking scotch in stately homes amid bevies of butlers, officers' messes filled with Crimean veterans (the sergeants' mess is quite another matter!), and colonial governors, bedecked with plumage, whose actual successors, though by no means less fatuous, are no longer so in this picturesque, engaging way. All these are merely caricatures; and when Giles's interest slips so does his pen, and he draws hideously. For other social groups that don't really interest him, he devises stereotypes—though sometimes he catches up on visual reality with a time-lag of a year or so. Thus, he's not at his best on Teds or teenagers (he doesn't like either and entirely misses the real horror of the one, and the real elegance of the other) or on their habitat (a Giles 'coffee bar' is far more terrible than any in reality), or on women's dress in general (unless it's squalid: if not, he exaggerates grotesquely). He's also (like so many English 'comic draughtsmen'—a rather nasty, masochistic trait) very ready to poke quite vicious 'fun' at artists, who are always presented as scruffy, pretentious 'bohemian' frauds. He doesn't much like (or try to 'understand') foreigners (though Frenchmen and Spaniards fare rather better than Germans or Italians—particularly Germans), and social outcasts in general (for instance, people who—as he imagines them—frequent 'Soho dives') get a rough handling. In short, he disapproves of, and goes for, anyone who fails to conform to his ideal norm of a safe, comfortable, unashamedly philistine—albeit 'independent' and eccentric—basic respectability.

Politically, Giles's 'Father' would seem, then, to be a Tory Radical, or of the Labour Right (it doesn't much matter which —though I suspect he actually *votes* Labour, if he remembers to vote at all). He is, in fact, what is known as 'non-political' (that is, one who accepts, consciously or not, the current majority opinion); and Giles's cracks are directed as much at the 'upper classes' (always depicted as lah-di-dah nitwits of the

Burlington Bertie vintage, and never as in any way *dangerous*)
as at trade unionists (when their activities inconvenience 'the
public'—a characteristic consumer's viewpoint), or at particular
politicians of either party (Cripps used to be a favourite
target—as he was of the Crazy Gang). Even his son George, a
sort of faded crypto-Bevanite, would appear to have no political
activity of any kind. Giles himself is, in his art at its best,
a critic and an original: and in his ideology, a humorous
conformist.

To this we must notice three important exceptions. The first
is Giles's attitude to the 'colour question'. On September 7,
1958, he came out with the best and most categorical cartoon
published by anyone on the 'happenings' at Notting Vale whose
full shame and disgrace we have none of us yet adequately
accepted, let alone redeemed—that is, if we ever can do. This
picture showed three Teds walking out of a surgery where their
self-provoked wounds had been patched up by a 'coloured'
nurse and doctor. Giles's rightness about this, and his silliness
about 'foreigners' in general, are an echo of the *Express*'s own
confusion: of their very creditable anti-racialist line, which
accompanies—without any consciousness of inconsistency—
their old-fashioned 'imperialist' propaganda.

The next two instances are more ambiguous. Giles, as has
been said, is 'pro-American' in a rather mindless, 'tolerant' sort
of way. He allows his US characters to call us 'the natives', and
British troops to call them 'the occupation army' (in cartoons
where RAF personnel polish up their rockets for them, or do
guardsman's foot-drill, while sleek US personnel do all the
technical work). But although in these and in a (perhaps
significantly large) number of other cartoons about rocketry,
there may seem to be, and probably only is, an amiable if
defeatist acceptance of the 'inevitable', there is also something
of a hint of a gnawing resentment: which took more tangible
form in a cartoon (September 22, 1959) of Krushchev's reception in America which, though not particularly flattering to the
perambulating Chairman, was certainly not so at all towards
the conduct of his hosts.

The other ambiguous exception is *The Bomb*: something of an obsession with Giles, whose 'children' are always exploding home-made ones (when they are not manufacturing sputniks, rockets, weapons of war in general or, rather ghoulishly, hundreds of live crawling mini-kids in test tubes). *The Bomb*, for Giles, seems to be a rather 'serious' joke; and on September 15, 1959, a junior Giles wrote a letter to his aunt Vera in which the infant had some fairly perspicacious things to say about it—though the overall tone was still quite 'humorous'. Perhaps it is dawning on Giles, as on so many of his countrymen, that if *The Bomb is* a joke, it's about the most hilarious yet devised by man.

★

Socially and politically speaking, the world of the Barry Appleby family is a complete blank: neither George nor Gaye has a single idea of any description in their heads other than the practical material: though on this level their observations (or their creator's) are often shrewd enough. It is true they possess a copy of *The Pilgrim's Progress* (which Gaye once used to hide a 10s note in from George), and that George *can* read (detective stories when he's ill in bed). There was even a dreadful moment when Gaye bought an object of 'modern art', of which the less said the better; and the 'joke' in one cartoon hinges on George's imagining that the question 'can you paint?' means can you paint a wall.

It is the Gambols' sexual life—or the absence of it—that horribly fascinates most of all. We know they have no child; and of the three families, the Gambols is the only one that sleeps in twin, separate beds (except on one of their seaside orgies when the tactless management gave them a double one). George isn't allowed to see Gaye undressing or, if he accidentally does so, ogles her with a libidinous, surreptitious leer. If her 'slip shows', or the dress falls off her shoulder in a public place, there's a little 'scene'. George's chief—in fact seemingly only—'thrill' is to 'zip Gaye up':[1] a recurrent episode in the

[1] *Later*: And never 'down'.

household. (I have even wondered whether Barry Appleby's insistence that the little niece and nephew, Miggy and Flivver, are cousins, not brother and sister, may be to lift from their infant frolics any horrid hint of incest.)

They are, in fact, a couple of sexless sparrows (if one can imagine any such sparrows) in their suburban love-nest: where the major events are the annual 'spring clean', the summer tending of the garden (a sympathetic touch, pleasantly contrasting with the infant-slaughtered foliage of the Giles back lawn), and the domestic dramas in the kitchen—where Gaye 'cooks' largely out of tins, and George 'does the dishes' wearing, needless to say, a (female) apron. George talks in his sleep, and Gaye, who sobs easily, will emit, when afraid of a mouse (or the dark, or almost anything), a desperate cry of 'Eek!' (One would really love to know—or rather, hear—what the Giles couple, and the Appleby, would think of each other's domestic customs. Gaye would, most probably, say 'Eek!' And Giles's 'Father'?)

George and Gaye are, of course, very *nice* people: that is undeniable. But outside their tiny world of consecrated mediocrity, nothing exists whatever. It is therefore most disconcerting to discover that Barry Appleby (whose own wife, he tells us, helps him with the cartoons) has an enormous fan mail, so that any slight deviation of his hero and heroine from acceptable suburban behaviour must most carefully be explained away. In 1951, the *Express* held a competition (with a £25 prize) to find the 'sporting, happily-married, middle-class couple most like George and Gaye'. There were 4,000 entrants (including, it would appear, two Caribbeans), and the prize was won by a proud pair whose photograph—he, of course, wearing an apron and washing up—was duly printed by the delighted journal. Of Appleby's actual *drawing*, it only remains to say that it is entirely without quality, since the cartoons are mere ideograms: but none the less effective, as we have seen, for that.

*

The supreme Lancaster gift is to use Maudie (and, to a much lesser extent, the dimmer Willy) as a vehicle for her creator's tart, apt, shallow and, above all, fantastically *swift* commentaries on the social scene. Within his range of sympathies and of ideas, which is severely limited, Lancaster is off and away a split second after the gun goes, outpacing almost any rival. His wit, which is thought to be 'sophisticated', seems to me not so much 'undergraduate' exactly, as 'sixth form': sharp, irresponsible, often rather mean, and waggish: 'boyish', in fact, as so many English Tory anarchs are (Lancaster on Hailsham and his bell-ringing, for instance, was one sixth former on another).

As a draughtsman, his line is consummate on the best English amateur level (cf Lear, Haselden, or the anonymous illustrator of Belloc's *Cautionary Tales*); and his observation of *what interests him*, devastatingly acute. Thus, for example, the Knightsbridge fashionable, 'clubland', the clergy, and bourgeois intellectuals, are pinned down exactly; while his teenagers and Teds (like Giles's) are inaccurate or dated—the Teds mere ogres and not the dreadful ingrown *mess* they really are, and his 'teenagers' in point of fact not Soho exquisites, but 'Chelsea-set bohemians'. (His comment on Notting Vale, by the way, was anti-Ted but not, like Giles's, essentially *for* their victims.) His family are Tory hedonists 'redeemed' (but then, Tory hedonists often *are*) by a certain 'style': by a cynical detachment towards themselves, and towards modern society, in which—despite their fall from power and, relatively speaking, riches—they are still very conscious of playing a key part. To art itself their attitude, though well-informed, is frivolous and modish (though it is rather touching to learn that they can both play—and do in private—the piano). On the literary scene, Lancaster mocks the 'Angries' (as who doesn't?), but is not, one feels, very interested in differentiation or analysis of their ideas and personalities. Sexually, his Littlehamptons are, of course, in a worldly sense uncritical, but there is no hint whatever that Maudie and Willy are other than faithful to their marriage vows; and one is certain, at all events, that their family life is—if the word can be said to fit the Littlehamptons—'sacred' to them. (In bed, Willy still wears his monocle: there is something infinitely reassuring about this).

As social critics, they (or their creator) lash out—or stab out —in all directions: though often at fairly obvious targets like traffic jams, dirty railways, 'inconvenient' strikes and so on. Politically, the chief Lancaster dig, on the home front, is that *all* politicians are confused, self-contradictory and self-deluded (as indeed they are); while overseas, the foreigners revert to their traditional role of being 'funny'—without, as in the case of the English victims, being sympathetically so. Germans are monsters (there is real venom here), the French *very* French indeed, the Russians ludicrous in the extreme (great idiotic, dangerous bears). For the Americans, Lancaster shares with Giles, though in a different way, a thoroughly ambivalent attitude: which fairly accurately reflects the love-hate of English top persons for America—love of the rich, the dispenser of good things (but resentment at their own acceptance of these gifts); and love of the powerful, the 'protector' (but jealousy and fear of that power). Thus Americans are people who take bribes, and who also entertain the parasitic Littlehamptons lavishly in New York. American senators and business-men are amiable, if droll, John Foster Dulles (who tried to implement their policies) a nuisance and a menace. As for *The Bomb*, it is a most unpleasant thing, and because in American hands it is unpleasant of them, too, to have it . . . but then, there are those funny Russians to consider, so the best thing for Maudie to do is have another bathe, change into something even more glorious, and go out (*with* Willy—he is almost as uxorious as George to Gaye) to a diplomatic party where she can make aw hip-crack about it all.

*

We have seen how, in the lives of all three families, the emphasis is on their highly-developed faculty for *consumption*: and, as a corollary to this, that none of them, profession-ally speaking, *makes* anything—or hardly anything. Willy

Littlehampton, perhaps, may do a spot of legislation at the Lords, but that's about all. George Gambol is concerned exclusively with *marketing*. As for the Giles family, though, as I've suggested, there seems to be a business of some kind in the background—which may, in fact, be of a manufacturing description —we see nothing of it, or of whatever it produces. It is true that, so far as 'do-it-yourself' 'production' in the home goes, the Giles family of all generations is outstandingly gifted and resourceful. But they produce nothing for the *community* and, in a general way, an outstanding feature of these family sagas is that all three sets of lives are centred on 'the home' (and on any visitors to it), and not very much on anything else that goes on outside. (In fairness to Giles one must also allow that his 'non-family' cartoons are very often set in factories, docks, warehouses and so on.)[1]

We have also seen that, with variations, all these three families are philistine materialists—even, in essentials, the 'cultivated' Littlehamptons; and all of them, incidentally— which is quite sympathetic (and even a little *daring* on the part of the moralising *Daily*—or, at any rate, *Sunday—Express*)— are drinkers, gamblers and (though quite inactively) 'sports lovers'. We may further observe that, in each family, the woman is the dominant partner: as indeed she usually is—though not, most emphatically, in the 'Andy Capp' cartoon in the (slightly more) proletarian *Daily Mirror*. Another reflection is that although George and Gaye (and their inventor) may imagine they are 'middle class' (whereas no one could conceivably be more lower-middle), we shall find that, in point of actual fact, the present problems and aspirations of the professional middle classes, which once governed (if not ruled) England, and which still, in their sharp decline, produce most of what's left of its cultural élite, find no place whatever in this triple family portrait of contemporary English life.

[1] *Later:* And in justice to Appleby, it would appear Gaye belongs to a 'women's club'—though the chief reason for its existence is to provide Gaye with the 'feminine' observations she tells George about her fellow members.

Nor shall we discover (in this most bang-on, alert 'newspaper for the millions') that any of the newly erupted social groups of the 1950s—born of the 'new prosperity' and of the cross-fertilisation of English classes—is anywhere represented: two of the families are archaic, and the third (the Gambols), though of today, is simply the 1930s petty-bourgeois with a bigger pay packet and less fear of the sack. There remains to be noticed one virtue—albeit of a static, not very positive kind—which all these three families possess. And it is that they are all of them, basically, *patriots*: they 'love' England, or their particular fragments of it—sardonically (Giles), or mindlessly (Appleby), or sentimentally (Osbert Lancaster). But this patriotism is of the uncritical 'Dunkirk' kind which was England's strength when time was on her side, and is now her dangerous weakness when, as at present, time is no longer on her side at all.

New Left Review, March 1960

IN THE NEXT PIECE, we return to the world of juvenile pop music; and I do not apologise for re-introducing this theme, because it does seem to me that the teenager is a key figure for understanding the 1950s; and that song is, and always has been, a key indication of the culture of a society.

POP SONGS AND TEENAGERS

THE EDITOR has warned me some readers may not know what pop discs are. So: pop=popular; disc=gramophone recording. In short, the elegantly boxed records of the High Street music stores which, last year, sold 50 millions of them. The music-fodder of the juke-boxes, the radios and radiograms. To the vast mysterious majority, the only kind of songs there are.

I sense a shudder: 'Oh, he means jazz.' No, he doesn't. True

jazz is, to pop music, what the austere harmonies of the Wig-
more Hall are to the lush tremulos of the Palm Court and its
gypsy violins. 'Then he means crooners.' That's a bit nearer,
though the word's twenty years out of date and at once
betrays the cultivated person who's never listened to a pop—or
even, for that matter, most probably, to a crooner (unless perhaps to Crosby, *circa* 1932).

Warming to my theme, I'd like to say I think the abysmal
ignorance of educated persons about the popular music of the
millions, is deplorable.[1] First, because pop music, on its own low
level, can be so good; and I must declare that never have I met
anyone who, condemning it completely, has turned out, on
close enquiry, to know anything whatever about it. But worse,
because the deaf ear that's turned, in pained disdain, away from
pop music, betrays a lamentable lack of curiosity about the
culture of our country in 1958. For that music *is* our culture:
at all events, the anthropologist from São Paulo or Peking would
esteem it so, and rightly. Alfred Deller, yes; but what about
Lonnie Donegan, he'd say? They're both of our world, and
there's no doubt which of these siren voices penetrates and
moulds more English hearts and brains.

But in England, pop art and fine art stand resolutely back
to back. For all the interest educated persons take in the pop
arts of their own people, they might be settlers among the tribes-
men of darkest Ruanda-Urundi. No, no, not even! In that case,
they'd certainly have collected a few native masks and ivories.
But how many of my gentle readers possess, I wonder, a pop
disc? The point isn't that you've got to like this music, if you
can't. It is that, if you don't know it, you lose a clue to what lies
behind those myriad faces in the bus and tube—particularly
the young ones.

★

[1]*Later:* This declaration was scornfully refuted by a columnist in
one of the grimmer dailies whose special talent—being himself bereft
of any marketable notions about such fragments of our world as his
myopic eyes can visualize—is to pinch ideas he is incapable of
inventing, and sneer at them in shop-soiled journalese. For a parallel
with this kind of activity, please see the essay on the ponce that follows.

Let's open our *Melody Maker*, and scan the list of the Top Twenty: of the recordings which have had the highest sales to our fellow-countrymen and women. What will it tell us of their tastes and dreams? In the week I write this, plenty. First, only three of the singers are over thirty, and a third of them are less than twenty-one (the youngest, Laurie London, is fourteen). The modern troubadours are teenagers, and the reason's not far to seek: the buyers are teenagers, too.

Gramophone recordings are one of the many industries that have come into being, in the past few years, to absorb the tremendous buying power of the young. We are in the presence, here, of an entirely new phenomenon in human history: that youth is rich. Once, the *jeunesse dorée* were a minute minority; now, all the young have gold. Earning good wages, and living for little, or even for free, like billeted troops on poor harassed Dad and Mum,[1] the kids have more 'spending money' than any other age group of the population. Farewell the classic, century-old pattern of Youth the industrious apprentice, penniless, nose glued to grindstone, and Age, prosperous, authoritative, in fair round belly with good chump-chop lined. Today, age is needy and, as its powers decline, so does its income; but full-blooded youth has wealth as well as vigour. In this decade, we witness the second Children's Crusade, armed with strength and booty, against all 'squares', all adult nay-sayers. An international movement, be it noted,[2] that blithely penetrates the political curtains draped by senile seniors, as yet unconscious of the rising might of this new classless class.

[1]*Later:* Who have thus, in point of fact, actually been *subsidising* their kids (whose surplus 'spending money' is so much higher than their own). For it's rare to find a teenager handing them over more than £2 a week, which is certainly well under the real cost of board and lodging for a hungry, light-leaving-on youngster. One reason for this may be that while Mum and Dad, traditionally, expect *something* from a son or daughter wage-earner, they're too proud (or innocent) to charge an economic figure.

[2]*Later:* The first spectacle I saw (after the Stalinist Palace of Science and Culture) when, with Kenny Graham, I visited Warsaw in the summer of 1959, was that of jean-clad teenagers; who on introduction, at once led us to a jazz club.

What are these teenage pop discs like to listen to? Let's look more closely at a typical best-seller in the Top Twenty, Mr Paul Anka's *Diana*. Paul Anka is a Syrian-Canadian who was born in Ottawa sixteen years ago. He wrote the words and music of *Diana* himself, it has sold over a million copies in England alone, and its world sales are said to have netted more than £100,000 to its young composer-singer. The tune has a slick, quick blare and beat, with crescendo passages of agonized ecstasy, and Paul puts it over with smack attack, total conviction, absolutely minimal subtlety, and a triumphal, unrestrained, juvenile animal vulgarity.

In this essay, alas, I cannot reproduce the voice and tune—only the lyric. This, on the whole, is undistinguished even by pop standards, with couplets like

> I love you with all my heart
> And I hope we will never part

yet there are some lines that hint at the reasons for its teenage appeal. It opens:

> I'm so young and you're so old . . .

And closes:

> Oh, please stay by me, Diana!
> Oh—please—DIANA!

Even the amateur psychologist can deduce, from this, the teenage triumph and the teenage yearning. It's wonderful to be 'so young' because it's *I* who am singing the song, I who am 'sending' my fellow teenagers by my singing, and yet . . . there is the underlying longing for the older woman (could it be the mother-figure?) whom the singer addresses, unequivocally, as

> Oh my darlin', oh *my lover*.[1]

What's most striking of all about the whole tone of this song, and of young Mr Anka's delivery, is its overall mood of world-

---

[1] *Later:* But the word 'lover' was used at this time in certain (not necessarily perverse) north American circles as a synonym for 'friend'; so I may have misread the young lyricist's intention—though I don't think so.

weary languor, as if it were a *cri du cœur* of a man saturated by an excess of experience. And it's startling (for anyone over twenty) to read, in the pop musical press, that the girl he originally had in mind when he wrote it was *eighteen years old*. Also, that he himself has announced that he proposes to retire when he reaches that same great age.[1] No doubt about it: teenagers—in some senses, at any rate—ripen more quickly than they used to.

★

Continuing our examination of the weekly lists of the Top Twenty we shall find some other changes, during the past year or so, in the type of song and singer that's most liked. We've already seen that English kids no longer want to rip the drape suits off the backs of oldsters like Frankie Laine and Johnnie Ray; now they demand minstrels of their own age. But there's another reason why such singers are in decline: they are Americans. For what's sensational about the list I have before me is that no less than half the performers are British—something unthinkable a year ago.

Now, the pop song of the past decade is an American invention, and the best pop singers were (and still are) American. Moreover, practitioners like Elvis Presley (of whom more soon) are still dearly beloved of English fans. But there has been a shift of emphasis: English singers have gradually captured a place in the pop market. And they have done this by learning to sing the American pop style in a manner quite indistinguishable from the real thing, so that we have the paradox that teenagers like, increasingly, songs sung *by Englishmen in American*.

Let's make a comparison between two stars of the Top Twenty—transatlantic Elvis, and our own Tommy Steele, both of whom swam to glory at the height of the rock 'n' roll craze, now mercifully in decline. With no less than four discs in the current list, Elvis must still be regarded, despite his relative antiquity (he is 23), as the teenage *stupor mundi*. In contrast to the 1940s ideal of the crew-cutted, athletic, out-of-door

[1]*Later:* He hasn't.

American boy, Elvis represents something of a reversion to the Valentino era with his sleeked, slick locks and sideburns, and his baleful, full-lipped Neronic glare. His songs seem, melodically, absolutely identical, with words, where comprehensible, that are loaded with mildly smutty innuendo. You may not admire the frantic agitation of his hunched shoulders as he laces his electric guitar with loving arms, or the equivocal motion of his over-expressive shark-skin slacks, or even, for that matter, his ear-cracking, plexus-shaking voice. But there's no denying the punch, verve and gusto of his performance—its utter certainty that what he gives, they need.

His act, in short, has all the frenzy of a jungle dance and war cry without their dignity. In complete contrast is England's Tommy Steele. If Elvis is the teenage witch-doctor, Tommy Steele is Pan. His tunes, originally derived from 'rock', but increasingly melodious and even, on occasions, tender, are an invitation to the forest, to the haywain, to the misty reaches of the Thames at Bermondsey from whence he comes. Not that Tommy cannot 'send' the kids with agitated, blue-jeaned leaps and caperings, and gollywog mop-shakes of his golden hair. But the whole effect, to use a silly word, is so much *nicer*. His voice and his cavortings are sensual, certainly, but in a strange way innocent, even pure. His speaking voice is that of a descendant of a long line of Cockney singers—Elen, Kate Carney, Chevalier—sardonic and sentimental. But when he sings, it's as if he spoke another language: for though the teenagers may accept a thoroughly English *singer*, they are indifferent to a contemporary English *song*. Indeed—except for old-style sentimental ballads— no such thing may yet be said to exist in early 1958.

At the risk of boring the reader with instances of this strange duality of the teenage mentality, I'd like to describe another American-style English singer—Lonnie Donegan. The reason I harp on this so is that I think a study of pop music may help to show in what ways young English boys and girls are 'Americanized', and in what ways they are not. Lonnie Donegan is a product of the skiffle cellars, and he has achieved a feat which is, in one sense, even more remarkable than that of Tommy

Steele—that is, to become a top pop singer not only in his native English backwater, but in the transatlantic land of make-believe as well.

In case there's anyone who doesn't yet know about skiffle, let's recapitulate. Skiffle (onomatopoeic) music has existed in America certainly since the last century and, in its original form, it was played by groups of amateur musicians who sang traditional (and sometimes newly-created) ballads accompanying themselves on home-made instruments—many of these, like the celebrated washboard, domestic utensils. It was thus, at first, a 'folk art' of sorts, and the reason why primitive instruments were used was simply that there was no money to buy real ones. A few years ago, for reasons that remain mysterious, and coinciding with the eruption of the coffee bars (and still more, their cellars) all over London, skiffle groups appeared and spread like mushrooms till there are today[1] certainly many hundreds of them, several of which have won commercial fame. The movement is, of course, a 'mannerist' one—somewhat similar, in a way, to the revival of English folk-dancing some decades ago. That is to say, the teenagers in the groups are reviving, artificially, a musical style that was once spontaneous —though I'm not at all denying their enthusiasm (or, for that matter, the sincerity of the dactylographs and clerical workers who cavort in Morris dances at Cecil Sharp House).

But what's odd is that the ballads the skiffle musicians sing are American, and their singing accent even more so. Songs about transatlantic gals and jails and railroads, intoned in a nasal monotone, seem entirely convincing to Cockney kids from Camberwell and Wood Green, sitting huddled in the Soho basements—and their idol, Lonnie Donegan, has sold some of these back to the Americans with resounding success. And not only on records like his *Rock Island Line*, but even by himself in person, barnstorming triumphantly across the Limey-despising United States. What's odder still is that, as the process continues, some of these ballads will have crossed the Atlantic

[1] *Later:* That is, in early 1958: skiffle is long quite dead, fading as rapidly as it arose.

three times: from here to America in colonial days, from there back again to the London skiffle cellars, and now, with Mr Donegan and Miss Nancy Whiskey, over once more to the US.

★

I come now to two minor changes in pop disc fashions, and the first is the decline of the female singer: for in the list before me, only two of the Top Twenty songs are sung by women.

Now, I think there's no doubt that in the whole dreadful, wonderful pop song canon, among the top practitioners of the art women outnumber men by at least two to one: for every Sinatra there's a Clooney or a Lee, for every Eckstine, a Vaughan or a Horne. But not in the Top Twenty of the teenagers! May this suggest that, if the adult dream figure is a woman, among the kids it's the wolf whistle of the adolescent male that 'sends' them most? And may we not see an analogy with the pop art of the films? Can anyone imagine, for example, that some female James Dean[1] could have been, in the middle of our century, the emblematic figure that he has become? At all events, as the 'personal managers' and recording company talent-spotters prospect the jazz clubs and skiffle cellars for new adolescent gold mines, it's boys they almost invariably select. Even Tommy's younger brother, Colin Hicks, has been pressed into service,[2] and it would seem that the unbroken voice of fourteen-

[1]*Later:* I thought at first that Bardot, when she came up, might fill the equivalent female role. But on reflection, no: for BB's essential appeal (witness her films) is to older men; and though Continental European and (less adroitly) some English teenage girls have modelled themselves on her (to the hallucinating degree, at times, of becoming exact physical carbon copies), their target, like hers, is adults hungry for the child-woman: and not—as that of the male 'teenage idols' is— the boys and girls of their own age.

[2]*Later:* But one must not mock this development. Matilda Alice Victoria Wood (or Marie Lloyd), of whom Tommy Steele seems to me to be, in so many striking ways, the popular reincarnation, had several gifted sisters who succeeded in their own right on the Halls: among them, Alice Lloyd and Daisy Wood.

year-old Laurie London[1] is no bar to favour with the kids. Could it therefore be there's something *tribal* in the teenage ideology? Among adults, I think there's no doubt this is a woman's age; but perhaps the kids have reverted to a more primitive pattern. The sight of two London Teds, out with their girls, is perhaps in this connection of significance. The boys walked ahead, their expressionless faces, surmounted by Tony Curtis hair-dos,[2] bent in exclusive masculine communion. Ten feet behind them, ignoring them completely but following on, come their twin Ted-esses. I've seen an identical sight among the Kikuyu.[3]

The other minor change is the teenage aversion (or indifference) to 'coloured' pop singers.[4] While 'coloured' artists certainly remain popular among adult fans, in the list of the Twenty there is only one—Belafonte. It's true, of course, that there are other 'coloured' singers, not in the list, whom teenagers admire—'Fats' Domino, for instance, and the incredible, hypnotic, hysterical 'Little Richard'. But they're not generally esteemed, it seems: and I very much doubt if it's teenage purchases that have lifted Harry Belafonte's sentimental rendition of West Indian calypso to so high a place in the Top Twenty. At all events, I think the real reasons for his state of solitary splendour are twofold. First, that most 'coloured' artists simply cannot bring themselves to sing the sort of number the teenagers like. But even more, I think it is that young people wish, increasingly, to identify themselves *personally* with the

[1]*Later:* Young Mr London's most amazing feat was to climb—in face of knife-edged competition—to the top of the American Hit Parade with his (religious!) ballad, *He's Got The Whole World In His Hands*: the first time a British artist had achieved this distinction since Miss Vera Lynn conquered America with her rendition of *Auf Wierdersehen.*

[2]*Later:* How fast teenage fashions dated in the 1950s! For the new male hair-styles of eighteen months later—and for the critical distinctions between Teds and teenagers in general—see the subsequent piece, *Sharp Schmutter.*

[3]*Later:* To whom all apologies for this comparison.

[4]*Later:* But not—may I make very clear—among teenage jazz connoisseurs to 'coloured' jazz performers: exactly the contrary, in fact. It is of the teenage pop (not jazz) public I was speaking.

singers they admire. It's not for nothing, after all, that Tommy Steele gets 2,000 letters a week, 150 of them proposing marriage.

★

The time's now come to draw—on, I admit, very slender evidence—some tentative conclusions about teenagers. But try to draw them I think we should, because the 'two nations' of our society may perhaps no longer be those of the 'rich' and 'poor' (or, to use old-fashioned terms, the 'upper' and 'working' classes), but those of the teenagers on the one hand and, on the other, all those who have assumed the burdens of adult responsibility. Indeed, the great social revolution of the past fifteen years may not be the one which redivided wealth among the adults in the Welfare State, but the one that's given teenagers economic power. This piece is about the pop disc industry— almost entirely their own creation; but what about the new clothing industry for making and selling teenage garments of both sexes? Or the motor scooter industry they patronize so generously? Or the radiogram and television industries? Or the eating and soft-drinking places that cater so largely for them?[1] Putting it at its lowest, there may well be

Kids of 15 to 23	Each with annual 'spending money' of	Making an annual teenage kitty of
2 millions	$£3 \times 52$	$£312,000,000$[2]

With this they can influence English economic—and therefore social—life. For let's not forget their 'spending money' does not go on traditional necessities, but on the kinds of luxuries that modify the social pattern.

And so, just as it's absurd for old Bournemouth belles to

[1]*Later:* I left out a key teenage (male as well as female) industry, that of cosmetics; also the growth of specialised travel agencies for youth.

[2]*Later:* Though this bit of uninformed statistical guesswork seemed to me, at the time, such as could scarcely be credited by serious readers, it turned out, when accurate estimates were published later, to be more than half too little.

decry the Welfare state itself, as if what's done could ever be undone, it's equally vain to suppose that teenage *power* (for that is what it is) can suddenly be withdrawn. Short of a general economic collapse, the teenage 'spending money' is here to stay. And make no mistake of it, the kids are very well aware of this. They may not have the vote (or particularly want it), and they may be subject to certain legal restrictions. But as anyone who read the accounts of the recent law suit over Tommy Steele's earnings will have realized, though the eminent lawyers spoke of Tommy in somewhat disdainful terms (as lawyers, those naïve realists, love to) as being an 'infant', it was the twenty year old Bermondsey boy, with his colossal fortune, who held the key position in the wings (or rather, on the studio set where he was making, at the time, the second film about his life, *The Duke Wore Jeans*). The hostility of some adults to teenagers—which often takes the form of a quite unbalanced loathing of their idols, particularly of Tommy and poor Elvis —is as sterile as is that hatred educated people often seem to have for television: a morbid dislike of these symbols of popular culture which they feel are undermining not so much culture itself, as their hitherto exclusive possession of it.

★

And what are they like, the teenagers? What do they think and want? How much will they alter when they become wives and husbands? Here the anthropologists have a lot of work to do (very much neglected, it seems to me). Meanwhile, I offer these inexpert impressions.

1. They are much more *classless* than any of the older age groups are, or were. In the days when I was a teenager,[1] it was impossible to step outside your class unless you joined the army, or went to jail; but now, the kids seem to do this quite effortlessly. An analysis of a jazz club membership would, I

[1]*Later:* A misnomer. In those days there were big boys and girls, or young men and women—but no such thing as a teenager: who, one must insist, is a new kind of person, chiefly on account of his economic power.

am sure, reveal the most varied social origins; and the point is, the kids just ignore this topic—they seem genuinely uninterested in it. In contrast with the earlier generation (say, now aged 23-35) that was emancipated by the Welfare state and who, in spite of economic gains, still seem almost ferociously obsessed by class, the kids don't seem to care about it at all.

2. They are not so much hostile to, as blithely indifferent to, the Establishment. In the two copies of *Fling*, the teenage weekly put out by the *Mirror* group and, most unfortunately, suppressed, an extremely detailed poll was taken among the kids about Altrincham-and-all-that; and their answers suggested the boys and girls just weren't concerned by all that nonsense. In the same way, I have the impression that a play like *Look Back in Anger*, with its cry of protest that so shook the old and staid, would seem quite meaningless to them. What is all this about outside lavatories and having to open sweet shops when you've got plenty of 'spending money'? What are the difficulties of meeting those who read 'posh' Sunday papers when you can dance with as many of them as you like at the local jazz club (with that splendid natural democrat, and old Etonian, Humphrey Lyttleton, presiding)? John Osborne's play exists within the context of the old order, and only takes on its meaning by being, in a sense, a part of it. To a teenager, it would seem thoroughly old-fashioned.[1]

3. They are *not* 'Americanized'. I say this despite all the evidence I've adduced to the contrary. The paradox is that the bearded skiffle singers with their Yankee ballads, and Tommy Steele with his 'rock'-style songs, seem so resoundingly, so irreversibly, English. I don't at all deny an *influence* (which, incidentally, has been going on ever since ragtime hit this country before World War I). But the kids have transformed this influence into something of their own . . . in a way that suggests, subtly, that they're almost *amused* by what has influenced them. Put an English teenager beside an American, and you'll see the difference: our version is less streamlined, less

[1] *Later:* But for an estimate of Osborne's vital break-through in the theatre, please see the subsequent preface to *A Taste of Reality*.

pattern-perfect, and more knobbly, homely, self-possessed. The last word on this was said by Tommy Steele himself. When asked, by an interviewer, if he was going to the States, he said (in characteristically transatlantic idiom): 'I don't dig America'.[1] And whatever they may take from there, I think that goes for his admirers, too.

4. I think they are more internationally-minded than we were; and not, as we were, self-consciously ('Youth for Spain', and so on), but intuitively. They are as much at ease at the Moscow congress as at the jazz festival in the local Trocadero. Teenage songs, and even styles of clothing, are carried across Europe, it would seem, by a sort of international adolescent *maquis*; and it may be that this post-Hiroshima generation has realized, instinctively and surely, how idiotic are the lethal posturings and deadly infantile bluster of their elders, as they wave bombs and rockets and satellites at one another.

5. In their private lives, they don't like to be *told*. Because of their economic power, and perhaps because those born in the war years were forced towards independence at an early age, they're undoubtedly more mature than youngsters used to be. How profound, psychologically, this maturity may be, I do not know; but on the surface, at any rate, they face the adult world with an almost alarming aplomb, and a touch-me-if-you-dare look on their impassive faces.

They're undoubtedly *cleaner* than kids once were: and in them the English people, which loves to sneer at Continental filth, but is actually the dirtiest race in Europe,[2] has at last had

---

[1]*Later:* The word 'dig'—already archaic (or used ironically) at the time of writing this footnote, among jazz addicts and teenagers who borrowed it from them (as they did so many other terms)—has, of course, in certain contexts, a double meaning: as when Tommy uses it here, with the dual implication of 'like' and 'understand'.

[2]*Later:* If this seems a snide smear, please consider, notably, pubs and cafés (and the finger-nails of so many honest toilers serving in them), railways, parks, and the fantastic paucity of public places you can wash in; and if you served in 'the forces' fifteen years ago, recall the feet (and underclothes) of military exquisites whose sabre-creased slacks and highly-boned boots were the exterior pride of their officers, and such a source of civilian admiration.

a collective wash-and-brush-up. And the improvement is not only on their persons. Dry cleaners, rare twenty years ago except in bourgeois quarters, now abound. The bright, coloured jeans and sweaters worn by both sexes invite the laundry, and lend themselves more readily to it than did the drab 'men's wear' and 'frocks' of yesteryear. With their hair, they take immense pains—the boys as well as the girls; and though this excites the scorn and envy of prudes and sergeant-majors, I find it attractive—perhaps, of all the idiotic parallels that have been found between our own age and that of the first Elizabethans, the only real one.

They don't drink;[1] and have thus created yet another industry, that of the non-alcoholic beverage.

As for their sex life, it's mysterious. Their gregarious sociability, their ease with one another, their interchange of clothing and the frank sensuality of their music and their dancing, suggest promiscuity[2] without pain. But whether this is so or not, is hard to determine. My own guess is that while their social life is very uncomplicated as between boy and girl, it's not particularly 'immoral'.

In general, they're gayer than English people seem to have been for fifty years at least. Contemporary England is peculiar for being the most highly organized country, in the social sense,

[1]*Later*: A paradox here is that police figures of juvenile drunkenness have *risen*: but police statistics, which refer only to court charges, can be quite misleading if one's looking for a total picture. Increasing 'juvenile delinquency' can—and I think has—accompanied a vast general improvement of social behaviour among the young. 'Fringe' groups like the Teds have become more anti-social, and violently so, as the conduct of teenagers as a whole has become more happily adjusted (which may explain why each group so fervently despises the other). The best evidence is that of one's own eyes, if reasonably wide-ranging. Characteristic teenage haunts, like jazz clubs and coffee bars, don't sell liquor at all; and in pubs and drinking-clubs this age group—save in its manifestly delinquent minority—is conspicuously absent.

[2]*Later:* 'Promiscuity' is the wrong word altogether. Teenagers who are 'steady' will 'go together': but together only. Promiscuous behaviour may well be more usual among their (more confined and more frustrated?) elders.

for ensuring the moral and material welfare of everybody—
pullulating with decent laws, with high-minded committees,
with societies for preventing or encouraging this or that—and
yet it has produced, in consequence, the *dullest* society in
western Europe:[1] a society blighted by blankets of negative
respectability, and of dogmatic domesticity. The teenagers
don't seem to care for this, and have organized their
underground of joy.

★

This is, on the whole, an optimistic view. But it would be
equally possible to see, in the teenage neutralism and indifference to politics, and self-sufficiency, and instinct for enjoyment
—in short, in their kind of happy mindlessness—the raw material
for crypto-fascisms of the worst kind.[2] I don't sense this
myself at all, though I may very well be wrong. What I am
certain of, though, is that adults who wish to remain aware of
their own world must study the teenagers, and get to know
them: for never before, I'm convinced, has the younger
generation been so *different* from its elders. Therefore, let
moralists—especially political moralists—take heed. England
is, and always has been, a country infested with people who
love to tell us what to do, but who very rarely seem to know
what's going on.

The Twentieth Century, February 1958

[1]*Later:* Except for that of the Federal Swiss Republic.

[2]*Later:* In the Notting Vale riots of 1958, the worst offenders—
initially, at any rate, before the big strong men joined in—were boys
who were technically (if not 'ideologically') teenagers: though the worst
by far, in hateful fact, were those countless respectable adults who
just stood and *watched*. After the Kelso Cochrane alert of 1959, real
teenagers (that is, not just teenage Teds) were more, and more
disastrously, in evidence. In complete and wonderful contrast to this:
round about London you can now see teenagers of both 'colours' in
close and casual communion; perhaps because, by now, so many
English-born kids of either racial origin have shared school desks and
football fields (and a crafty contempt for 'teacher'—and all adults)
intimately for years together. So that now (1961) the 'activists' of the
teenage population may be poised between social choices leading to
life or death; and the attitudes of the *ex-teenagers* (young adults now,
kids in the 1950s) may be the decisive factor in the new decade.

AN INTERLUDE NOW, to recall an attempt to initiate a campaign for restoring to their owners the Parthenon marbles at present lodged, like stolen goods at the receiver's, in the British Museum. My efforts were a total failure: though in Athens the editor of KATHIMERINI withdrew from his daily column and reprinted the ensuing piece in full.[1]

GREEKS AND VANDALS

It is the Large Elgin Room of the British Museum. The Lecturer has just introduced the marbles. An abominable Oriental approaches him, and says:

Oriental: But why, sir, are these monuments here in London?

Lecturer: That surely sir, is what I have been explaining to you in my recent discourse. Nevertheless, to recapitulate ... In 1802, Lord Elgin, then British Ambassador to the Porte, duly equipped with the legal authority of a *firman*, and at immense personal cost to his own fortune, began to remove the marbles to this country where, in 1816, the Museum purchased them for £35,000.

Oriental: The Turks, then, sold these marbles to the British?

Lecturer: Indirectly, you might say so—yes.

Oriental: A question: what of the Greeks?

Lecturer: Well what, sir, of them?

Oriental: These marbles, you have said, are their creation.

Lecturer: Evidently, they are. I would however remind you that, at the period in question, the Greeks were a subject people of the Turks and, moreover, totally indifferent to the fate of Pheidias's masterpiece. The Parthenon was rapidly falling into ruin and, had not Lord Elgin rescued the sculptures for posterity, neither you nor I would now have the privilege of viewing them. I would further point out that the presence of

[1]On 2nd August, 1957, under the title 'The Loot of the Scottish Lord'.

the marbles in a convenient centre like London has enabled thousands of scholars from every country to examine them; and indeed, as I have already said in my short lecture, the architecture of the Parthenon is such that, were many of the figures you see here replaced in their original positions on the building, they would in fact be quite invisible to the public.

Oriental: Thank you. Some further questions. The Greeks are now no longer a subject people of the Turks?

Lecturer: Obviously not.

Oriental: Are the Greeks not now actively restoring the whole complex of the Acropolis?

Lecturer: So I believe.

Oriental: The city of Athens: is it not now as convenient a centre as is London? And, for a serious scholar, would not an examination of these marbles, here in London, have necessarily to be complemented, in any case, by a visit to the Parthenon?

Lecturer: No doubt it would.

Oriental: A final question, please. If a sculptor sets a work of art in a position on a building where it is visible to gods and not to mortals, should this intention of the artist not be respected?

Lecturer: So one might argue, possibly . . .

Oriental: What, then, do you conclude?

Lecturer: My dear sir: I perceive that your question, like so many questions, is in fact an inverted answer. Your own conclusion, I imagine, is that the Elgin marbles . . .

Oriental: The Parthenon marbles, sir . . .

Lecturer: Very well, that the marbles should now be returned to Greece.

Oriental: So it would seem to me. Yes. Resold by Great Britain, of course, for cash, if this financial consideration should be thought important . . .

Lecturer: That really, if I may say so, is a somewhat offensive remark.

Oriental: 'Offensive.' A question. Have you, sir, any conception, may I sincerely ask you, of how deeply offensive it may be to many visitors at this Museum to see the cherished creations of their ancestors exhibited like trophies? To see religious relics torn brutally from their holy contexts? Looking around us here, sir, at these masterpieces stuck on stands like carcasses on butchers' hooks, do you not feel at all the overwhelming *vulgarity* of this *Elgin* Room?

Lecturer: Pray calm yourself. Voices, in the Museum, should not be raised.

Oriental: Forgive me: I am calm. Proceed: I listen.

Lecturer: I invite you, then, kindly to ponder the alternatives. Would you return all works of art in all countries to the places of their origin?

Oriental: By no means. Not in all cases.

Lecturer: Ah! No?

Oriental: No. For instance. If works of art exist in great abundance, I would not return them. Mummy-cases, for example. I would not return all the mummy-cases in the world to Egypt.

Lecturer: All those *I* would gladly return. Hideous things.

Oriental: Nor would I return a work of art to a country whose present inhabitants bear but little relation to the ancient peoples who originally created the works of art in question.

Lecturer: So we may hope, under your kind dispensation, to retain some of our Assyrian and Babylonian antiquities?

Oriental: Certainly. Again, I would not return works of art to a people who, even if the direct heirs of the cultures which created these treasures, are manifestly incapable of looking after them today. Thus I would not deem it necessary to restore a plundered sculpture to the Easter Islanders.

Lecturer: I really, at this juncture, must be allowed to object to your term 'plundered'. Certainly, some of the Museum's treasures came into our hands in historic circumstances whose morality would not bear too strict an examination. But many others—indeed, most of the works of art here—were purchased legitimately, and were often actually discovered by exploration and excavation conducted by British scholars.

Oriental: Good sir: do you not see that to buy something that no one has a right to sell is exactly the same as to steal it?

Lecturer: I confess the distinction does escape me somewhat.

Oriental: The more so when those who sold the ancestral treasures that no man has a right to sell were often, in fact, unaware of their true value?

Lecturer: It is a nice point, I admit. Pray permit me, however, a rejoinder. Is there not much to be said—for reasons of safety, and of the greater diffusion of learning throughout the world—for the wide distribution, in every country, of works of art of every culture?

Oriental: That is a proposal which would naturally occur to one, like a Briton, who, coming from an island that, historically speaking, has produced relatively little, is anxious to enrich his culture by works of art by older civilizations that have produced much. As for the scholars, nowadays they can fly to whatever countries they wish and, indeed, often do so. It is the scholars that should now be distributed, not the works of art.

Lecturer: Quite hypnotized, if I may say so, by the subtlety of your dialectic, I see I must fall back upon the brutal argument of 'what we have, we hold'.

Oriental: I am glad you are now using an argument that is at any rate devoid of hypocrisy. Lord Elgin took the marbles, in spite of the denunciations of Lord Byron, and you side with the diplomat against the poet. Very well, then; but may I ask you this. Does this art imperialism, if you will allow me to call it so, conform to the ideas that you hold now in England about imperialism in general?

Lecturer: You are taking me somewhat out of my depth, I sadly fear. I am—please recall it—a museum official.

Oriental: Even as such, do you not see an inconsistency between your political attitude to India, let us say, or to Ceylon, or now to Ghana, and your attitude towards works of art of these and other countries—works which you possess thanks largely to your former imperial power? The inconsistency, that is, of restoring former colonial territories, while keeping the works of art you have removed from them?

Lecturer: No. I confess the thought has not occurred to me.

Oriental: But does this thought perhaps not strike the mind of the Asian or African who has won his independence? Or the minds of other peoples whose countries, until recently, were dominated by Europeans?

Lecturer: That may well be . . . Which European (as Asians never tire of reminding us) can hope to penetrate the oriental mind? But what bearing, may I ask, has all this on Greece, and on the marbles of the Parthenon that are now in the Museum?

Oriental: Simply, I imagine, that a European people will no less resent—will perhaps even more resent—your removal, in times of its own weakness and your strength, of any sacred work of art that was designed specifically for a particular building that is still standing and still cherished. No sophistry can disguise from anyone with a sense of what is just, and what is fitting, that there is only one place in the world where the sculptures that surround us now can stand with dignity and honour: I mean the Parthenon.

Lecturer: Good sir, you really must excuse me. The Elgin marbles now await your scrutiny, and my colleagues expect me in the basement for a restorative cup of admirable oriental tea.

The Twentieth Century, July 1957

'SEE YOU AT MABEL'S'

IT'S FIVE PAST THREE in the afternoon, the London pubs have closed, you're dying for a drink. What happens?

You head for 'the purlieus in the vicinity of Shaftesbury Avenue', as a judge called them recently, and visit Mabel's place, or one of the other drinking clubs. These resemble in no respect the port-and-leather palaces in Pall Mall, or the honest social and sporting clubs about the country. The drinking clubs —in the words of Mr Arthur Seldon,[1] 'essentially public houses

[1] In an article called 'Club against Pub' in the *Manchester Guardian* of 30th June, 1956, an excellent short guide to the legal intricacies.

outside the licensing laws'— are remarkable for their numbers and variety of atmosphere, and for the very fact that they exist at all. These clubs conform, more or less, to the letter of the laws that govern them; yet it is clear that Mabel's was not the kind of club imagined by the legislator, and that she and her resourceful colleagues conduct their clubs in ways quite different from those that were intended. In a nutshell, the paradox is this: though hundreds of these places are technically 'members' clubs', they belong in fact more absolutely to individual owners than any public house does to its licensee.

Here are the theory and practice of the matter. To open up a 'members' club' you gather together twenty-five ratepayers, as reputable as may be (really, they should approach you, not you them), and you apply to the chief inspector of police of your area for permission to open up. The inspector—or in fact his minions—look into you and the twenty-five and, if all is well, in three months' time or so a permit, costing five shillings, is granted by the Magistrates' Court. Meanwhile, you have rented premises which the sanitary inspector (and the police once more) must examine and approve. Then you stock up with booze, hang out a neon sign, and a new club has joined the 500 odd that are said to exist in the district round W1.

Somewhere or other, you should display (though you will probably put it away among the empties) the rules and regulations of the club. These, except for minor details, are standard, and can be bought in printed form at a stationer's. Chief among their clauses are:

> 'The Club's objects are the promotion of social, sporting and recreative intercourse' (this last phrase, if anyone reads it, is always good for a laugh).
>
> There will be a General Committee, appointed by a General Meeting, which will select a Wine Committee of three persons.
>
> 'The club is a mutual co-operative concern carried on by the members collectively, not for trading or profit.' The prices of the drinks will therefore be fixed in such a way as to 'prevent any loss or surplus accruing to the Club'.

In practice, things, to say the least, are otherwise. Who, for instance, has ever attended a General Meeting of a drinking club? Who, when buying his gin and tonic, has ever enquired if the price is such as will 'prevent any loss or surplus accruing to the club'? Though all the apparatus of committees and so forth may exist, these clubs are owned, conducted, bought and sold by individuals. If they were not, few would exist at all.

★

No club is typical, but this is the basic set-up. Mabel's place will be located either on a first floor or in a basement (ground floors are rare). Behind the bar will be Mabel herself, her friend, male or female (or *vice versa*, if Mabel is a man), and a barman or, less usually, a bar-woman (one cannot, in this context, say a 'barmaid'). In addition, there may be a 'host' (male—he probably gets free drinks, but no wages) who radiates bonhomie and stimulates the urge to spend, one or more 'hostesses' who do the same, a pianist (sometimes a small band), a cloakroom attendant and a doorman (often the same person, and potentially the chucker-out). In size, most clubs are small—generally one fair-sized room with 'offices' adjacent.

Even if there is no doorman, directly you go into Mabel's place one of these pairs of eyes will spot you (probably Mabel's own, which are at the sides and back of her head as well as the front). If you're an interloper, not a member, you'll be met with an icy 'Can I help you?' and hustled out. If a member, greetings will be general, and it is etiquette to bestow on Mabel's cheek a hearty, sexless kiss. Should a friend be with you, not a member, you'll be asked at once to 'sign your guest in' (both of you should sign the form)—an important ritual, though ninety-nine signatures in each hundred are totally illegible. Non-members may not drink till this is done, nor may they buy drinks: most clubs are strict about this (though there is nothing to prevent your pal handing you the money). If you want your friend to become a member, he fills in an application which must be 'posted in a conspicuous position in the Club Room for the space of forty-eight hours'. Subscriptions range from 10/6d up to two guineas, but are often waived in the case of persons who are thought likely to become 'good spenders'—though, according to the regulations, this shouldn't be, unless an 'honorary membership' (whatever that may mean) is granted. In many clubs, it is by no means automatic that the application of a newcomer—even if vouched for by a member—will be accepted until the proprietor has looked the candidate over on several visits. Sometimes a member deemed, for various reasons, undesirable, may get 'barred'; and since different people get 'barred' at different clubs, it can be a delicate matter, if you're taking a party out, to find a place where everyone is welcome.

In the more squalid joints, the prices of drinks are much the same as those of public houses; but in a place like Mabel's beers will be 2/-, and spirits 3/6d the nip. Credit, according to the regulations, 'is illegal', but is often given, since the illusion of getting drinks for free encourages further spending. By her native wit, discreet questioning and gossip, Mabel assesses the sum to which she thinks she can safely let you go before gentle, then sharper hints are dropped that a settlement would oblige. In spite of this, she is certainly often left with bad and quite unrecoverable debts. The belief is strong, among club *habitués*, that the 'bill', when finally presented, is always inflated beyond the sum actually drunk; but if this is so, one can only say that as Mabel in fact is lending you money without security, she's entitled to interest on it.

In a very few clubs, you can drink 'after hours'—that is, after 11 pm when all clubs should close. But most are seriously-conducted places, if only because they don't want trouble. Not being, like the pub, a 'public' house, the police, in theory, cannot go into a club without a warrant; but police officers have a way of going where they want to, and from time to time they pay the clubs a call. These officers grow less and less like their caricatures and are increasingly difficult to spot; though two indications of what they are—even if he is wearing a crew-cut and drain-pipe slacks, and she a clinging garment and a beaver stole—are that they will stare at you with a persistence found nowhere in Europe north of Spain, and that if you talk to them, however boring you may be they will listen with an endless

fund of patience. The legend is that, on the whole, 'the Law'
is not hostile to the clubs, if only because they provide splendid
founts of information, and are the places where the wanted
person of each category is most likely to be found.

★

The reader, if not a patron of these places, will now be asking
why hundreds of people go there every day. 'I can understand,'
he says, 'your wanting to drink between three and half-past-five.
But why, when the pubs open up again, do you prefer standing
tight-packed in a stuffy room paying 7/- for a double Scotch
you can get outside for half the price?'

One answer is that a lot of drinkers dislike public houses
very much. Speaking for myself, I am fond of clubs and 'caffs'
but loathe espressos and, with few exceptions, pubs. I think the
'friendly English inn' is a much over-rated thing. The word
'pub' conjures up for me no vision of a cheery mine host and
rollicking regulars. I see instead grim-faced citizens with their
hats on, swilling slowly gassy pints, flanked by tight-skinned
women sipping gin with a dreadful air of decorum, the pair
staring silently and censoriously at nothing. Even worse are
the ghastly saloon bar wits, belching with hard unfriendly
laughter, or public bar athletes getting in everyone's way with
that inane game called darts. The service is slow and slovenly
(will they *never* wipe the counter, as they do in every civilised
country, or, if they can't, manage at least not to put the packet
of fags you've bought in a puddle of ale?). The food (unless the
pub is Jewish) is a disgrace (withered pork pies and leaden
sausages are a luxury; the best you can usually hope for are
potato crisps, peanuts, aspirins and breath-pills), and you can't
get a coffee,[1] so that your wretched non-drinking companion

[1]*Later:* If the pub-owners had had the gumption to serve coffee
(on which the profit is proportionately greater than on liquor), as all
the Continental licenced cafés do, there might never have been the
spawning of the coffee bars and a further drain on the pubs' shrinking
clientele: especially dangerous in the long run to the publicans, as
the coffee bar public's mostly young. However: the notion of the English pub dolled up with Gaggias and Kent-grown 'tropical' plants is
even more horrible than the coffee bars themselves.

has to drench himself in fruit and vegetable juices. To add to
these delights they've now installed the telly; and if you ask
for a drink, they gaze at you as if you'd screamed in church.
They make you as drunk as they can as soon as they can, and
turn nasty when they succeed. In short, these places are like
branches of a bank that happens to sell liquor instead of
overdrafts: hideous, respectable and unwelcoming, with inconvenient opening hours.

A drinking club, by contrast, is a club: the clients are all
acquaintances, or soon get to be so, and if Mabel knows her
business behave themselves nicely, even when high. Mabel
and her like, although they're out to get your money, are hosts
in a way 'mine host' is not, and doesn't seem to want to be.
(Perhaps the fact that more and more licensees are merely
managers of the brewers who own the pub has a lot to do with
it.) Club owners are various in temperament, but it's in the
nature of their job that they must be patient, obliging, firm,
shrewd and tactful—all attractive qualities. As for the profit
they make, if you work out, even roughly, what their wages bill
must be, add rent in an expensive quarter and other likely
charges, it's clear it can't be terrific. But the charm of their
calling is the life: the constant exercise of social flair. In the
words of one of them (now retired), 'It's a perpetual party where
your friends pay for the liquor.' And it's a tribute to their
popularity that the club is always known not by its real name,
but by theirs: the 'Tar Lake' thus becomes 'Headley's', the
'Military Pickle' is known as 'Cuthbert's', and the 'Noon-day
Hour' is simply 'Mabel's place'.

*

The membership, though in some clubs it is mixed and varied
(they are the nicest), is often composed of those who have
common interests: professional, racial, or sexual. Yet even within these categories, it's striking how faithful the members are
to a particular club. In Brecht street, Soho, for instance, there
are three coloured clubs, but in one you will find sleek GIs, in

another rumbustious Africans, and voluble West Indians in the third—yet with little interchange of custom between the three. In clubs whose clienteles have no such apparent bond of minority sympathy, the membership of each seems even more watertight: you can drink a dozen times with Adam in one place, as many with Eve in another round the corner (or even in the same building), but never see Eve in Adam's club, or him in hers. Because of this, and because the decoration of each club is so individual and often peculiar, to visit several in a single evening is like seeing, in sequence, the scenes from entirely different plays.

Let's make a tour. At the 'Tar Lake' Headley, the Trinidadian proprietor, will greet you with melancholy charm. In his hey-day twenty years ago, Headley was an adagio dancer much sought after for afternoon parties in Mayfair. Now he is sad, wise and peaceful, though capable of shrill violence if offended. Immensely tolerant of amiable eccentricity (erotic dancing, uninvited musical turns, or impoverished pals who buy nothing all night and wheedle drinks from more prosperous customers by a lavish expenditure of winning smiles), he is strict about true breaches of nice conduct (shouting, swearing, even wearing a hat) and entirely fearless in correcting them. In the kitchen, behind his bar, is a sombre African who cooks meals till four in the morning[1] with a great air of disdain: the pair seem on the worst possible terms, but their destinies are linked by some mystery—probably financial—indissolubly together. The membership is kaleidoscopic: Siamese students in splendid sweaters who shake everybody's hand and speak not a word of English; young French boys and girls singing melancholy songs, in dim corners, to a guitar; vivid West Indians who jive white girls slowly round with disdainful masculine languor; women getting ready for duty on the streets ('No, I won't have another now, dear—I'm going "out"');

[1]*Later:* Slightly confusing, for I said earlier that the clubs (if 'legitimate') shut at 11 pm. The explanation is that some of them close (and ostentatiously lock up) the *bar* at 11, but remain (quite legally) open for food and 'softs' till daybreak.

odd couples of all sexes whose ambiguous glances recall the limerick line, 'Who does which, and with what, and to whom?' . . . What lures these disparate spirits into 'Headley's place'— whose decorations are drab in the extreme (crude murals, plastic palms, and furniture of the kitchen variety)? Undoubtedly, the atmosphere that Headley's magic presence somehow engenders: which puts everyone on their best behaviour and makes them eager to snatch small joys from the jealous evening, and spread what affability they can.[1]

The 'Military Pickle' is quite otherwise: most resplendent. The stair is carpeted, the cloakroom attendant calls you 'Sir', albeit with a leer, and the decorations are like those of the embassy of a nation about to go into voluntary liquidation: 'old master' paintings on flock wallpaper, Knole chairs, and a flower-decked grand piano. Cuthbert, its owner . . . but *is* he the owner, or is it that Indian restaurateur who slides in sideways, like a piece of purposeful driftwood, never buys anything, bullies Cuthbert in a soft, high-pitched voice, and takes his leave finally with an undisguised sneer at everyone? Cuthbert, one gathers, was a military man, complete with gin-drenched moustaches and an egg-bald crown; but in what regiment he served is never specified. He attributes to favoured members ranks of his own selection ('Good evening, Colonel,' to some youth of 23), and says things like, 'Parade dismissed, gentlemen,' at closing time. He has a huge and special glass ('my beaker') in which he pours all drinks that clients offer and, when cashing a cheque, produces a wad of notes as thick as *The Times* folded octavo, saying, 'I shouldn't have all this about me —the town's full of footpads and besides, I'm a bankrupt.' Who *are* his members—these dozens of men and women expensively dressed, with currency falling out of their ears and infinite leisure, who only rarely admit to an occupation? When

[1]*Later:* A drinking club *is* its owner. It is striking to notice how when he, or she, is momentarily absent for some reason, the whole 'temperature' of the place (and the consumption of liquor in it) sag. Which is why an owner can never really sell his club at its full value, since he can't sell himself with it; and a change of ownership may mean an almost total emigration of *habitués*.

Cuthbert finds out what your own 'line of country' is, he says you must meet old So-and-so (naming someone at the apex of your profession)—'a former messmate of mine'; and occasionally he does effect the introduction, though six months or more after he first mentioned it. His eyes are pale blue, almost as pale as the whites, his lips pink and rapacious, you mistrust him on sight . . . yet though you feel certain he's defrauding you, you never find out how. He has a flat above the club ('my orderly room') and invites chosen members up there after hours for 'a little kit inspection among ourselves'. He is unalterably affable, and in moments of confidence tells you, 'I'm a villain, yes, but such a nice one, as they go.'

And what of Mabel's place? Mabel's a character often met with in films and fiction, but oh! so rarely in reality: the platinum-tough girl with a heart of gold. Sharp, hard, ruthless and aggressive, she's generous, forgiving, considerate, and rather shy. Quite ignorant of the inner operations of the professional worlds of all her members, she can nevertheless assess, with uncanny accuracy, their intrinsic talents and current reputations. In appearance she's a *belle laide*, bulky and perpetually radiant. Her conversation's witty and salacious, her capacity for absorbing spirits without ill effect apparently limitless. She's always glad to see you ('Sweetie! Come and kiss mother! You're a cup of tea!'), and just as glad, when the time comes to tot the takings, to see you go. Her barman, Henri, who's French (though of convenient British nationality), must be the only man in the world who's never been seen to be rude; and when one reflects on how dreadfully silly and irritating barflies are, this grace of nature seems to raise Henri, in spite of his trade, to the heights of a sort of saintliness. But the greatest charmer of Mabel's place is the pianist, called Angelo, from Grenada. He breaks off his current tune to play each new arrival in with a theme-song he's chosen for them—either flattering, like *You Go to my Head*, or (if he thinks they can take it) one loaded with innuendo, as when he greets some notorious couple by *Mother Nature and Father Time*. Angelo sees everything, says nothing, and can produce at will an effortless, all-embracing smile which, if it doesn't come from the heart, always seems to do so.

Of course, the spell of the drinking club is partly morbid. To sit in Mabel's place, with the curtains drawn at 4 pm on a sunny afternoon, sipping expensive poison and gossiping one's life away, has the futile fascination of forbidden fruit: the heady intoxication of a bogus Baudelairian romantic evil. As the gins slip down your throat, and the dim electrics shine on the potted plants and on Mabel's lurid colour scheme of emerald green and gold, you feel like the fish in the tank above the cash-register —swimming aimlessly among artificial water-weeds, mindless in warm water. The pub, drear though it may be, is certainly more bracing—it offers none of the spurious comforts of this infantile hankering for the womb . . . And is it, you wonder, as night falls all too abruptly, because of war memories that club addicts are so fond of cellars? Is it that life underground is appropriate to the atom age?

★

In England, the war between Cavaliers and Roundheads is eternal. All English institutions reflect the compromise between the saints and sinners, between the Salvation Army and the Music Hall views of life. Our lunatic licensing laws are one of the crazy cease-fire lines drawn up between the contending parties, and the drinking clubs, a typical British absurdity, a truce agreement in the struggle. Mr Seldon estimates that clubs—'legitimate' social clubs as well as those purely for drinking—now account for one-eighth of the national drink bill and, in Wales and the Midlands, a figure as high as a quarter or even a third. Clearly the clubs, if ever challenged in strength, are vulnerable, and their status fragile; but it's probably because of the tacit agreement between the puritans and merrie Englanders not to disturb the balance of blackmail, that no one has yet gone gunning for them on a major scale.

Encounter, March 1957

FOUR YEARS have passed since I wrote this, and the guns are now being limbered into position: for at the time of writing there are parliamentary proposals to 'clean up the drinking clubs'. What this will no doubt mean is that the 'well-conducted' places for the rich will be allowed comfortably to continue, and the 'dens of iniquity' for the less rich forced to close: just as happened when the abolition of the 'bottle parties' made London night life available only to the socially restricted public of a score or so tolerated 'night-clubs'. Anyone else who wants to drink after 11 pm (and who, even if he has the money, doesn't want to 'dress' or doesn't care for the 'plushy'—the columnist's word catches them exactly—permitted night-spots) has the miserable alternative of pitifully squalid west end clip-joints or, if prepared to take a chance, of the innumerable nocturnal speakeasies that have sprouted in the drearier of the inner suburbs: places far more 'undesirable', and far more difficult to 'regulate', than the frank 'bottle parties' ever were. London must be the only capital city of the western world that rivals those of Marxist countries in its censorious disapproval of the noctambule. And England remains what it always has been: a playground for the monied, and a place where the un-rich must enjoy themselves at night illegally, or out of sight indoors.

HAMLET AND THE GHETTO

THE GIST of Mr ———'s[1] piece on *The Anglo-Jewish Writer* is, if I've correctly understood it, that 'the misfortune . . . is that Jewish writers are cutting themselves off from the best of their material' (that is, from Jewish themes), and that when they do *not*, they write 'about an East End Jewish world which no longer exists, presented in terms of a

[1] *Later:* I have omitted the name of the writer whose study I was criticising, since his essay may not be so well known to present readers as it was to those of *Encounter*—who could thus fairly judge between our points of view.

tradition which was built up and died in Eastern Europe.'
Mr ―― cites, as one of his two examples of this, the art of
Bernard Kops, and says that in Kops' case 'it is really a question
of blowing on the embers of a fire which went out with the death
of Israel Zangwill.' In choosing the work of Bernard Kops to
sustain his theorem, Mr ―― could not conceivably have
done so more ineptly.

The best-known play of Bernard Kops is *The Hamlet of
Stepney Green*. According to Mr ――'s notion this must,
then, be what one might call a 'ghetto' play: that is, one which
is about, and whose author is emotionally-intellectually
involved in, a dying life (that of Stepney Jewry), and which is
expressed in a dead tradition (that of Zangwill and of East
European Jewish writers). *The Hamlet of Stepney Green*
is exactly the contrary of all this.

The first clue is provided by its title. To think of Hamlet is
to think of many things; but among them, instantly, that he
was a man devoted to his people and its best traditions, but
hating everything they had both been twisted into, and desperately anxious himself to break out of—and, if he could find
the strength, transform—the whole situation. 'Denmark's a
prison'; and Elsinore is, in fact, Hamlet's ghetto, and he
loathed it.

The next clues are in the names of the three chief characters.
These are Sam, the father; David, his son; and Hava, David's
girl: that is to say, Samuel the prophet, David the warrior who
will be king, and Eve, the eternal recreative mother of the race.

From these clues alone one might expect to find (even before
one had read or seen the play) that it is to be profoundly respectful of Jewish life itself; hostile to everything that recalls its
imprisonment in the ghetto; that Sam will be the prophet in
this predicament—praising the true essential, castigating the
mis-shapen form; that David will break out of the ghetto walls
triumphantly; and that Hava will help him to re-create a new
life outside it in the larger world. And this is precisely what
will happen.

★

Let us examine the actions of each of these three characters, to see how they achieve their—and their author's—purposes. Sam, the father, it will be recalled, dies at the end of Act I, and reappears in Acts II and III as a very voluble ghost. In Act I, when he is still alive, but dying, we learn that he is profoundly dissatisfied with his life in Stepney Green. For instance:

> I've been poisoned by someone or something. What's the odds? By my life or my wife. But my wife was my life; so my life poisoned me, so my wife poisoned me.

He knows (as his author very well does) that Stepney Green is finished:

> Stepney Green is dead; Whitechapel is dead. What am I waiting for? Whatever became of Whitechapel? Teeming with people, so gay, so alive . . . where are they?

For his son David, whom he loves but doesn't yet fully understand, Sam is prepared to make sacrifices quite unusual for a poor Jewish merchant. David, he knows, wants to leave Wentworth street market and become a singer; and though anxious and disturbed about this, Sam can bring himself to say:

> Look, Davey, all right I'll help you; go and study music, learn all about notes.

And even:

> Or you can take a world trip before you begin.

And Sam's ultimate message to his son, before he dies, is:

> Time presses; they decide to make the most of a bad job. Don't settle for the second best like your mother and I did.

Now for David, the son. The first thing that strikes us about him is that, though still stuck as yet in the Stepney ghetto, his *language* is so different from his father's: not just the shift of speech of generations, but the whole mood and tone of each are strongly contrasted. Compare Sam and David in their first solo dialogue in Act I. Sam says:

> Na Davey, what can I say to you? All these years I wanted you to work in the market with me, then I told myself—'Don't worry, Sam, he's looking for something better'—well—what are you going to do?

And David answers:

> Why should I work when I've got my health and strength? The thought of having to spend the rest of my life looking at the heads of herrings and the heads of hungry people makes me sick.

We soon learn why David wants to be a pop singer, that 'he started going up West when he was 17', and that his most profound ambition is to reach out, as a musician, to the entire world.

> I want to make people happy—I'VE GOT TO MAKE THEM LISTEN.

Then Hava, the girl. Though still a teenager, she's already been to Israel. But:

> I couldn't seem to settle down. England's where I belong.

We hear from her own father (Mr Segal) that the pretext for her return to Stepney was her mother's death, and the duty of looking after her widower father. The real reason—immediately apparent to the audience or to the reader—is that she's come back to get David. And (jumping now to Act III) she says so herself specifically:

> Then I went to Israel to get away from you but when I found you weren't there I came back again.

*

The death of Sam, at the end of Act I, and his subsequent spectral return until almost the final curtain, are, of course, symbolical—a 'symbol' so evident, in fact, that the term is almost over-emphatic. Sam has died, and the old Stepney ghetto with him: his task in Acts II and III will be to warn and guide his son David so that, while denying nothing essential in himself, he breaks out of Stepney Green forever. Thus, in a dialogue with his son, the ghostly father apologises for having nagged him, while alive, to become a business-man ('God forbid. I must have been mad'). He encourages his son to make the break complete—even from the *thought* of the old life:

> Some people never leave home; even when they put a thousand miles between them and the street door; when you leave, really leave.

He tells his son how to keep the will to independence burning:

> Commit arson every day in your imagination, burn down the previous day's lies, have a little revolution now and again in your heart.

Samuel the prophet's final message to the young warrior David, his message to the audience—and, one cannot but feel, the author's own message to the Jewish people—is:

> Make the most of your life—because life is a holiday from the dark—make the most of the world—because it is YOUR WORLD.

Surrounding these three key characters are the Jewish comicals: the only ones remotely resembling (and oh! how little) those of Zangwill or of old East European memory. These relics the author mocks—but with an infinity of kindness and, essentially, tact. As he presents them to us, it's impossible not to like the poor old fossils still embedded there in Whitechapel: whence they, with it, will so shortly pass away. Even Sam's daughter (David's elder sister), we learn too, had already broken out before the play began: but at the cost of marrying a man who contrived to unite in himself the disadvantages of being a Gentile, *and* a Communist, *and* a Catholic, *and* a vegetarian, *and* an inhabitant of Leeds! Desperate 'integration,' on the poor girl's part, indeed: which the author satirises every bit as strongly as he does the 'integration' of the ghetto.

What is most amazing about this play still remains to be said: and that is, the profundity of love and respect for his people and for their ancient *permanent* traditions by which the author is enabled to praise all these things while being totally irreverent about all the distortions—both sterile and 'sympathetic'—that the ghetto period (now dead, thank God, forever) forced upon the Jewish people throughout the twilight centuries of their life in Europe. Thus, the passage at the end of Act II, Scene i, in which the mourners (so picturesquely grotesque but a moment or so before) pray in the Kaddish, with the ghost of Sam, whom they are mourning, joining in—invisible and inaudible to them—with a voice solemn from beyond the grave . . . is a most wonderful human, religious, and theatrical triumph. The next minute, or almost so, these same characters become once more the sagacious lunatics of wild, poetic farce, and the author is busy taking the mickey out of *that* archaic aspect of Jewish life.

The Hamlet of Stepney Green is a lament for the bewailing past; a respectful dirge for it, with a tear but with no regret; and a hymn of confident affirmation that young David and his Hava will go out into the *English* world, there to live out their lives as *English Jews*. Hamlet has become Fortinbras: and the ghost of the prophet can say to the prince his son, as the old king never could at Elsinore:

> Well, Davey, it's all over. Hamlet is dead and may flights of angels sing him down the stairs.

Encounter, May 1960

THE PIECE that comes now, about my scamper round Nigeria, was written there in Kano at the only hotel I've ever stayed in that turned out to be the 'dream hotel' which travel writers seem so often, and so happily, to discover on their professionally ecstatic journeys. This was the International: run—although most efficiently—by its extravagantly delightful staff as if everything they did for you was part of some vast and humorous theatrical performance. All their initiatives on their guests'

behalf were prefaced by an engaging, conspiratorial, 'Let me...'
As: 'Let me seek out the vendor, and say to him you need all
English-speaking newspaper.' Or: 'Let me introduce you to
your bedroom neighbour: elected Miss Kano, second prize, in
last evening's competition and celebration.' Or even (when I
ran a fever, which hotels don't like), 'Let me tell Thomas and
Sylvester to bring up some dishes privately for you here: I
shall silence personally the chief cook's objection.'

Faced with the crazy task of trying to convey the heady
aroma of a vast country—its heart-wrenching charm, and its
enormous exasperations—in one preposterous 'article', I knew
that if I didn't get it down somehow before I left Nigeria, I never
would be able to. So though playing truant as often as I dared
among the fascinations now to be described, I clocked in regularly at the International for the horrid struggle between the
dear reality of recollection, and the hateful one of words:
solicitously spurred on by Thomas and Sylvester ('Sir: I think
you require more letter-paper, also some fresh biro: let me . . .')
and I trying desperately not to step out on the balcony, suspended treacherously over Kano and its wonders, for more than
three-quarters of each working hour.

WELCOME, BEAUTY WALK

The Booma Boys

The Nigerian warriors came home from the Burma war filled
by the same impatience with the past that flung their English
comrades into Clement Attlee's grim embrace. Among them
was a residue of restless souls whose misconduct in Lagos won
them the name of 'Burma boys'. When the late 1940s raced into
Nigeria (as they never did to war-sodden, static, 'welfare'
England), this name became 'Booma,' and the 'boys' really
boys: for a new generation of good-bad lads sprung out of the
Lagos pavements who were too young to have fought overseas,

but old enough to demand that the future happen quickly now. Many of these vivid scamps, innocent as rogues under twenty-three can be, were suddenly gripped by a deep urge to know the world; and as swallows do, they took off from Africa for England with nothing but a compelling instinct as their baggage, stowing away, signing on and deserting, sometimes cajoling minimal fares from rightly reluctant families. Their landfall was in the big English dock cities, and they loped ashore blithely confident that the world loved them and owed them a treasure.

This was the first mass exploration in reverse: the encounter with Englishmen and women not as they appeared in Africa, but as they are. It lasted until the early 1950s by which time the Anglo-Booma boys had prospered, floundered, died or drifted home, and Nigerian emigration had become regulated, with motiveless journeys hindered by both governments. Properly so: for these English Nigerians were good citizens of neither country—only of a precarious realm of their own creation which had nevertheless the beauty that in spite of squalors, it was the only honestly integrated Afro-English society. It was because they had 'no reason' for coming to England that these wild ones had the best. Never again will young Nigerians know this shock of a first confrontation; nor will young Englishmen.

Into the London chapter of this community I happened a decade ago without conscious intention, and I cannot remember how: only that one summer day I knew no Nigerians, and a few months later, scores. From these exiles I heard constantly of Africa long before I went there, so that names of tribes, regions, cities and even streets grew familiar though unknown. One day in this novitiate, a Yoruba friend brought with him an Ijaw countryman who said (not exactly 'asked') he was looking for a place to stay, and how about if he stopped with me for a while? This was Hawton, who was brave, intelligent, generous, selfish, and slothful save in emergencies . . . the ideal temperament for a soldier and a leader, which he would have been if his manhood had come in other times than tired peace. With him as guide and guarantor, I learned the bush paths of

Afro-London, and how to address its denizens appropriately on strange occasions. After a year of staying for a while, Hawton 'cut out' from London and settled in Manchester, Moss Side: the most homogeneous and least unwelcoming African reservation in the Black Man's Grave. Two years ago now, pneumonia (which is for Africans what malaria was for us) drowned one of his lungs, and the other the next day; and life that he enjoyed so much, and scattered so much on his friends, abandoned him in thirty-six hours, surviving only in his infant Afro-Mancunian daughter.

Lagos Interiors

Lake Street, Lagos, was as Hawton had evoked it in his tales of waterfront scallywaggery—a comfortable slum behind the Marina, blocked from sight of the lagoon by modern offices. I passed several times before the house wondering how, or whether, to announce myself. I knew Hawton's mother lived there with his elder and younger brothers Easter-day and Eugene, but not if they knew of my existence or would welcome memories. Faltering along Broad Street, my doubts were resolved when with a great shout of 'Collins!' Jimoh erupted, a cherished old-timer of the London scene, the first of many I re-met in Lagos who belonged to the old boys' club of Tottenham Court Road before the deadline when the Paramount was closed down. Jimoh, who knew Hawton, made off to Lake Street to explain matters, and next day I found myself facing Hawton's mother: she uncomprehending and remote. It seemed I and my story had scant reality, did not connect up with the reluctantly believed and unproved fact of her son's death in that place 'England'. I told her what I could, which Jimoh 'translated'—that is, re-phrased in Afro-English, for he being a Yoruba and she an Ijaw, no intimate translation of my words was possible.

Later I met the brothers and a seaman cousin, and everything fell into focus—thanks greatly to this seaman relative. All I had told the family about my friend convinced them I knew Hawton well . . . and yet some token of physical reality was missing. Eyeing this mariner, I suddenly recalled that Hawton once brought home to Camden Town a relation from a ship who saw I was limping with a dislocated toe, asked leave to look at it, and had immediately (and without permission) seized it and set it straight: an incident I could scarcely have invented and he fail to remember. It was indeed the same man: incredulity vanished, and this cousin became the essential witness who had seen Hawton and me in London when he was still alive. Afterwards, by their unspoken wish, I had separate sessions with each brother. Easter-day is a good man carrying a sorrow: which and why? He had gone into the police force where Hawton's father had been a prominent and successful figure, had come unstuck, and the love-affair with a career—perilous for a young man—had turned sour on him. My guess is that Easter was born a trusting man, and that this instinct had been shocked and wounded . . . so that though he exudes confidence and strength, it is Samson's when his locks were shorn. He was deeply and patiently concerned about all the circumstances of Hawton's death—and obsessively so about his daughter. I was soon manœuvred into the role of emissary to the Lancastrian mother, to ask her if the child could be surrendered and adopted by its African relations. I asked Easter-day had he thought if the girl herself would like to be in Africa? An infant Mancunian suckled on telly, cold rain, and rock-salmon with soggy chips? And I warned him not to expect her to be grateful, or to be astonished if she hankered for England later on . . . Easter-day bowed his head to all this European sagacity, and asked me to write him when the child could come.

Eugene, the junior brother, is a Nigerian angry young man (non-literary): startlingly like Hawton physically, but with more practical energy and less glamour. Independence delights him, as it does everyone in the Federation; but the emerging political-social set-up makes no appeal. Again and again I heard this from the young: good work is scarce, all wages are too low: the drop in status from the few rich to the poor millions is catastrophic; and they are looking beyond the national revolution to the economic, and despise the new Nigerian bourgeoisie.

It is sad so late in the day—and after it has fulfilled its historic task so valiantly and done so much for one and all—to have to write yet again with disparagement about this persecuted class; but I must record that the Lagos bourgeoisie is quite sensationally unattractive. To begin with, because aggressively vulgar ostentation coupled with complacent ignorance of everything except export and import prices, is so uncharacteristically African: for though Africa has known brilliant traders always, commercial suburbanites are a horrid novelty. Worse still is that though technically a 'bourgeoisie' in the Marxist sense, this Lagos lot is culturally petty-bourgeois in the extreme: their social tone corresponding conveniently and disastrously to that of the outgoing managerial 'expatriates' (polite local term of hostility) whom they imitate in many ways while striving to eject these helpful aliens more rapidly ('Nigerianisation'). Of new-rich clubs in the federal capital, I append this last malicious vignette: of the sight of dozens of stout young men robed in shapeless curtain material, thickly bespectacled in little bonnets set at jaunty angles on fat heads, shouting at servants and laughing loud and heartlessly before rolling off too fast and noisily in tank-like cars: the international hall-mark of the philistine parvenu in every rich society, irrespective of its political belief. (Car owners of the world, unite: you have nothing to lose but your manners and someone else's life.) In spare, tense contrast was Eugene, his voice kind and furious, plagued visibly by a frustrated idealism and a dangerous generosity. What independent Nigeria offers to the youth it has excited, is bureaucratic posts which many will delight in; but Eugene and his sort peer over the heads massed in celebration, scanning Africa for a vision.

The night I left Lagos, he took me late over to the mainland to see Rose, Hawton's beloved sister he spoke of so often as if of a guardian angel. We reached the house after midnight, and Rose and her husband and two children were already sleeping. After a minute or two of knocking and of parleying with Eugene, the door was thrown open and there they all were: children tucked tidily away, wife and husband dressed and ready for conversation, all in one room: a deft illustration of three African graces—the faculty for instant, unconditional hospitality; the effortless cohesion of the family unit, the children always in evidence but never in the way; and the sublime ability to receive you wherever they are, simply, without any 'explanation' or apology. Rose as a young matron is superb: as a girl she must have been a startling beauty. She is also, as not so many African women are, engaging in her manner; for most of her sisters lean heavily on the stark fact of being female to amaze the male. (It is not surprising to find policewomen rampant in the largely non-Muslim south; bossiness from a static position of strength coming naturally.) Rose, once initial courtesies were cleared away, was concerned only, as her brothers were, with Hawton's child: she brushed aside politely any hint of legal obstacles, and told me to get things moving, please. I am struck by the paradox of this family's instinct to retrieve part of their flesh, and of their neglecting, for two years until my arrival, any practical measures to ensure this.

Boy Born to Riches

The Yoruba are the chief tribe of the Western Region, numbering millions, and they are incontestably one of those peoples born exceptionally gifted, like the Jews or Greeks. Their culture is as ancient as our own (I speak here of the English), their arts and social organisation complex and sophisticated, and their society traditionally urban: most of the big towns in Nigeria are theirs, and Ibadan, their present (though not historic) capital, is the third city of the continent. I think that to understand their culture one must realise that the Yoruba have known 'primitive', 'advanced', and 'decadent' periods long before Europeans made any contact with them. This fact reveals itself, in their company, by a characteristic blend of energy and nonchalance, of avid curiosity and languid self-assurance, of a passion for novelty coupled with an attitude of 'we've seen it all before'. Many of the Nigerians I knew in London had been Yoruba: and among them Afolabi of the

Ambrose Campbell band. Ambrose ('Bless you, my brother'), a man of generous temperament and of great authority among English as well as African musicians, led for many years the best Yoruba group in London, of which Alofabi was a drummer. The fame of these exiled artists travelled back to their native land through their recordings, and a few years ago they went home to perform on tour; but alas, in their country these prophets had little honour, and they came back disconsolate amid the alien London maize, leaving Afolabi behind in Ibadan.

He was out when I called, but burst in on my siesta at the Paradise Hotel with a cry from outside the door of, 'This rascal! I know he has come here to rob us;' and when he came in, 'Lord have mercy! You make me twenty years younger. Look! I have put on my European dress so as not to frighten you.' We filled in the gaps of several years, and I learned that Afolabi, though he does arrangements for younger musicians and sometimes sings on the radio or television, is no longer a full-time professional; but works in the Lottery department ('Loitering department') of the Treasury. How had this happened—to one who had sacrificed so much, as African musicians must in London where there is little understanding of their art? Afolabi told me he had stayed in Africa because 'they spoke to me of my old mother, whom I would never see again if I went back to England, but look! I have grown older and she is the same as ever!' I sensed a deeper reason—a pang of disappointment at the band's reception; and as I walked round Ibadan with Afolabi in the next days and nights, I felt the sorrow of his position. He is an artist in a country where artists now have no status: have lost the esteem of the old tribal society, and have not yet won respect (and decent incomes) in the new one: no longer bards, and not yet stars, they are simply entertainers underpaid by upstart café owners. But at this point one may pause to blush and ask—what have we Britons done for them? Nigeria is outstandingly rich in dancers and musicians, especially the majestic drummers whose subtlety and dynamism make Latin-American and even jazz performances seem monotonous and pallid. (I believe their technical 'secret' is that they can create melody at will, even as they make fantastic rhythm.) Except for incidental performances by visiting Nigerian troops at English military 'tattoos' (how truly a British way of presenting 'colonial' arts!), we have seen and heard nothing of these glories in the years when we held power in Nigeria. This is disgraceful: the more so when one remembers the immense success in Europe and America of the African artists brought over from (former) French Guinea by the initiative of a local impresario (who has since become a minister in the independent government). However, recalling that no major exhibition of Indian art took place in England until after independence, I predict a growing vogue for Nigerian dancers and musicians shortly after 1st October, 1960.

'Yes, indeed,' said Afolabi, 'they did not give me the correct name—"born to riches"—at my christening. Never mind—this is the City Hall: you wish to write your name on the roof?' We entered, escorted by a tropical copper, passed by a meeting of a sub-committee in session on the concert stage (whose members paused in their deliberations to exchange cordial greetings with Afolabi), and climbed up to the heights where the copper provided helpful chalks for our roof-top vandalism. The view was superb: Ibadan, like Rome and Kampala, is a hill city whose generous dimensions are due to its ancient urban status; and from any of its hilltops, splendid panoramas of card-house corrugated iron roofs rise and fall in groups of Chinese elegance. At night, from these summits, the town glitters like a nest of fireflies from electric flares and street vendors' oil lamps, car lights always at full blaze and, indeed, from fireflies in person. 'Lord have mercy,' cried Afolabi, as we returned from a late night visit to a Yoruba combo of drummer-singers, entirely traditional (yet as entirely contemporary) save for the accepted anachronism of the leader's electric guitar. (I beg some qualified person to explain why this instrument, in the past two decades, has become the queen-siren of pop music everywhere.) 'Lord have—take care, please, of that bullshit there!' He had seized my arm as I had almost trod, at the dark intersection of two highways, on a bowl of charms set out by someone to do something to somebody. The mystic silence of this encounter was shattered, round the next bend, by the mystic din of a band of hooded, gesticulating Engungun men accompanied by ambulating drummers and a throng of followers: 'masqueraders' they are frankly called these days, but were once apparently authentic spirits, and still may be such to some. Outside the hotel Afolabi told me, 'Well, I shall not walk home through all this magic,' and he borrowed some small change for a part share in a taxi.

Scholar, Priestess, and a Holy Man

Ten years ago Ulli Beier, a Berliner who completed his education in London, joined the University College of Ibadan as lecturer on phonetics, and then in the new department of extra-mural studies. Asked to unfold to Africans the splendours of European literature he soon found that, lacking points of reference and comparison with anything of their own, his words had little meaning to his students: whereat, with unacademic brain and imagination, he set about searching in the traditional arts of the Yoruba people to see if he could find any helpful analogies; and by a study of their songs and oral literature he found so incomparable a richness that very soon (as all—that is, few—good teachers do) he was learning from his pupils. He has since become joint founder and editor of *Black Orpheus*, the only literary-artistic revue yet to come out of Nigeria, and which embraces all African (and indeed Caribbean and US Negro) arts in general; and also of *Odu*, a journal specifically of Yoruba studies. The colonial, and then Western Regional governments, which provided publishing facilities without perhaps quite realising yet what they were publishing, passed, in their reactions to these periodicals, through the phases of indifference, alarm, and then, as their world-wide reputations became apparent, an attitude of possessive pride.

Ulli Beier and his wife Susanne Wenger entertained me for a day in Oshogbo, where they live in a 'Brazilian' house of fine proportions—so-called because this neo-baroque style was originally brought back to Africa from Latin-America by descendants of those sent there as slaves. I had ventured to 'date' this house at first sight of it as late 19th century, and was disconcerted to learn it was in fact mid-20th: so exactly have the Yoruba craftsmen conserved a rustic Latin elegance of building. I had met Susanne Wenger for an instant when she had shown in London the cloths she has designed and made in Oshogbo, using re-discovered techniques of dyeing and of printing that have been largely ousted by those of imported fabrics; and much more strangely, depicting in them emblematic scenes which reveal her deep knowledge of Yoruba pre-Muslim and pre-Christian religions. For though this may seem incredible, Susanne Wenger is not 'merely' a remarkable artist who has penetrated so far as any European probably can into some of the recesses of the Yoruba soul, but she is even accepted, I was told, by such Yoruba as still adhere to them, to be a priestess of their antique cults. She is a familiar of their holy men, and is admitted to participate in the mysteries of their most sacred surviving shrines.

I am sorry to record that my sojourn in Oshogbo consisted almost entirely in disputations with my hosts. The difficulty, of course, is that to assess the entire value of Susanne Wenger's work—and even that of the less hermetic activity of Ulli Beier—one would need to know as much of Yoruba culture as they do. It is also apparent that to have studied, lived with, and brought honour to ancient alien arts and cults—ignored by Europeans, and rejected or forgotten by so many of the modern Yoruba themselves—is a rare and brilliant feat. However: my own obsession (since one is oneself) happens to be to try, in so far as a writer can at all hope to do so, to stick to the lurching European ship and help it by self-awareness to find courses that may keep it off the reefs among fresh trade winds and new currents; and not to wave it a censorious farewell from the refuge of any enchanted isle. Susanne Wenger, if I understood her, thinks our continent is doomed, and that such real life as may survive can best be re-found in old religious wisdoms. Ulli Beier's position, I believe, is somewhat intermediary, since his encouragement of modern African arts is as active as are his investigations of the old ones. What at all events seems to me indisputable is that the instinct both he and his wife share to make us learn from Africa, and for heaven's sake stop 'teaching' it, is wholly right: for the almost total absence of curiosity about, and of respect for, African cultures (I mean as something immediately valuable, and not merely as supposedly dead material for curious examination) is the greatest and most obstinate European fault; and the vulgar contempt for its social, but non-mechanical, cultural achievements is a shallow betrayal of what, in European culture itself, has worth far above our practical schoolboy skill in gadgetry.

In the afternoon, Ulli Beier drove me to Ede nearby, where Susanne Wenger has decorated two Yoruba shrines with mural paintings. Of these I must say that while they seemed to me splendid both as works of art and in the tact with which the murals were married to the exterior shrine walls (of their religious iconography I cannot, of course, speak at all), they also seemed to me to make these shrines less shrines: to be, by their foreign exoticism, yet one more indication of the decay of this old faith. While these subversive thoughts were passing through my brain at Ede, the priest himself suddenly appeared: 'appeared' is the word; for at one moment he was not there and, at the next, he was: an old man of 'oriental' more than African physique, stepping towards us with a sort of dainty, enamelled simplicity, totally dignified and enfolded in a sly, cordial, distant courtesy. (Anything less like what might crudely be called a 'witch-doctor' it would be impossible to imagine.) There were bows, murmurings, and graceful genuflections; and from the priest emanated what I can only call a most apparent tenderness. He disappeared into his cavernous house, and returned bearing a gift of kola nuts. I immensely admired the dexterity with which Ulli Beier contrived (with only two hands) to take the proffered bowl, remove the nuts without dropping any, hold them securely, and yet then grasp, as is the custom, both the priest's hands in a gesture of gratitude and farewell. (And I also could not but wonder how the precursors of this holy man might possibly have greeted us in the days when their status could inspire in strangers other emotions besides respectful pity.)

To give myself a last word on all this: the day before my visit to Oshogbo, I had been present, in Ibadan, at the opening of an exhibition which Ulli Beier had organised of photographs and of carvings from adjacent Yoruba shrines. This was inaugurated by the Timi of Ede (for a highly-placed chief, a highbrow, who contributes learned studies to *Black Orpheus*) amid a gathering of Yoruba and European personalities and television cameras. As an exhibition it was wholly wonderful: the photographs, in particular, of priests, chiefs, children, and of domestic and ritual architecture, taken by Ulli Beier himself, were a revelation; and yet . . . In Europe, we have come to accept that exhibitions and museums of 'primitive' cultures rise from the very ruins of these old arts, and almost feed on the sad fact of their decay. Was this not happening here in Ibadan in an even more cruelly poignant manner? Where not far from this British Council building was still be to found the exhibition's just surviving raw material—the arts and people and the holy sites themselves?

High Drama in Old Calabar

I flew far east to Calabar partly because of its name, and partly because Mrs Elspeth Huxley told me to. In the salt water days before land and air transport, it was a chief port of the country; but now, being landlocked between the Cross river and the mountains of the Cameroons, it is in woeful decline. To the casual visitor it has the aspect of a township in the Somerset Maugham country: wide, turgid river overhung by authentic 'jungle', battered steam ferries amid photogenic clusters of Efik trading boats, 'torrential' rains, and a decayed architecture of immense tumble-down balconied and shuttered wooden palaces. Film companies should abandon Zanzibar immediately and cross the continent: they would find their sets and supers waiting for them.

I was driven from the airfield to a hotel which I must call

(it will soon be apparent why) the Star of Ind. This seemed ex-sumptuous and vaguely derelict; and oddly in the charge only of two grave Efik youths, one of them, he told me, called U C Ukpong: no owner, no manager and, still more bizarre, no manageress. Sprawled about in the most comfortable easy-chairs there were seven or eight decorative young Africans, relaxed but somehow seeming interlopers; and no other guest whatever. 'Thank God you have come,' U C Ukpong said fervently and mysteriously as he demonstrated the mosquito net.

I walked into the old town which totters steeply downhill to the river. From a passing truck a voice shouted, 'White man die here!' and I caught sight of the gesture of a finger drawn expressively across a throat. Disturbed, I entered the rococo Zorro Side Bar: three-quarters given over to palm-wine drinkers, with a little sector reserved for beer lovers, strangely enmeshed in wire net. As I cautiously ordered something, one of the picturesque youths from the hotel appeared. I was full of questions, and he readily sat down to solve these perplexities for me. The wire-netting was to protect the beer customers if the palm-wine addicts hurled any bottles. Did they do so often? No, but there were 'many ruffians' in the town. And he and his friends at the hotel? They were musicians of the Rogers Jumbo and his Top Bop orchestra (I am not inventing any of this except for the hotel's name), engaged to play at the weekly dance next evening. He himself was Charlie 'Parker' (rather confusingly, since he played drums) Jegbefume, his father had been a chief, he had 114 half-brothers (I thought he was kidding me, but I checked later and this is not impossible), and he had abandoned his studies in agricultural science to follow the call of jazz. The Rogers Jumbo group were wandering minstrels from various tribes and regions, who worked along the coast (in 'France'—i e, the Cameroons and Dahomey—as well as in Nigeria) wherever they could find engagements. And things at the hotel, I asked? Ah! Here was the scenario. The owner, an old Indian (rare in Calabar, where most Asians are Syrians), was lying ill and abandoned . . . ('Ill of what?' 'Ah . . .') at the

Star of Ind, what time his wife, a local Efik beauty, had made off to 'another house he has built for her' (it would seem imprudently) to join her stalwart Efik lover, who has told one and all that he is now owner of the hotel! From his sick-bed the Indian has riposted by warning the police his rival must be kept off the premises at all costs. And at the dance tomorrow night, Charlie 'Parker' foretells, the lover will appear in glory with the erring mistress.

Next night he indeed did: a sullen, peremptory Don Juan, who opened the ball with the handsome and equally command-ing wife. The Jumbo band played energetically, terrific in the rhythm section and in its vocalists, highly defective in the melo-dic brass—who played in tune all right, but in what seemed to me different tunes . . . but maybe my hearing was defective, because an untrained ear can mistake deliberate 'discordancies'. Visually, at all events, they were delightful: Rogers Jumbo himself with an Ellingtonian princely bounder's dominance of his excited public, the singers casual and intent, the drummers self-hypnotised, and pint-sized David 'Chico' Nwagu out in front of the band, neatly shaking his maraccas and tracing a deft pattern of infectious footsteps. The dancing, as African dancing is unfailingly, was a joy to see: the couples moving face to face not touching (yet so much seeming to), then each hiving off to perform little individual solo sequences, connected nevertheless with the counterpoint of their partner's equivalent embroideries: subtle and sensual without a blush—indeed sex, for Africans, after dancing, must be an anti-climax. I was forced by fatigue to leave reluctantly in the small hours, and found on my pillow a note (the first of several) from U C Ukpong. It was touching and futile—the story of his young life and hard times, and could I find him a job or, alternatively, give him a substantial sum to make his fortune with? It is impossible for a European to 'resent' or to feel condescending about such requests: for to U C Ukpong I was a multi-millionaire, and any European is known to be a dispenser of jobs and perquisites. I know no people like the Africans who have the gift of asking the most outrageous favours entirely without abasement, or apparent resentment if these are not forthcoming. (As Kenny Graham, who knows them as a jazz leader far better than I do, once so exactly said to me: 'They ask you for anything, but they never give you a hard-luck story.') Saddened and frustrated by the thought of U C Ukpong's hopes, I retired, but not to rest. For at first I was woken by a party of boozy fellow-countrymen (Scots, need I say) who shouted through the door that they had driven in from a distant oiling station to the dance, and wanted to drink my health; I declined, and they tried to climb in through the ventilators. The next disturbance was a really colossal row outside the hotel, as if of an uprising. I disentangled myself from the mosquito net and staggered anxiously to the windows, whence a seething mess of cars, bicycles, quarrelling customers and onlookers could be seen deployed. The cause of this (I learned next morning) was that towards 2 a m the Top Bop combo, having played for six hours non-stop, called for the habitual refreshments from the management. The owner's wife (or the usurping owner?) sent them four half-bottles of Krola (soft drink) for eight musicians. Rogers Jumbo, in the finest tradition of the recalcitrant jazz artist, had spurned this meagre offering, requesting something adequate, or else. When no more was forthcoming the band had downed instruments, at which the frustrated dancers demanded money back and, on refusal of this, had streamed angrily into the outer air amid the crash of breaking glass. But as those who have witnessed African public rows will know, there is usually a strong instinct to fight with verbal weapons and with a kind of non-lethal lurching, scrumming, and wild gesticulation, before any fatal issue is unfortunately joined. To look at, the scene seemed perilous; but no blood was shed, and when the customers' rights and energies were vindicated and appeased, the din suddenly subsided and their rage evaporated in the night.

I spent the next day with the musicians who were in some doubt whether a state of strike or of lock-out existed at the hotel, since the wife had arrived in the morning (without her lover) and had silently impounded all the instruments (which belonged to the hotel), leaving the critical matter of payment in suspense until the next day. Charlie 'Parker' had now adopted me as 'his' European: to whom, when they do this, Africans are solicitously protective, which one may attribute to interest or affection, as one pleases. We visited together the City Bar to see a performance by The Austin King Joe of Fedral, a magician colleague of his; but though arriving at the advertised time, and lingering for an hour after it, we saw no more than preliminaries by a boys' band of singers, all with little drums like tambourines. Charlie 'Parker'—I could see it coming— dreamed of visiting England: a Mecca I should have thought shop-soiled by now, but it would seem not to be so yet: for 'London-trained' is advertised as a recommendation for almost anything; and your own London address, so often earnestly requested, seems to be cherished like a talisman. As he laid bare his hopes, and told me the frustrations of an African jazz troubadour, his voice was soft, wily, insinuating and candid. He had about his whole person that particular grace and *chic* which is a gift to so many Africans from their gods—of movement, of gesture, and of dress (even when this is minimal; and what other people could ride their bicycles in the rain with mackintoshes intelligently worn back to front, or bear an umbrella hooked practically over one shoulder, or twine a piece of cloth round their middles and seem neat—and dressed!— without looking absurd—and, in fact, looking exactly right?); and elegant most of all by a quite indefinable attitude in human intercourse that one can only call, for want of an apter word, 'distinguished'. His favourite phrases were 'Exactly!' (agreement of spirit beyond reason), 'It matters not' (to brush any care in the world aside), and 'At all' (meaning something like, 'Think nothing of it'). He introduced his odd European friend easily into African interiors (and from his point of view, I reflected, how strange my own arrival in the midst of this little crisis must have seemed!) and though gentle to a degree, cracked down in sudden fury when, for instance, an inquisitive immigration official (so he said he was) accosted us in the street importunately. At the airport there was one of those farewells to which I had become accustomed—for over the joy of an

African greeting there soon hangs a sorrow at the thought of your departure: which, if it is not authentic, seems so much so that there is no difference.

A People and its Poet

Of the Eastern Region, the capital is Enugu: not an old city like Ibadan since the Ibo, chief tribe of the east, were a village people, and the town was at first a railhead for the nearby mines. But the setting, backing on mountains, is attractive, and for a new city it could not have found a better time to build itself. During the last decade, the 'modern' style—which seems custom-built for Africa—and the notion of generous town layout, have become a happy commonplace; and Enugu has profited by both.

Before I came there, I knew little of the Ibo and was told that they are, so to speak, the Lowland Scots of Nigeria—go-getters lacking graces, with a passion for commerce and for education. If this is as true as any racial cliché, one must surely allow that the Ibo virtues are vital ones for modern Africa: indeed, one may even have the impression that this people has been waiting for the late 20th century fully to deploy their inborn gifts. It is of course delightful to be received, as a visitor, by practised charmers; but no less so to find men who in practical affairs are brisk and accurate. Their hunger for knowledge is most evidently worthy, and one is much abashed to find one's hotel 'boy' studying shorthand or arithmetic when one summons him to wash some socks. (Bookshops in Enugu— as indeed throughout both the southern Regions—are as plenti-ful as sweetshops in England; and none I entered had nothing at all worth reading.) As for the love-affair with money, this has its vexatious aspects, certainly; since it would seem to be the custom to confront the luckless European with a demand not for two or three times what the thing or service may be worth (which would be fair enough), but (I do not exaggerate) for up to twelve times or more. This necessitates not Port Said haggling exactly, but perfecting a tactical technique whereby one manœuvres, if one can, one's rapacious adversary from a position of strength (in which Africans are not always, I think, at their best) into one somehow vulnerable. (How often, during such exercises, I recalled the explorers' tales of endless arguments over lengths of copper wire.) I do not know whether, in international as in petty local trade, it is African practice to propose to foreigners a starting price 1,200 per cent above what may ultimately be expected: if made to Europeans, such demands might be regarded as a partial restitution of percentages no less extortionate extracted by white men in the past; but if the custom should be general, I imagine it must cause to any prospective foreign buyers whose pasts are innocent, a good deal of bemused surprise. In small transactions, at any rate, the notion that if you offer a fair price you win and hold a customer, does not seem to have caught on at all. I would add to this that, in so far as I could see at second hand, though not so wildly exacting to one another, Africans, who are outstandingly humane and lavish in their human contacts, can also, in financial contexts, be ruthless and blatant exploiters of their fellows. I must also make haste to add that these tetchy generalisations by no means apply exclusively to the Ibo people.

Unburdened of this characteristic European (and tourist's) grouse, I turn sharp about to record that my first visit in Enugu was to an Ibo whom I admire extremely, and this is Chinua Achebe, whose book *Things Fall Apart* may be called, with no excessive praise at all, a classic; and I implore any reader who may not yet have the good fortune to know of it, most instantly to procure a copy (Heinemann, 1958). *Things Fall Apart* is the story of Okonkwo, a tragic village hero at the end of the last century, whose life is defeated by the weaknesses of his strength, and whose downfall is the symbol of the disruption of Ibo life when we Europeans first brought to it our blessings and our curses. To evoke tribal existence so that it seems at once life-loving and wanton, and to describe the white incursion without malice though with fitting irony, is an amazing feat for so young an author; all the more so when one reflects, almost with a start of disbelief, that the measured lyric prose is that of a writer for whom English is not the mother tongue.

In this journal some time ago (*Encounter*, October 1959), Mr Dan Jacobson, whose opinions I respect as greatly as I do his novels, suggested that writing by Africans in English is unlikely to be fruitful. I can hardly believe this, for the chief reason that while so many African tongues themselves are (I am told) entirely adequate vehicles for a writer, there also now seems to me to exist an 'African English' just as there does, for instance, an American or a Caribbean: each of these new English languages having been re-fashioned out of the old primal one by a local genius, and being in no sense whatever 'bad' or 'broken' tongues. African English is the fruit both, I imagine, of happy transpositions from indigenous languages and, even more, of a dexterous joy in verbal wit that no ear can possibly mistake: the old English tongue is taken, turned inside-out by lively and inventive brains, and magically re-formed: a process which our language, so flexible and hoveringly imprecise, most readily abets in the mouth of anyone who really loves to use it. I do not, of course, speak of African political-journalistic English, which is almost as dreadful as our own, nor of African 'Babuisms', nor even of the kind of oddity that so many admire (often with inner patronage) in the work of a 'natural' like Amos Tutuola; but of what is by now an entirely autonomous linguistic re-creation. One may also observe the sensational flowering of West African prose and poetry written in French, and perhaps be allowed to deduce that if so much has not yet been written so well in English, this may be due to the very different kinds of encouragement that French and English educators and 'authorities' have given, in their former African territories, to any literary endeavour. One will also see that in fact, whereas even five years ago very little had been published by English-speaking Africans, in the last few years (thanks, among other causes, to the germinal presence of Ulli Beier) a great deal by playwrights, novelists and poets very suddenly has: of which *Things Fall Apart* is one of the most striking instances. No one who has frequented Africans can have failed to notice their delight in verbal play, or to admire their Grecian skill at its performance. It is quite possible among them—and even on quite critical occasions—to score a resounding victory by apt speech alone (one reason for the civility of African disputes already noticed). It is true that this talent has sometimes the defect that an artful sophist can mask acceptably the superficiality of his ideas by deft verbal gambits; and one must also record an almost Krushchevian aptitude to settle any serious intellectual argument by using the sledge-hammer of some hoary proverb. Nevertheless, the true gift is there; and with no disprespect to any creation there may be in the African tongues themselves, I pray that writers in English—since they have so much to tell us of which we know less than nothing—may grow in strength and prosper: so that Orpheus be black, and not only called so by sympathetic Europeans; also revealing Africa to herself in ways only a writer can: for it is sad for a gifted nation to admire none but politicians and athletes, the only public heroes at the moment.

Rascal City by the Niger

This was how Toby, 'boy' (as a matter of fact, in this case he was one) at the hotel in Enugu, described the celebrated market town of Onitsha, when I told him I was going to drive there. Though large tracts of the old open-air market still survive, its centre is now a vast Italianate emporium packed sky-high with bewildering cascades of goods, mostly consumer and imported. Stumbling through avalanches of textiles and perfumery, beset by hordes of insistent siren salesmen, I suddenly came out on the Niger: a wonderful moment, for it looks so exactly what it is, one of the great rivers of the world; and while many lose their hearts to seas and mountains, I know no excitement like the first meeting with an illustrious river. A terrace of huge steps, which the waters mount and cover at the ending of the rains, falls in a wide arc down to the fast, wide, yellow-ochred stream, with craft and busy watermen abounding on it. In Onitsha, more than anywhere as yet, I was made conscious of how cos-mopolitan Nigeria is, since traders from all its tribes of thirty-six million peoples make their way there. The market seethes: and one senses its age even as one is struck by its modernity: in one of the new roofed stalls a galaxy of gleaming tools, in a plot outside, a lad with an alarming glare selling charms in his little area of magic. From a bookseller's mat I bought tales enthusiastically misprinted by local moralists intoxicated (as our own were after Caxton's day) by access to a press; and among them, *The World is Hard, Drunkards Believe Bar as Heaven* (both by S O Olisah), and *Young Harlots a Shame to a Country* by Miss Shalma (whom I strongly suspect to be a man). Quotes (all from *The World is Hard*):

> Wife argued before husband, 'I shall not part with you unless you renew my body as it was before.'
>
> He became poor because he could not manage his property. Secondly, he was confused by the attractive skin of his wife.
>
> The wife said, 'I don't care, you caused my breasts, which pointed as nails, to collapse.'

But in E Uba's novelette, *The Broken Heart*, is much Babu:

> After the refreshments had been taken, we repaired into his inner enclosure amidst series of kisses and compromising mutual irregular motions of the flesh and displays. It was all satisfaction.

On the journey back to Enugu, Andrew, the piratical driver in a Homburg, alarmed me by turning 180° to admire attentively any succulent young wayfarer (and aroused grudging admiration by the enterprise with which he turned the car I had hired into a district bus for such suppliants as could meet his price). The constant procession along the road verges in Africa is an everlasting pleasure; best enjoyed, of course, on foot, when one can sense more intimately a vivid instance among so many of that peculiar plasticity of African movement. The women with babes at their back and ant-loads on their heads (but nothing antlike in their motions), the men in robes, shorts, or next to nothing, the trick-cyclists with gowns billowing like butterflies, the republic of children (often carrying each other), and the auxiliary goats and laden donkeys, all weave and glide among themselves with the ease of swifts in flight, making patterns alternating endlessly as the birds do. The white man is greeted with 'Good morning' (irrespective of the hour of day) or, most attractively, 'Wel-come!' (If he stumbles, there are—even more pleasurably—immediate cries of 'Sorry!' from persons in no way responsible for his mishap.) The children—to whom it would seem we are at once figures of fun as well as of possible menace—cry out shrill choruses of 'white man' or 'European' in whatever is their language; and heal any vexation this might cause by waves or bold sallies to extend a confident or cautious hand. Of African children, it is hard to write with moderation: their charm is overwhelming, since they combine tremendous self-assurance and an air of 'You may be bigger, but look! I am I!' with almost histrionic deference when this is felt to be appropriate. Europeans are apt to attribute such African infant —and adult—graces to a gift of nature: well they may be, but so much hints at immense care in upbringing, mastered through centuries, and made of a sage blending of intemperate love and severe discipline. For example: Ulli Beier has told me that though African parents are most strict, no child must ever be punished privately; but hauled into the open where a throng of witnesses gathers instantly to whom the enraged parent must justify the punishment to come. An intercessor will appoint herself counsel for the defence, and the mother's wrath must be publicly agreed to be well-founded before she strikes the child in front of this communal jury; and if there is no such general agreement, it is not unknown for a parent deemed unjust to be forced to apologise to the child: a contrast, to say the least, with our own canings by appointment behind closed doors, and quite evidently a procedure of great psychological and social wisdom. Where polygamy exists (I quote Ulli Beier once more), a young mother will not approach her husband again until the child is weaned, so that all her emotive and even erotic love is centred on the infant: young Oedipus without a rival—or a complex. While this custom is not perhaps transferable to Europe, undoubtedly a great many ancient skills of African upbringing most profitably would be; and I long for the day when among the fatuous piles of books about Africa that explain nothing but their writers' pre- or misconceptions, there will appear just one well-informed study of African education in the home;

with a companion volume to explain to us how Africans contrive to respect their old men and women and find them honourable tasks without having, as we not occasionally do, to banish them into single rooms and public 'homes.'

Back at Enugu, I was changing for supper when through the window came strains absolutely unmistakable: those of Victor Silvester and his saccharine strict-tempo dance music. When listening, in England, with fascinated horror to his radio programmes, I had always found it hard to believe that the endless fund of letters from his fans in Africa, quoted and mispronounced so confidently between one-steps and cha-cha-cha, could ever really have been penned by so many distant Nigerian lovers of the English ballroom style. Throwing open my windows, I could doubt no longer. For there, on the concrete open-air dance floor of the hotel, an exclusively male class of Silvester addicts was in session: some sailing round in pairs, some moving with solo preoccupation holding an instruction sheet, others being admonished and encouraged by a plump instructor. They performed these ghastly gyrations, I must say, very prettily indeed; and as for their invisible mentor, I must allow his was the only English music of any kind I heard extensively in Africa. And yet I shuddered: will the day come, I wondered, when Africans in white tie and tails, and with numerical placards plastered on their backs, will twirl dark belles in leg-revealing tulle and flounces around huge palais, as may be seen in English temples of the Silvesterian art—occasions which resemble a vast terpsichorian congress of head-waiters and female hairdressers? Will this be the new English cultural penetration to carry on, in even more insidious form, the ground-work of the missionaries and of the British Council? I fear so; for Toby, who now appeared, said admiringly, 'Just like we saw it in the film! And to think that my grandmother danced like this!' Whereat the little monster sketched a grotesque parody of an African dance (which is, with Indian, the finest in the world): I had to remember his long hours bent over his shorthand manuals to forgive him.

Soon Gabriel Okara arrived, the Ijaw poet, and at dinner I

asked him much about the strange delta country that he and Hawton come from, where the great Niger splits and spills into a thousand creeks and estuaries as it soaks itself finally into the sea: a Jeremy Fisher land of dreamy birth-streams that I long to visit—and indeed, the Ijaw are believed to be the oldest inhabitants of Nigeria, driven among their islets and lagoons when peoples like the Yoruba and Ibo came down from the east and north. Britons in Africa love to 'pick' tribes, as they might football teams, and constitute themselves their supporters; and if I am to do this too, I renounce tribes more strikingly alluring and elect the Ijaw, moving among their salt and fresh water swamps in canoes and launches (and even, as I imagine them; at times semi-submerged—though Gabriel Okara deprecated this fantasy). We went together afterwards to a boxing-match of hammer-and-tongs ferocity, where I was as much struck by the referees (changing at each bout) as by the dynamic pugilists. Their skill, patience, fairness, and ultimate authority over the boxers and the at times frenzied audience, were absolute: watching them, who could doubt for a moment that Africans know how to rule themselves? When a notable local champion, Francis Ibe, made, amid shouts of rapture, his triumphal entry, I found I was surrounded by a wild nest of his juvenile supporters: one of whom, trembling with joy and admiration, wore on his head a cap bearing on its front the new Nigerian flag and the magic date in October, and at the back the date of independence once again with, underneath it, the words BEAUTY WALK.

In Quest of the Fulani

From the east I flew up to the largest and largely Muslim Northern Region whose chief city (though not its capital) is Kano, well known now to travellers as an international air junction. Kano is four towns, really: the old city, still enclosed by twelve miles of crumbling walls; a squalid but vivacious 'township' built a mile away for the exiled immigrants from the south-east and west; the (former) European 'reservation' (the word makes one think of the Red Indians); and a new light industrial city—which, it is not difficult to predict, will soon become the real Kano as the old city declines into a sort of decorative and derelict Soho or collegiate Oxford. Linking all these are vast avenues leading in the wrong directions, so that the contrast of extreme modernity and of deliberately preserved antiquity recalls that of the ancient cities, with their new French annexes, in Morocco. It would seem that the European is fated to fall heavily for the glamour of Islamic culture, or else to be repelled by its hermetic timelessness. I must confess to belonging to the uncomprehending party, though the visual attraction of an old Muslim city has, of course, an immediate four-star Michelin appeal.

Kano City, seen from the air or on Cinerama, looks terrific; close to, architecturally, it is something of a disappointment—a red mud town, to be quite frank. But this impression may soon change again: for the size and homogeneity of the orange and cream buildings are impressive, and the new mosque, which one may at first view condescendingly with superior memories of old Islamic glories, does gradually win you over: its size and scale and siting in a huge open space are so very right, and its green dome and twin white minarets look sensational from anywhere, with vultures, so unsavoury from near to, wheeling like sail-planes far above it in the blue. But it is really the perpetual spectacle of the inhabitants that seduces you, if you're going to be seduced at all. These are the Hausa, the great tribe of the north, tall, tough, and at first approach seeming haughty—a notion due, I believe, more to their flowing robes and stately mien than to any undue severity of nature. They are great traders, as the sight of them sitting protectively on chests of bullion on a bank's mosaic floor, or their cordial man-handling of you if you venture inside their markets, will bear witness. The rich, who till recently owned camels, now chiefly own U S cars: thus switching, in a decade or so, from the most ancient and disagreeable form of transport known to man, to the most disagreeable and contemporary. There is also a great vogue for luxury bicycles, shining like those of circus artists: a Pepsicola vendor told me, with no modest pride, that his tall, glimmering machine cost him £40. When not working (which seems fairly often), the Hausa drape themselves in comely groups and postures upon mats. (Africans sit on their spines, not on their buttocks, and use their bottoms as a cushion.) There are also the poor, hordes of them, toiling desperately like . . . like themselves; and of lepers, and the deformed, and the blind led by boys with bowls, there is a terrible profusion. I contrived to sleep in the old city (all the hotels are in the new towns) to see what the interiors of the red mud warren might be like. You enter the 'compound' wall through a porch whose inner door is hidden from the outer one, are leisurely examined by a guardian armed with a torch, and make your way through an intricacy of starlit courts into a womb-like maze of small roofed halls from which rooms may be entered through low corrugated iron doors covered with hanging curtains. The inner room itself has uncovered mud walls (very hard), a minute Lady of Shalott casement window, mats or linoleum on the earthen floor, and the nocturnal couch is of course the daily divan: nothing is more than a foot high, and you must recall from childhood how to live close to the ground. Rain plopped gently through the mud and lath ceiling of the one I sampled, and the illumination was by oil; but this may not be typical. It seems very cosy, agreeably simple, and slightly claustrophobic.

I must now reveal that my chief purpose in coming north was to visit, if possible, the Fulani. This is a tribe by which one can, if not careful, become obsessed much as many Europeans in East Africa are by the Masai. The Fulani have the peculiarities that they are the only tribe which entered Nigeria from the west (although they probably came originally, like everyone else, from the distant east); that they are honey-skinned, very tall indeed, and somewhat 'Roman' in their countenance; and that a century and a half ago, under Shehu Usman Dan Fodio (1754-1817), they suddenly erupted in a Jihad, conquered almost everybody, and then withdrew abruptly to the wilds and obscurity again—leaving their descendants as dynastic rulers of a great many northern tribes. Being cattle-breeders, and wanting little modern society has to offer, they do not come much even into small and distant towns: which means that anyone inquisitive about them must leave his base and go and look for them.

I accordingly flew 450 miles north-west to Sokoto, where Dan Fodio himself lies buried in a tomb still the object of pious pilgrimage; for though this is a Hausa city, I was told that the Fulani might be found nearby. Sokoto is called disparagingly, by those who do not like such places, a 'bush town': which does mean, for the visitor, that he must rough it just a bit. A touristic digression now on African hotels. There are four types: anonymous international luxury in a few of the larger cities; more modest but attractive and substantial places, mostly frequented by Africans (and strongly recommended); ultra-minimal establishments as in Sokoto; and then, in most towns, what is called the Catering Rest House (CRH), intended chiefly for government officials (of all races, but in fact still chiefly used by Europeans), where any seemly traveller may also stay. It was sheer pig-headedness on my part, in the interests of culling 'authentic' experience, not to lodge, in Sokoto, at the CRH there: since the African inn whereat I floundered was in any case located not among Hausa (let alone Fulani), but in a southerners' annexe-township comparable to that at Kano. The disadvantages of such a choice were the lack of filtered water (or indeed water of any kind, when the yellow Sokoto river failed, as it so often did, to pour from the outside taps); the absence of European food—and try hard as I have for years, the only African thing I cannot love is what comes out of the kitchens—so that I found myself eating meals of *bouill-abaisse* and Edinburgh shortbread out of tins; and the rich profusion of insect life—those crazed liberty-takers simply haven't learned yet that man is master of creation; and I believe that, for a European, getting used to Africa is largely a matter of becoming reconciled to an autonomous insect world.

Though Kano market has been famous since the Middle Ages ('Morocco' leather really came from there by 1,000-camel convoys over the Sahara), I much prefer the market of Sokoto:

Kano's is cramped and stuffy, but in Sokoto it extends under trees over a vast irregular field with camels, donkeys, and horses with silver saddles resting in a parking lot nearby. The proportion of local (i e, non-European) goods on sale is also higher: varieties of animals and their skins, and of fruits and vegetables and spices displayed in jewelled assortments on the ground. The movement is restless and continual, and you are soon sucked into it: people assemble, confront one another standing or squatting down, and then drift away, re-grouping again, yet all part of one whole. There are musicians who sing accompanied by melodies beaten on large steel rings, snake-charmers (who also sing, and who had a trick I didn't like of hurling specimens abruptly among the onlookers), dervishes (is that the word? —amiable, menacing, half-naked leaping men), soothsayers and (I believe) prophets, and on the special market day (Friday, also the Muslim sabbath) there was a girl who pranced naked, which none took any notice of save for a dozen children and an expatriate. You yourself—whether you like this sort of situation or not—are one of the accessory attractions: I saw no other European in the market on any day I went there.

This can be something of a strain: even more so in the new 'exiles' section of the town than among the indifferent Hausa. The state of affairs, I think, is this. An immigrant southerner—Ibo, or Yoruba, or whoever he may be—comes north not because he wants to, but in hopes of making, by his skill and enterprise, a modest pile with which to return and set himself up at home. Thus the rapacity, already noted in the south, quadruples (so far as the white visitor is concerned) in the alien north. With this goes a restless curiosity about you. Africans (to generalise once more) are, I would say, inquisitive but not nosey; and one must remember, if one finds this at all trying, that the cult of 'minding one's own business' is English more than typically European (let alone Anglo-Saxon); also that to know who the stranger is, and what his business, was, until very recently, a vital matter in daily tribal life. As well as this, the 'modernised' southerner has, most naturally, an insatiable desire to find out from a European, if he can, about how the whole white 'thing' works. All this leads, among the less naturally discreet, to importunities—which a white electing to stay solo among Africans quite legitimately invites; and into my room at the Charity Hotel there would come at all hours visitors who would seat themselves uninvited, and put me through an inexorable third degree. It was maddening at times, but very rarely irritating: for to exasperate without actually arousing rage is yet another African achievement— probably because it is all done so very frankly. What one must try to keep in mind, I believe, is that if one admires any quality a people has, one must accept any defect that is its natural companion: one cannot just pick and choose. Thus Africans, divinely unselfconscious, can be inconsiderate to a degree; generously affectionate, they can also be oppressively possessive.

Days passed at Sokoto (I was marooned there for a week by the Mondays-only aircraft), and I had still seen no Fulani. To my dismay, I found there were no taxis to be hired (according to the southerners, because the residents fear that their women would be kidnapped; much more probably, because anyone who needed a car there, had one). Through Mallam Musa, my most promising Hausa contact, I had been negotiating for a private hire, but we were still playing cat-mouse-cat over prices (which had a way of attracting, once agreed on, supplementaries: 'And also the needed shillings for the petrol, so my friend says,' etc, etc). Hearing from rival sources (unbeknown to Musa) that the Fulani might appear at the village of Shuni, eight miles distant, on its Wednesday market day, and when a shattering dawn thunderstorm that morning had rinsed out the torrid air, I set off on foot for Shuni. The walk there was a delight: the fresh sky limpid, a breeze, and splendid vistas of the gently rising landscape. (My chief memory of Sokoto is the glory of its pearly dawns and evenings that redeemed the sticky sweltering in between: all life in Africa is made of moments of pure wonder soaring from tracts of trial and fatigue.) I overshot Shuni, which one reaches up an unsigned track; and when I made it, found it to be a walled village hidden in a glade. I had hardly entered its gates when a man of substance spotted me who, rising swiftly from the shades, beckoned me commandingly to follow him. He led me to a fortress-like dwelling into which he disappeared, first parking me in a lofty entrance hall among suppliants and pairs of sandals. I realised I was to be presented to the Ardo, or chieftain, whose abode this was. After a fitting pause, and preceded by an inaudible fanfare, the Ardo made, across the courtyard from his inner dwelling, an Old Vic entrance, flanked by six counsellors or so, and strode slowly until he towered before me (the ground was sloping) with an interrogative and red-toothed scowl. With a clumsy European bow, I said:

> *MacI:* Worthy Ardo, I am a traveller
> Who to famed Shuni's mart has come,
>   seeking
> The wild Fulani.
> *Ardo:*   And where is your cook?

This disconcerted me, for I had none: nor car, nor any companion; indeed nothing but myself and a white plastic bag containing a raincoat, spare underclothes, and miscellaneous pills. This modest accoutrement seemed not to please the Ardo; who told me, nevertheless, that the Fulani might be expected at some time between dusk and midnight (it was now midday). With this he called on two hefty minions, and signalled to them to bear me off. Our destination turned out to be a circular thatched hut, and my intended fate to sit there for six hours eating spiced rice the Ardo had kindly ordered for me; but I was dying for a drink, and implored them to let me buy some Pepsi. Rashly—being used to finding the dreadful stuff on sale everywhere even when little else was—I had not foreseen that only well water would be available. To drink or not to drink? Five years ago, on a journey to East Africa, though strictly observing every medical admonishment, I had returned home nearly to die after months in a tropical hospital: so what now the greater risk? But even so, the far call of the white witch-doctors was too powerful; and I bade them a brisk adieu and started tramping back to Sokoto. By now, of course, the refreshment of the storm had vanished, and I tottered on like a character of PC Wren's. Three miles from a Cola bottle, a huge limousine drew up and I found myself exchanging small-talk through parched lips with an affable minister of education, Northern Region; who told me, with impeccable lack of accent, of his pleasurable sojourns in 'the UK', and that himself several times a pilgrim (but by air surely?) to Mecca, he appreciated the English passion for 'a trek'.

Two more days went by, and when a treaty with Mallam Musa for a car had at last been initialled, signed, and even ratified, we set out further afield for Wamakko. This expedition seemed more promising, for we soon left the roads and bumped and scuttled over tracks, rivulets and, I regret to say, local crops. At Wamakko, the same ceremony with its Ardo was enacted; but he seemed a kindlier man (or was it the reassuring presence of my escort?), and he had a wooden throne brought out for me—which I insisted (though I fear violating protocol) that he sit upon himself: anyway, he fitted it, and it him, superbly. He heard us out, and Musa encouragingly whispered that our visit and our purpose pleased him. A guide was appointed, and we departed again over fields (and more crops) to a distant village near which the Fulani and their cattle were encamped. I am most glad to say our incursion among them was an entire success: marred only, from my own point of view, by the prompt disappearance of the Fulani women, of whose striking beauty I had heard so much. But the headman (not chief, for the Fulani—like the Ibo, and unlike the Hausa or the Yoruba—are elective democrats) did us proud: gazing down on me benevolently (I am over six feet), he seemed overjoyed to do the honours. He showed us round the encampment, followed by its male inhabitants, and I was presented to the cherished cattle. Cordial messages, twice interpreted by Musa and then the guide, passed to and fro, and there were constant halts for yells of delighted laughter, which I believe and hope were not entirely due to my behaviour or appearance. The headman was most impressed to learn that the gesture of removing my cap in his presence betokened respect: a custom that must indeed seem odd to a people whose own heads are swathed in decorative cloths, the whole sometimes encased in an enormous bell-like covering of heat-protecting straw. When we came back to the car, I asked if there might be any sick among his followers to whom I would be allowed to make an offering. Two ancient, stalwart invalids were instantly brought forward who accepted their gifts with gestures and glances that seemed (can one ever tell?) unaffectedly and genuinely grateful. I shall never, at all events, be able to forget the gaze these old men gave me as they clasped my arms chattering, seeming to look right across hundreds of miles and centuries at a fellow creature.

Beauty Walk, Farewell

Even from these cursory notes of a random excursion, it will be clear that in Nigeria what is taking place is not just a 'national' revolution of one people in our historic European sense but, together with this, a political junction of diverse races in the short space of a half century. We Britons, who took ages to achieve this among a mere half dozen peoples, should therefore, I think, speak circumspectly: avoiding, while remaining lucid, that hateful kind of glee with which publicists have pounced (to its entire indifference) on Ghana, while feeling no obligation, as protectors of a Commonwealth conception, to examine as censoriously whatever may have taken place in Pakistan, or England, or elsewhere. And if Nigerian politicians and journalists say odd things, we should remember our own say odder, and that the dignity of a people is never to be assessed by the provincialisms of its public notion of itself; but by its faculty for personal self-criticism, at which Africans —sensitive understandably in the public sector—have well-developed gifts; and mostly, of course, by this people's deeds. Thus we should not expect from Africans any 'gratitude' what-ever: they see no reason at all for this, deeming our profit from the encounter of our two nations vastly to exceed their own; and being above all (to a degree few Europeans seem to have discovered or imagined) indifferent to us—far, far less preoccupied by our thoughts and customs (save for those that are manifestly practical) than we, who have been so greatly obsessed by theirs. It is their friendship that we should now rather hope to win: which I believe will be given readily enough if we try to help where needed—not at all forgetting our legitimate advantage—and above all, do not meddle. African heroes henceforward will be Africans of the present and the re-discovered past; and it is in Europe that the monuments to Lugard (and to Sir James Robertson, and perhaps to Harold Laski) should be erected—with possibly a *denkmal* somewhere for Adolf Hitler, since the war accelerated sharply the time-table of change; and in Asia, fitting tablets to the real fathers of independence everywhere from British colonial rule— Ghandi and Nehru, and Jinnah and S C Bose. And I think most of all we must realise that, in 1960, all Nigerians are preoccupied by social and political alterations in their lives of a swift intensity we can scarcely understand from any similar experience; and that this leaves them with little time or inclination to think up points for cordial abstract chats.

Contradicting my own precepts, I present two fragments of unsolicited advice; but as these are commercial, not political, they may perhaps be acceptable to any roving African eye. Films: when will these be made by Africans for Africa (and elsewhere)? Everything is there ready to hand. The cinema diet at present is Indian and tattered transatlantic: a minimal investment (of money though not, it would be hoped, of talent) could surely yield huge dividends of cash and reputation. Tourism: except in Enugu (American students), I met no fellow tourists whatever in six weeks, ten cities, and 4,000 miles. Yet most aircraft and Kiplingesque trains I travelled in were half empty (in the trains, above third class), and so were all but a very few entirely adequate hotels. Facilities exist, and the attractions—despite a stiff initial air fare or sea passage—are varied and prodigious. Once again: would an initial investment not quickly multiply?

To the rag-bag of reasons why Africa exerts—when it does— so deep a fascination on the European mind and heart (additionally, that is, to our hope of making money there), I now offer up my contribution. Africa is Eden: loved for what is lost, hated because we have lost it: longed for by distant recollection, despised because by ourselves rejected. Out of the Garden, its last inhabitants now make ready themselves to come forth forever. May they carry into the world a closer memory and warmer gratitude than ours.

Envoi

I end by quoting one of the many farewell letters I was handed by friends made so quickly in places that I came to knowing no one.

I hope you will not be so much irritated for informing you that I shall be proceeding to Lagos unfailingly tomorrow.

Because yesterday I was phone that my Mom is seriously ill and I am sure I shall be back recently.

I thank you very sincerely for the hospitality you have been rendering to me.

May the almighty God be with you surely he will assist you in all your deliberations and undertakings.

May the almighty be with us till we meet again with the greatest joy and happiest amen.

Encounter, October 1960

It was Henri Thomas, who knows and loves London as only French intellectuals do, who asked me to write this recollection of Alice Fleming. I did so, he splendidly translated it, and it was printed: whereupon I lost my copy of the original English text and, on appealing to Henri Thomas (by now improbably transplanted to Waltham, Massachusetts), he wrote back that his copy 'is in a wooden box in Cargese, Corsica,' and that he could not extract it from its island prison for me 'without asking an old woman there to open the box, which would be disastrous.' I have therefore had the bizarre experience of translating myself from his translation.

AUNT TRIX

MY AUNT TRIX, like St Francis, spoke to the birds. I have seen her, at the Edinburgh zoo, addressing cynical macaws who strolled courteously along their perches to listen to her. Herself like some rare bird, with her large, prominent eyes, her sharp nose scenting the air, and her fingers clutching it like restless talons, she spoke to them in high, piercing, affable, pedantic tones until a crowd of curious Scots gathered round her, keeping far enough off to show their superior disdain for an eccentric, but sufficiently near to observe if the birds would bite her when she popped chocolates through the bars into their huge, slow, lazy beaks. When birds and Scots were all assembled in sufficient numbers on either side of the metal barrier, aunt Trix would turn to tell their human brethren what the birds were thinking, as if she were the interpreter between two portions of the animal kingdom. At this point, the more prudent citizens of Edinburgh would steal off in some alarm: but others remained, glued to the spot by my aunt's shining eye as was the reluctant wedding-guest by the piercing gaze of the Ancient Mariner. After one of these performances, I said to my aunt Trix, 'If you'd lived two hundred years ago, they would have burned you as a witch.' She eyed me with a gay and guileful smile and said, 'I know they would have done, my dear.'

When she was still a young woman, my aunt Trix wrote a novel[1] about Anglo-Indian life in Simla—that Versailles of imperial British splendour set in the odorous freshness of the Himalayas. In this book there are two subsidiary characters, called Lilian Myles ('a dark-haired woman with pretty eyes, and

[1] *Later: A Pinchbeck Goddess* by Mrs J M Fleming. Heinemann. 1897.

a suggestion of picturesqueness held in check by severely conventional garments'), and her husband Gilbert ('he had a good face of the plain, straightforward type, and the brown hair was beginning to recede from his square forehead') who bullies and punishes his young wife—too much addicted, for his liking, to the honest worldliness of Simla—by refusing to speak to her for days. Thus:

'Good-night, Gilbert. Oh, do speak to me!' she added, after a moment of absolute silence; 'do, dear!' and she laid a light kiss on his forehead.

'Pouf!' he said, grimacing.

She went quickly to her room, and began to undress, humming a tune the while; but the little show of bravado soon ended in helpless tears.

Was this, I wondered, a faithful portrait of the earlier years of aunt Trix and of her husband, uncle Jack, who now sat face to face with her, day after day, at the breakfast table of their austere Victorian mansion in Edinburgh? If so, what a lesson for tyrannical young husbands, showing them that time, in a marriage, gives to the woman, when both grow old, a terrible vitality! Uncle Jack seemed the perfect caricature of the Anglo-Indian colonel he had been: with his lean, bony body, his pair of 'frantic moustaches' (as Colonel Lawrence once unkindly described those of Marshall Foch), and with his total appearance —now that he was bereft of the protective support of uniform and regiment—of pathetic vulnerability. He was that much mocked, admirable personage, the English—or Scottish— military gentleman: kind, good, honest, unimaginative and timid. And how aunt Trix teased him, cruelly almost, like a cat with sharpened fangs! Always arriving late for meals (which exasperated him), her breast clattering with necklaces, her fingers glittering with rings, she talked, and talked, and darted witty shafts, and chattered on and on until he cried out in despair, like an Old Testament prophet in the depths of torment, 'Oh, woman! Woman!' Whereupon who wore a sweet smile and raised her brows.

From my remarkable aunt, uncle Jack, indeed, had suffered much. During her sojourn in India, she had become interested in its mystical arts, and had experimented in their perilous techniques: to such a point that withdrawing one day, in spirit, from her bodily shell, she found to her horror, when she had wished to return, so to speak, inside herself, that powerful occult forces barred her way: which had kept her painfully suspended in the cosmos for many years leaving only, as a companion for uncle Jack, a body without its soul. Uncharitable persons may find a simpler, more rational explanation of my aunt's astonishing disappearance; but all I can say is that when she finally returned to inhabit herself again, it appears she was exactly as before—if not even more so; and also that when she described this experience to me, she did so (though the details of her voyage into space seemed vague, not to say incomprehensible) with a total and sincere conviction. In her old age she had abandoned these practices, although she sometimes produced a crystal ball and invited me to gaze into its depths. 'What do you see within, dear?' she asked, when my eyes had remained fixed on it until they filled with tears. 'I see only the lamp on the ceiling, reflected upside down.' My reply was deemed to be facetious; and rebuking me more with pity than with anger, she took the ball herself and told me the fate she saw there for me: though never, I am bound to say, anything I found very useful or, indeed, precise. Nor did I ever see the phantom which, she assured me, roamed about the house—although the room I slept in (which she called 'the Galsworthy bedroom—ugly as a bad dream, but quite comfy'), with its gaunt mahogany furniture filled with Victorian menace and denial, was sinister enough for such an apparition.

I should perhaps explain that aunt Trix wasn't my aunt at all: but, more precisely, my first cousin twice removed; or, as she wrote herself in a letter—filled, like her speech, with metaphor and literary allusion—'Dear and amiable White Knight twice Removed, or any other move on the chess board which suggests the two-step of our complex cousinship.' It was perhaps this very dilution of our consanguinity, and the fact that fifty years separated us in age, that enabled us to converse like members of one same, intemporal generation. On each such occasion, however, it was to me that almost always fell the role of listener. With her hands fluttering like butterflies, but with her body in repose, she would look somewhere over the top of my head, or round the side of me, as if it was my shadow, or my guardian angel, she was addressing. The most beautifully constructed, precisely enunciated phrases fell then from her lips as if she'd learned the intricate sentences by heart; and so far did she often adventure into a forest of conditional clauses, and of parenthetical embroidery, that I wondered if she would ever conclude these Proustian periods with sufficient syntactical clarity. Not once, however—rather to my disappointment—did she fail to do so. And if, as sometimes happened, the thoughts that passed so rapidly through her agile brain outpaced even her capacity for expressing them, then, while she stopped a moment to dispose her ideas in a harmonious sequence, she would utter a high-pitched 'And . . . ' like the sharp cry of a bird in pain: an 'And . . . ' destined to prevent me from interrupting, rather as someone leaves his hat on a seat in the train to show that, even though he's not occupying it himself, *you* must not. On such occasions, I found that the only way I could break in on her was to put my hands over my ears and shut my eyes. The sound would then cease; and when I looked up again I'd see aunt Trix gazing mildly at me, and hear her saying in kind, gentle tones, 'Yes, dear? Have you something to say to me?' 'Aunt Trix: I want to *speak*.' 'Then *speak*, dear. Pray speak.' This I would do; while she waited, her eyes averted and her thoughts probably elsewhere, until, when I paused for an instant, aunt Trix, in whose mind a great backlog of thought by now accumulated, would give a slight smile, say, 'Yes, dear, yes . . .' and begin again.

Those who have read the terrible and secret autobiography of her brother, Rudyard Kipling, or his atrocious story, *Baa Baa, Black Sheep*, will know how cruel was the exile from India that the young brother and sister suffered together in the 'House of Desolation' at Southsea where they were boarded out; and will understand, I think, many things that seem obscure about aunt Trix (whose real name, by the way, was Alice —'Trix' was a family invention[1]) and about her illustrious brother. (They will also have noticed the warning given in the autobiography to 'weaker brethren—*and sisters*' about those who would travel the 'perilous Road to Endor'). Certainly, aunt Trix's whole life was made of exile: born far away in India, her childhood spent in England (how hard, when one thinks of it, these separations of Anglo-Indian families must have been, whose children were always sent home to 'their' England for many years to avoid the rigorous climate in the country of their birth), then her mysterious departure to the infinite, and finally her retirement, with uncle Jack, to Scotland where he was born and which she never loved, in what she called 'sunny, showery, drizzling, gleaming Edinburgh' with its 'straight steel continuous rain'. Sometimes, it is true, she escaped to London, which she adored. On one such occasion, we went together to a luncheon of the Kipling Society at which she was one of the guests of honour. Imagine some hundred people sitting with that rapt look they have when full of lunch and the sense of a great occasion; and imagine one of the speakers—an eminent literary theologian—addressing them. Sitting beside aunt Trix, I became aware of her growing agitation: the twittering of her hands, and her swift glances hither and thither; till all at once, first begging his permission, she broke in on the orator to correct—or amplify, I think it was—a quotation he'd just made. On which the churchman, rising to the occasion with an infinite and marvellous courtesy, began a dialogue with aunt Trix over the astonished heads of the lunchers, who sat listening to their hero's venerated sister with respectful awe.

Towards the end of her life, my cousin became a victim of diabetes. 'I suppose,' she wrote, 'when one is four score, one must "have something"—and diabetes, though incurable, is painless, non-catching and not disfiguring. Even at eighty, one doesn't wish to be uglier than need be.' And though she warned

[1]*Later:* In letters she signed herself 'Auntrix'—all in one word; until I devised 'Ancestrix', which she liked and sometimes adopted.

me, before I last went to see her in the year before her death, that she was 'white as wool and thin as a rake', I found her almost unchanged. 'I appear about eleven,' she said to me, 'fresh from my morning jag of insulin, ready for anything.' Seated in her spacious and frightful drawing-room, decorated with a singular mixture of Indian souvenirs of uncle Jack's, and of objects of pre-Raphaelite art belonging to her own family, aunt Trix discoursed as eloquently as ever, handing me, from time to time, the caramel walnuts she'd discovered which delighted her because of their extraordinary resemblance to the bald head of William Shakespeare. After her death, she spoke to me once more through the prosaic intermediary of her solicitor: who sent me a parcel containing one of the huge enamelled Persian plates she'd had and knew that I admired, and—proof even more cogent that she understood her young relative—a cheque for the fifty pounds that she had left me in her will.

Cahiers des Saisons, September 1956

THE ENGLISHNESS OF DR PEVSNER

DR NIKOLAUS PEVSNER first visited England in 1930, at the age of 28, on a research grant to study English architecture. In Germany, he had been assistant keeper of the Dresden gallery and lecturer in art history at Göttingen, specializing in British themes. In 1934, he settled in our country, teaching at first at Birmingham university, and later joining for a while a firm of manufacturers of furniture. In 1941, he became head of the department of the history of art at Birbeck College, and he was elected Slade professor at Cambridge in 1949. He delivered the 1955 Reith lectures, he has been editor of many architectural books and journals, and he was honoured for these services by the award of a CBE.

This splendid and unusual achievement, which has carried Dr Pevsner to a place of such eminence in the worlds of art and scholarship, has been welcomed by the most illustrious of his adopted countrymen—save for a few native rumblings of complaint to which I shall presently allude. But perhaps the very range and quality of his gifts as a scholar and as an art historian have partly served to mask two rarer, rather unexpected talents which are the subject of this study. The first of these is Dr Pevsner's quite extraordinary penetration as a sociologist of the English scene; the other is the astonishing skill of a man whose mother tongue is not our own, in becoming an English stylist of the highest order.

Nikolaus Pevsner's interest in ourselves and in our culture, before he even came to England, has already been referred to. Since he has lived here he has published (besides his books relating to European culture as a whole) several works that deal specifically with England.[1] It is in two of these—*Industrial Art in England*, of 1937, and *The Buildings of England: London*, of 1952 and 1957—that the particular qualities I am anxious to evoke are revealed most strongly. For paradoxically, I think that Dr Pevsner is even more perceptive about 'the English' when he is writing indirectly about us in surveys which deal, apparently, with pots and pans and furniture, as in the first book, and with churches, public baths and railways-stations, as in the second two.

Industrial Art in England is very reflective of its period which I myself, unfortunately, am old enough to remember—namely, the truly dreadful 1930s. It is frankly moral in tone, reforming in its aspirations, and it reminds us that men of good will, twenty-five years ago, were fighting a defensive,

[1]Chiefly, *Pioneers of the Modern Movement from William Morris to Walter Gropius* (1936); *An Enquiry into Industrial Art in England* (1937); *Matthew Digby Wyatt* (1950); *High Victorian Design* (1951); *The Englishness of English Art* (1956); and the monumental series of *The Buildings of England*, beginning in 1952.

almost a rearguard action, far from the seats of power. For example:

> To fight against the shoddy design of those goods by which our fellow-men are surrounded becomes a moral duty.

And,

> I have no doubt that beauty, both of nature and of things made by man . . . in the places where we work and where we live . . . helps to make our lives fuller, happier and more intense.

The question of good design, superficially a matter of aesthetics, is thus, in its fundamentals, a moral and social one:

> Not one of the subjects is less essential, not one can be neglected, neither slum-clearance nor the renovation of school buildings, neither the levelling up of class contrasts nor the raising of standards of design.

In the course of his survey, Dr Pevsner visited nearly 200 manufacturers, stores, art schools and designers. A sixth of the firms he wrote to refused to see him ('We are . . . not interested in the question of public taste in design'), and one manufacturer believed him to be the agent of a Foreign Power. But though he concluded that '90 per cent of British industrial art is devoid of any aesthetic merit', it is quite clear from his story that the astute and determined young investigator (Dr Pevsner was then 32) liked England and the English—was, indeed, quite fascinated by them. Firmly fixed in his mind was the recollection that in late nineteenth-century architecture and design, English artists had been creative pioneers. Examining the surprisingly progressive motor-car industry, he recorded that 'the manager of an automobile factory never seems to be the narrow-minded, badly dressed provincial bourgeois whom one meets in so many other industries'. Indeed, he is constantly amazed at the savage contrasts of excellence and ghastliness in different manufactures—some (chiefly the more modern) producing designs of high international quality (e g, watches and sanitary appliances), and others (eg, jewellery and carpets) of the very lowest. The English, it would appear, are dense and reactionary—and then, hey presto! in the work of another factory, bewilderingly the opposite: fanciful, unconventional and inventive.

When I first read this book—this record, one might say, of the initial direct encounter of Dr Pevsner with his future countrymen—I was at once reminded strangely of . . . *Gulliver's Travels*! In appearance, this study was about industrial design: and indeed, as well-informed and sensible as anything ever written on the theme in England. But the book also seemed to me to be the tale of an exploration by a curious, courteous, cultivated stranger of an inexplicable people, half Yahoo, half Houyhnhnm. And in spite of his later self-identification with us (to our own immense profit and enlightenment), I still feel that Dr Pevsner has preserved the rare and enriched dual vision of a thoroughly inside outsider.

★

For *The Buildings of England* series which Dr Pevsner was, is, and, it would seem, eternally will be writing, the only fit word is staggering. 'The series,' its blurb says calmly, 'which is written by Dr Nikolaus Pevsner, is intended to continue until all the counties of England are covered.' '*Written* by Dr Pevsner', please notice, not edited, or anything of that sort. All that he has described, he's seen: volumes on sixteen counties are already completed, including the first two on London.

I have myself, in Dr Pevsner's wake, perambulated around a good part of the streets whose buildings are described in the two London books. The effort left me wonderstruck and limp. It was quite something, please believe me, simply to have *looked* at all those buildings. But to have looked at *and* thought about them, studied their histories in the minutest detail, and penetrated inside almost all of their interiors (let alone then written about them), seems to me an achievement for which a new superlative adjective must be coined.

London, as is well known, has eluded almost every artist who has set out to describe her. There has never been a worthy film about London nor even, by the painters, a really adequate pictorial evocation. One reason may be that London being so formless and so hideous, yet so fantastical and poetic, she offers no meaning or shape herself, and this can only be found and made by a deeply gifted artistic imagination. The writers, of course, have fared somewhat better: Defoe and Dickens, obviously, Mayhew, and in his odd way, Firbank. I do not hesitate to say I believe that for a true apprehension of what modern London is, Dr Pevsner's two books, in this purely artistic sense, now impose themselves as absolutely essential reading.

Volume 2 (*London, except the Cities of London & Westminster* —actually written first) I like even more than Volume 1 (*London, the Cities of London & Westminster*), if only because its introduction seems to me more revealing sociologically (though certainly not architecturally) than that to the companion book. This introductory essay I would describe as a concise epitome of what our city was, is, and could be: an essay about buildings, certainly, but even more about the Londoners who live, work, worship, shop, bathe, study, get arrested or die inside them. Never does Dr Pevsner slip for a second into the 'aesthetic fallacy' which supposes—as so many architectural authors do— that buildings were built for art historians to contemplate. Perpetually, he interlaces his human and aesthetic themes: sometimes returning almost with a jerk from humanism to fine arts. Thus:

> . . . So one can say without undue generalization that well over one-third of the population of London in 1841 lived in slum conditions worse than anywhere in London now.
>
> Architecturally the outstanding feature of the first third of the century is the change from brick to stucco, or Roman Cement, as it was then called . . .

Briefly to list the virtues of Dr Pevsner's survey, I would describe them as arising chiefly from a living sense of history in which the past is seen constantly in terms of the present and, indeed, the future. Both books have a solid Roman foundation:

for London *is*, essentially, a Roman city[1]; and even when describing some masterpiece of a much later epoch, Dr Pevsner is always ready to dive beneath the sub-soil in search of tombs, baths, walls and mosaic pavements. On seventeenth- and eighteenth-century architecture he is superb: and I don't think it's too much to say that Wren, for instance, emerges from his volumes an even greater man—if that were possible: thoroughly English, yet firmly established as an international European figure. On Victorian building he is masterly—on the horrors, on the real originals like Norman Shaw and Voysey, especially on the docks, schools, hospitals and warehouses, and, above all, on the 'model dwellings for the labouring classes'.

To meet Dr Pevsner the social moralist, I specially recommend the chapters on the East London boroughs. It is soon apparent that the volumes have a villain—the late nineteenth-century undisinterested philanthropist. Describing some 'desperate early industrial dwellings' in Shoreditch, he writes

Alderman Sydney Waterlow gave the money for them and intended to receive 9 per cent out of this humanitarian gesture.

But the most abhorred monster is that even more celebrated philanthropist, Mr Peabody (and, as attendant demon, his favourite architect, H A Darbishire). I have traced, without help of index[2], in Volume 2 alone, eight acid references to their sinister joint creations; and in Volume 1, the final deadly shaft is neatly placed in poor Mr Peabody's bleeding heart. Describing his—indeed grotesque—memorial behind the Royal Exchange, the author writes simply of this benefactor of East London:

[1]Or, as I would say (though this is not Dr Pevsner's view, I think), essentially still a Roman-Victorian (or Roman-Venetian) city rather than, for instance, a Georgian-twentieth century one.

[2]Both books have indexes of artists and of places, but not of other names. The only 'improvements' I can imagine to the volumes are this one—plus, even more, a supplement on those buildings of London (already, of course, described elsewhere) that may be *seen from a boat on the river Thames*: since this is the nicest way of seeing them, and the way that so many were intended to be seen; and most of all, because the Thames *is* London.

Seated also and steadily looking w the bronze statue of Mr Peabody who established the Peabody Trust, by *W W Story*, 1868.

A paradox, among so many, in our society, seems to me to be the extreme difficulty, among the welter of informational media, of finding exactly what is going on: what England really *is*, and the lives of those therein. Films and TV tell nothing, radio very little, newspapers rare snippets, and plays and novels and social studies much, much less than they could. For any who may be likewise wracked by the pangs of a sociological hunger, Dr Pevsner offers a very rich fare indeed; for even when writing of life and art in distant centuries, it is always with the acute perception of a man very much of our own.

★

I come now to Dr Pevsner as an English writer: and I would like, initially, to make it very clear my praise is directed *not* merely to a scholar of foreign birth who has successfully mastered English, but to a stylist who—like Joseph Conrad, for example—has made of the English language a superb instrument of his own. This feat is partly possible, of course, because our splendid, fantastic tongue, flexible, evocative and imprecise, will lend itself, for anyone with a deft ear and who loves it, to endless happy manipulations and re-creations.

Dozens, literally, of Dr Pevsner's architectural evocations are like little epigrammatic poems. Quoting from Volume 2 alone, and rationing myself severely:

> A light interior wholly devoid of mystery. (*A church.*)
> PUBLIC BATHS, by *E. Deighton Pearson*, 1902, unusually jolly with short squat intermittently rusticated columns at the entrance and monstrously fat little columns in the gable.
> There is indeed plenty of chamfering of beams and quatrefoil piercing of parapets. (*A church.*)
> A charming exterior, white, with portico and cupola, and an exceedingly charming, neat, and light interior, with three galleries on two orders of slim columns, the upper order carrying the shallow tunnel vault of the nave. Box pews, classical reredos. (*A church*).

High slender circular piers into which the vaulting ribs and arches die without capitals. (*A church.*)

For the reader bemused (as so many 'educated' English people sadly must be) by the meanings of the architectural terms, each volume contains an admirable illustrated glossary. To turn to this from the author's descriptive vignettes, to find exactly what he means, is an absolutely compulsive act, and constitutes the least imaginably painful way of ceasing forever to be an architectural ignoramus.

Dr Pevsner equally delights in what one might call architectural ironies: deadly, deadpan sentences about buildings he dislikes. For instance:

> The upper bridge, 112 feet above the water, was meant for the use of pedestrians, while the lower bridge can be opened. (*Tower Bridge.*)
>
> Of park furnishings the most notable are the FOUNTAIN given by Baroness Burdett-Coutts in 1861, an elephantine polygonal structure with oversized putti and dolphins in niches, the whole in a Gothic-cum-Moorish style.
>
> WORMWOOD SCRUBS PRISON, 1874, by *Sir Edmund Ducane.* Built by convicts.
>
> Hearty, robust, and revolting. (*A church.*)
>
> No part of the walls is left undecorated. From everywhere the praise of the Lord is drummed into you. (*A church.*)
>
> Norman (ritual) E front with two stunted towers. Riding-school interior. (*A church.*)
>
> ST LUKE, Burdett Road, 1869, by *Sir Arthur Blomfield.* Big and dull without steeple.

Striking in themselves, what is even more so about these epigrams is that when one actually beholds the buildings they so trenchantly evoke, the words cling close and tightly to the actual stones—often with horrible effect.[1]

---

[1]Rarely before can a writer on architecture have kidnapped audaciously so many single adjectives not usually applied to buildings. Thus, in Volume 2, we may find the highly apposite use of: utterly crazy, silly but lovable, grim, lanky, papery, skinny, victoriously vulgar, picturesque and heavy-handed, ruthless and respectless, dear little building, unmistakable Teulonesque hamfistedness (Teulon is the

But it is really in his set-piece architectural abstractions on a larger scale that Dr Pevsner writes most powerfully. The verbal description of a building, inside and out, so as to reveal its essential *plasticity* (or the lack of it), is a testing feat, and I would particularly recommend, in this respect, the analyses of Greenwich Palace, of Sir John Soane's own house, and of the Royal Festival Hall. To read them is to understand at last what architecture means.

A certain current, or eddy, of feeling hostile to Dr Pevsner's achievement has been hinted at. The argument of the dissenters, to be brief, runs thus. Continental scholarship, and method, and laborious research, are no doubt admirable qualities: but about England and her art there exists some hermetic, elusive English *thing* perceptible only to the native born. To fathom this esoteric local mystery, the methods of a sort of architectural MI5 are inappropriate.

That this principle is not allowed, by critics such as these, to operate in reverse, is one of the curiosities of their attitude. For Ruskin, and many a latter-day English connoisseur of Continental arts, are blandly assumed, by suchlike of their compatriots, to possess insights even denied to the inhabitants of Continental countries thus honoured by the revelation of artistic glories. But the real idiocy of this parochial English viewpoint is, of course, that scholarship and method (and, one might add, very hard work) are all immensely valuable to anyone who also possesses, as our present author most undoubtedly does, an understanding of our country born of patient enquiry and affection.

---

architect), crushingly mean, deplorable utilitarian, rustic floridity, crushingly unattractive vaguely Italianate, frantic, non-committal, wild undisplined, busy, tidy, soapy hardness, almost naughty looseness, confident tastelessness, rum, starved, nothing special, quack chaste, inept, ill-advised, convincedly harsh, heavy cyclopic, aspiring but otherwise obscure, coarse, well mannered, unremarkable, ornate and irresponsible, horrible, abominable, desperate, playful, Grecian gone gaudy, clear and concise, gross and sumptuous, trustworthy (describing chimneys!), entertaining.

There's little doubt, indeed, that one very real aspect of Dr Pevsner's Englishness is that he has himself, from *Industrial Art in England* onwards, considerably influenced English taste. There is no doubt either that he has very greatly contributed to making us aware that buildings aren't just simply *buildings*, and that architecture is the queen of visual arts: for in his first English book he had already announced roundly that

> The modern movement means (thank heaven!) the superiority of architecture over the fine arts.

Since then, his restless and fruitful investigation of our cities, villages and customs—always, I think, just and generous in its appreciations—has helped to reveal us to ourselves.

Revealed us as what, exactly? As a people, above all, still of those contradictions that he saw as a young visitor twenty-five years ago: philistine and idealist, crazy and practical, infantile and wise. His portrait of each century of our building will confirm this. Thus, after the Fire, the chaos of the City Fathers, in their reconstructed mediaeval warren, contrasts with the later order of Lord Burlington, and the graceful ease of the planned squares and gardens in the West. Thus again, writing of Victorian England, he notices:

> The new parts of London, which had to house nearly two million newcomers, were provided with very few public amenities but innumerable churches and chapels.

And in 1960, the paradox remains. Of the buildings of the new London of the last decade, Dr Pevsner writes:

> It is a style of timidity, of playing safe, of introducing just enough of the C20 to avoid being ridiculous and keeping just enough of giant columns and other paraphernalia of Empire to stake the claim of remaining a great nation.

Yet he does not lose hope, and tells us in detail how '. . . a new City could arise as fascinating as the old and yet not, functionally speaking, obsolete . . .'

If the London books have a villain, symbolized by Mr Peabody, they also have an emblematic hero: appropriately, he is a

Roman. Though often generous in his praises (indeed, in spite of his apt acidities, one feels Dr Pevsner's natural instinct *is* to praise), in very few passages of his books does the author allow anything like a private emotion to intrude. An exception to this is his account of the memorial tablet to Gaius Julius Alpinus Classicianus, of which a replica is let into the splendid surviving fragment of the Roman wall adjacent to the Tower of London. Of this monument, Dr Pevsner writes:

> It is a stone tablet, over 5 ft long, which commemorates the great and humane administrator who saved Britain from vindictive punishment after the crushing of the Boudiccan revolt in AD 61. The victorious general, Suetonius Paulinus, wished to introduce a general reign of terror, but was prevented from doing so by the foreseeing and forbearing Procurator newly sent out by Rome to take charge of the distracted Province. He was a man much deserving of British gratitude, and it is one of the more fortunate circumstances of our history that his memorial has come down to us.

Gaius Julius, then, may symbolize the wise and practical technician whose inborn instinct was creative; and who, coming to us from afar, could guide and persuade the wild local authorities, bent on destruction, and teach us to mend and heal.

The Twentieth Century, January 1960

THE NEXT PIECE, on Ella Fitzgerald, is one of the very few I've written about jazz. Though I love jazz music and listen to it endlessly, and am fascinated by the whole jazz phenomenon, I don't really know very much about it. After all these years I still can't distinguish the sound of a tpt from that of a tmb, am never 'on to' the latest thing until everyone else is on to the next one, and I seem to take years to digest, more or less, the essence of any new style or interpretation of it by a new musician. What little I know I've learned by attending countless Sunday concerts in suburban super-cinemas, by plunging, with wistful determination, into jazz club cellars, by listening to discs for far too many happy hours, and by talking (though understanding only two-thirds of their language and less of its essentials) to clued-up persons and especially to jazz musicians.

Despite this, when the invitation to contribute to a special number on *Women* came from the editor of *The Twentieth Century*, I immediately chose Ella as my heroine. (Had I felt I could describe an angel voice, not just that of an angelic human being, I should have chosen Billie Holiday). I was staying, at this time, with Bryan Robertson, whom the reader will meet more fully a few pages later. I asked my kind host to help me, and he there and then jotted down two pages of notes on Ella Fitzgerald's particular magic. I joined these ideas of his both together, added some notions of my own, and posted the robbery to Bernard Wall.

ELLA

As soon as she appears, your spirits lift. Her body is ample, comfortable, and easily carried on her elegant sprightly feet as she steps up to the microphone, briskly professional yet with a sense of enjoyment like a girl's. In her face shine appraising sardonic almond eyes, the wide generous nose dilates, and the amused lips savour the situation of her presence there among you. About her whole person is an air of absolute indestructibility. And then, with a smack matter-of-fact attack, she starts to sing.

And how she sings! Ella Fitzgerald, if not 'the greatest', is certainly the most universal female popular singer of the English -speaking world: universal, that is, by the variety of the songs she sings in ballad and jazz idiom, by the original stylings that she uses in her interpretations, and by the different publics that admire her, ranging, as they do, from juke-box primitives to the Roman-suited hi-fi esoterics with their mine-detector ears. To be, in the mid-twentieth century, an immensely popular artist of the highest calibre is an astonishing achievement, partly explicable by her gifts and partly by her nature, each admirable as the other.

The voice itself, the actual instrument, is not remarkable: a 'healthy, rather ordinary voice' is how one of her own sleeve-notes describes it, not unkindly. But everything else she has, or has acquired. An inborn sense of rhythm, so strongly felt that she can vary the beat to a preposterous degree without ever for a second losing it. Clear, precise diction, and a sixth sense for pace. Easy, assured and infinitely flexible phrasing, graceful, undulating and vivacious.

Thus equipped, Ella can interpret her songs in the richest possible way. In one sense, she is entirely faithful to the lyricist's and the composer's purpose. She has an intense affection for the words and, above all, the meaning of each phrase, which she delivers with no condescension whatsoever, without smart twists of intellectualization, and with no concession towards intrusive sentiment. But in another way, she departs, or seems to, from the 'usual' interpretation of the number—until one remembers that no song exists until it is sung, that it is the singer who in a real sense partly creates it, and that there are no 'usual' versions of a song at all. For Ella, using her voice as an instrumentalist would his wind or strings, and possessed of a musicianship of a quality that enables her to transform the melody in a free improvisation, can recreate a song, making it seem, at first hearing, almost 'unrecognizable'. And not only change the song, but change her voice, or seem to. It is her chameleon-like self-identification with the mood and style of the number that leads to the variations of quality in her singing, ranging from almost hoarse, sharp, exclamatory teenage sounds to entirely mature (but always youthful) middle-register notes of velvety smoothness.

As one would expect, she is past-mistress of the throw-away technique: understatement may be sustained throughout a song, but without diminishing the urgency, the fluency of communication, the quiet excitement of the sound. Sometimes the whole conception of a rather meaningless number (a few too excessive love ballads, for example) is altered by a total throw-away, and a mad acceleration of speed, so that instead of falling into bathos by singing the ditty straight, Ella catches the mood the ballad-writer really intended by a roller-skate delivery of a sort of berserk enthusiasm, bowling madly along to save the melody from the death-kiss of a guffaw. Scat, or wordless onomatopoeic sound, often mildly indecent, she sings as nobody else quite can—delightfully and entirely convincingly. Singers' gimmicks are clipped to an absolute minimum: for instance, the slight catch in the throat in the middle of a word (much abused by her numberless imitators); the almost inaudible tremolo in certain sustained notes; and the occasional smokey shiver when she rises to the treble clef.

Reflected in these splendid sounds is a no less splendid personality. What is she most like to hear, to look at, to imagine? At moments, certainly, like Mom, a thoroughly reassuring character, but a Mom of a particular kind: that rare and admirable species who turn an amused eye upon the young, and who would tolerate from them just simply anything at all. For instance, when Ella has made us understand the real sense of an apparently familiar song, her attitude seems like that of an amiable and clear-witted schoolmarm teaching esteemed and very bright young people: with no patronage, and with affection and a lively interest. It is thus, too, that while nothing could be less morbid, and more normal, than her song, her style has a certain sexlessness, a sense of disembodiment from physical entanglements that is replaced by a general vague elation. She even, at times, contrives to guy sex, entirely without heaviness, in the manners of expert practitioners in this knife-edge art like Mae West, Sinatra, Marilyn Monroe and Groucho Marx. Yet nothing could be further from the bland inverted pallor of the now very popular Lesbian-type singers. She has, in short, an extremely light oblique touch emotionally, combined with a direct stylistic general frontal attack.

It is also the voice of a great lady with a wonderfully crazy streak to her: the *grande dame* presence with undercurrents of entirely uninhibited, unselfconscious mayhem. Often, in her songs, she seems most graciously to descend the stairs half way . . . then leap on the bannisters and slide the rest, though arriving always entirely the right way up at her destination. You can't describe her, really, as an 'actress', because the sense of a 'performance' in the usual way is altogether lacking. She's so good you only have to listen, it is the voice that acts. Nor, unless you see her, does her voice sound particularly 'coloured' —just as she seems any age between sixteen and forty (which is close on what she really is), so does her voice sound as if it might belong to either race.

In a word (or two), her outstanding characteristics are her radiant bonhomie as a human being and, as a performer, her agile swinging easy unornamental delivery, conveying a variety of moods of which the finest one is lyrical, glowing with warmth and light. The all-enveloping sensation that her music gives is of a relaxed acceptance of life—acceptance, not advocacy; and her criticism is confined to a mildly cocked eyebrow, or a sigh. To hear her is to be given, in the most telling and pleasurable form, that particular lift of the spirits that is the great gift of jazz, in its more positive moods, to our frowning, cross-patch age.

The Twentieth Century, August 1958

THE GAME OF TRUTH

'Anywhere in Galicia,' I said to the man in the ticket office. 'No train for a fortnight,' he said, slamming the little door.

We are in the Carson country, of which three books have now suggested the horizons; and many have long enjoyed Mr

Carson's occasional pieces that amid gnostic naggings in the *Statesman*, and the pile-driven pleasantries of *Punch*, have offered fresh gasps of welcome air. His 'I' character narrator has grown happily familiar as the sad, sagacious philosopher-clown in whose existence the bizarre is commonplace, hilarious and of disturbing meaning. And after laughter perhaps initially condescending to the antics of this comic hero and the talent of the humourist who made him, a suspicion now grows into a certainty that the 'entertainer' Anthony Carson is a serious writer on grave themes: is what great comic artists always have been.

Despite our self-admiring devotion to the humorous, the muster in this century of first-rate English comic writers is minute. High in a short list would be the names of Ada Leverson and Ronald Firbank, with each of whom Anthony Carson has some affinities—though I by no means wish to suggest an 'influence'. Each of these three—untypically in English literature—is a classic writer in the sense that Congreve was, or Wilde of the great play: their effects of feeling arise obliquely from deliberate abstractions of form and measured language. Each is a writer apparently 'uninvolved'—in tone urbane (Ada Leverson), or detached (Firbank), or anarchic (Carson)—but each really holds humane and even moral views that determine a whole vision. Each is a finely polished stylist: let no one be deceived by the easy, laconic throw-away of Ada Leverson, the casual inconsequentialities of Firbank, or by Anthony Carson's air of jotting it all down in an exercise-book between pork pies. And though as writers none could be more professional, each of these three has manifested a marked preference for life itself over the painful, elusive process of recording it. 'Everything gets killed by words sooner or later,' Mr Carson says.

So far as their reception by the world goes, a sadly significant further common factor is that each has been undervalued critically, and by the 'reading public'. If a 'humorous' writer has a vein of buffoonery, or facetiousness, or sentimentality, or frivolity, the problem of popularity is solved; and at that kind of level the list of our comic writers in this century is long. But if the comic vein is pure, even critical appreciation lags. It has taken us decades to realise how good *The Diary of a Nobody* really is, and that Wodehouse is an 'art' writer; it took Americans as many to measure the greatness of Thurber, and to disentangle the genius of Mark Twain. Despite the warning of past literary revaluations, in spite of our having grasped that nonsense can be wisdom and the jester judge, we are still prone to underrate comic talent and fail to see when the comedian is the alarming clown.

*

One could describe Mr Carson's three published works as a travel book with family portrait (*A Train to Tarragona* of 1957); a moral fantasy, or spiritual odyssey (*On to Timbuctoo* of 1958); and a confessional fragment of autobiography (*A Rose by any Other Name* of 1960). *A Train to Tarragona* is the most factual and literal of the three, which helps the writer to bring off the triumphant *coup* of enticing the reader to share his love for a region (Catalonia) very possibly unknown, and for a family (called Mir) who must be total strangers. Self-respecting readers instinctively resist such private infatuations of a writer; and the siren seduction is effected in this case because the place and people so clearly are attractive, and because of the author's descriptive potion of affection, candour, and a splendid ultimate indifference to anyone else's view of his obsessions. The emblematic episode of *On to Timbuctoo* is a journey by derelict submarine to the Azores, via Blackpool and Morocco. Here common-sense reality is snatched from under the reader's feet, he is press-ganged on a voyage of bewildering destinations wherein the writer re-makes his own reality by imagination. What this book, with its haphazard 'construction' and convincing inner logic, is really *about*, is no less than a journey of the human spirit in search of intangible truth and elusive beauty. The Azores, where both these may reside, are never reached . . . still less is Timbuctoo itself, whither the writer is still poised for departure on the last page of his book, as he was in its opening sentence. In *A Rose by any Other Name*, the factual and fantastic mingle. The method here is to print in sequence of the author's age, short episodes that evoke a life of pregnant misadventures.

Throughout these books, themes and qualities recur from which quotation can best convey the flavour of Carsonian talent and preoccupations. I have grouped these terse, aphoristic extracts in the order they appear in each of the succeeding volumes.

Landscapes

There was the quick smudge of sunrise in the sky, and the air was fresh as a new sheet.

The sea looked as angry as a jilted woman.

It was raining, and a little boy was crying with a burst balloon.

When the bus stopped I could hear the cackle of frogs and the watery flute of a bird.

There was a long procession moving down the street, black as an old frying-pan, and there were drums and chants and a last gasp of brass. (*A funeral.*)

In those days Sydney ended suddenly and a primeval world tapped at your heart, the pearly gum-trees guarded a million years of secret peace and a kookaburra cackled over a prehistoric joke.

When I reached the Spanish frontier a hot barbaric wind blew in my face, there was a distant sound of drums and a smell of crude olive oil.

The apples fell and the swallows crossed off the days.

Portraits

What amazed me most was the grace and the air of legend with which she moved in her wedding dress.

They bent over us like stricken trees, their hands creaking over the table, and they talked like breaking bones. Their eyes were the swamps of memory.

Andalusians like to shimmer in your eyes and disappear.

The civil guard are a secret hard-hatted race like ghosts with rifles who are really longing to be human.

The girls came over giggling, their bosoms blossoming, their aprons full of insults.

He could prune roses, make chicken runs, mend plugs and fuses and talk fluently about the reasonable things of this world.

I waited a week in a ruined boarding-house full of coughing old men, who read books from the public library about fertility dances, vampire bats and lost races.

The angry exalted faces of the Australians shone like back-block suns; their courage and male outrage sent the insects to the sky and toppled the houses of alabaster and silk. (*Aussies ashore at Sourabaya.*)

He looked like a cardboard hangman. Poisoned ink, paper-clip stillettos and suffocation by forms. (*Inland Revenue official.*)

She was dressed in white, and had black snapping eyes. When she got up her legs twinkled through the dining-room like swords.

Animals

It has two voices, one imperious and a trifle rasping, and the other diffident, tiny and subdued, a ghost of a little silver voice, like a beautiful boy holding a broken plate. (*A pet bird.*)

The streets bulged with camels. In the market-place there were about five hundred with hobbled legs dancing a sort of angry polka and belchingly roaring at their drivers.

Pigeons, those dull, unmysterious city unemployables, dressed in their grey secondhand suits.

It was night and the fish were leaping like knives in the river. They had sad little faces with tiny black spectacles. (*Seagulls.*)

Writing

If you don't possess an income, or are not practical, or young or particularly vigorous, or are not what is called 'religious', and, above all, have lived a life of complete sincere unrighteousness, magic is the most important ingredient. It is a blood-stream in the air, strong, durable, but also quite horribly delicate. The spiders who spin webs of this particular kind of happiness disappear at the slightest tremble, the slightest infraction of laws one can only dimly apprehend. This is the greatest misery. And what else does the act of writing contain but the shadow of the web?

'But what about the comic essence of the writing?' 'That is something which has to alternate. It is like the backwash of a wave.'

The only reason why people write is because they are not wonderful men.

The novel, with exceptions, was a bourgeois invention for tired businessmen, a sort of literary crossword puzzle for old ladies.

Life was the important thing, and it was the important thing to renew life in the book, so that it was like a living organism itself, incalculable and devious and never trying to make a point, or say So-and-so is, you see, like this; not like that. And not indulging in the businessman's trick of sticking to the point.

'Then I can't write a book,' I said, 'unless my publishers want a book about emptiness.'

Life

Inside a man, I thought, there is a brilliant reel of fantasy and the world pulls on the thread and it is soon run out.

I sat down near one of the windows, and tried to tempt the joy, like a bird, to come nearer. But it flew over the blue water to the sun.

Everybody, possibly rightly, was biologically against those who lose railway tickets, who are deceived by their wives, who are over forty-five and do not look prosperous.

No. No. Into whatever vileness man can sink, or if his eyes go like stones into the old back mud, the abstract heavens are not worth a spoonful of the salt sea and the striving.

. . . the welcome sugar and acid of human company.

I was obsessed by the magic of loving; I was hungry for present triumph among the world's flowers.

Inwardly I was waving to myself.

★

It is clear now that we are in the presence of a comic artist in the great tradition; that is to say, a writer who achieves his primary aim of causing laughter, yet never fails in his more important task of leaving the laugher pondering on the jest. Of all talents, this is the most attractive: for wishing to give wisdom wrapped in happiness betokens generosity of soul. Of spirits kindred in this quality to Mr Carson, the only name in our times that calls instantly for honoured recollection is neither English nor American, but that of Valéry Larbaud: one of the very few French elder giants whom the vogue for latter-day 'discovery' and translation has regrettably passed by. In Larbaud's comic fantasies there is the same spontaneous gift of fun and of revelation—the gracious offering of profundities within a mood of carnival that one might call Mozartian.

It will equally be clear that though Mr Carson's 'I' may seem a 'natural', no writer is more conscious of his own processes and intents than he. It is life that consists in tenuous encounters . . . the writer's record of them is diamond-precise. The 'vague' 'impractical' narrator, to whom all things 'happen', has a snake's eye watching in the sun and whip muscles to uncoil suddenly and strike for capture. It is indeed as a critic that Mr Carson, the fabulist, is so memorable: a critic of society, of human conduct and of literature itself, whose diagnoses are acute and final. And it is this inner thoughtfulness of a nature which, in other aspects, is poetic and fantastical, that gives his prose its jewelled astringency. No one is more a master of timing effects upon the page, and no one more ruthless in self-cutting (both sure signs of comic talent). Occasionally, one must allow, the pressures of periodical publication and of life's fatigues do mar and blur these built-in disciplines, and at these rare moments stories sag: their tone seeming sentimental, and their form contrived. But from these lapses, like the champion after three double-faults, Mr Carson always rallies to capture game, set, match and challenge cup (whose plastic pedestal he will, however, drop during the royal presentation) from his—and all writers'—perpetual adversary, the *ordinary*. Throughout his writing, what is most exhilarating, most admirable and most endearing, is his undying passion for discovery: to him the old world is new, there is no place nor moment that has not wonder hidden in it if this can but be seen and found.

I arrived in Valladolid. It was now winter and beginning to get cold. I had a hundred pesetas left. I went into a bar and ordered myself a brandy. I knew, but tried to pretend I didn't know, that I was trapped. I had travelled, I had seen towns and people, London was far away, I had written a few stories and a book on Blackpool. Now what? It was difficult to foresee. I stood there in the bar, sipping the brandy very slowly. The trouble was that I was not a businessman, I was still interested in truth and the game of truth. Particularly the game of truth.

The Twentieth Century, August 1960

THE OTHER MAN

THE FIRST THING to grasp about the triangle of prostitute, ponce and client, is that it's indivisible: in other words, if one doesn't like the idea of ponces, one must (with all the thousands of others who spend millions of pounds a year in England subsidizing 'the game') stop being a client. Some prostitutes, it is true—especially older, independent, business-like operators—don't have a ponce at all. But most of them do; and the relationship of the visiting male stranger, the local girl, and the resident male somewhere in the background, is probably as old as time.

Why should a prostitute want a ponce? The two chief reasons, as one would expect, are psychological and financial. The woman submits herself, however voluntarily, and perhaps a dozen times or more a day, to caresses that mean absolutely nothing to her; but which, unless she's utterly abnormal, must do violence to some part, at least, of her nature. For this, the ponce is the compensation: the lover, the man she really cares for, if only sexually. He is often, in addition, the more usual 'unmarried husband'—the man you have the daily natter with, and cook for, and bring his Guinness to as he sits in his shirt and slippers, watching the telly. I have seen ponce and prostitute interiors that have a thoroughly domestic, even petty-bourgeois atmosphere.

Now, as to finance. In some cases, the ponce takes everything (repeat, *everything*), and grudgingly returns to the girl the price of some contraceptives or a pair of nylons. In others, the financial arrangements have just the same order—or chaos—as those of any young couple living together. But whichever the case, the woman, being the earner, in a real sense dominates the man. Prostitutes could survive—and do—without ponces: never the contrary. This pleasure of *ownership* by the woman of the male has familiar parallels in the worlds of the gigolo and of the wealthy wife—and even (in various subtler forms) in many completely conventional unions.

At this point, I hear someone saying, 'But aren't ponces bullies who force women into vice, and bash them every Saturday night (or else more frequently)?' The answer is yes, this type does exist, and usually battens on young, or weak-minded or, possibly, masochistic girls. But he is very far indeed from being typical. In the first place, experienced prostitutes are usually tough and intelligent, and would never put up with such treatment unless (as may sometimes be the case) they wanted to. In the second, it is very often the woman who initiates a young man into the business (by physical favours and then small, and increasing, gifts) without his realizing at first he *is* a ponce—until it's too late for a weak-willed youngster to withdraw. In the third place, it must always be remembered that the woman has another ultimate, lethal weapon with which to dominate the male: and that is, that he's a criminal and she is not.

As the law is at present, the only person in the triangle whose activity is always illegal (even if the ponce and prostitute be married, as they often are) is the ponce. And of all the possible witnesses at his trial, the only one who could ensure his almost automatic conviction is the woman he lives off. Of course, if the prostitute were to 'shop' her ponce he might very well carve her up when his stretch is over, or otherwise damage her person and her reputation in 'the game'. But temper, liquor—and even love—thwart clear judgement: and the danger to the ponce that his girl will one day pick up the blower and say the dozen fatal words to 'the Law', is always there.

By now one can clearly see that the woman (as, indeed, in most of her relationships) is, in all essentials, the central figure. In their association, an element of psychological blackmail is always present: even if they are really fond of each other, and even if the ponce is a brutal terrorist. It's for this reason, too, that though ponces may fondly imagine they pick the woman, it's really the woman who picks the man, whoever may have made the initial overture. It's true that in the case of 'star' ponces, who enjoy a particular vogue on account of their acumen or general splendour, the ponce may momentarily call the tune; and there may also be a certain rivalry among the girls to hook him (just as there very naturally may, among the ponces, to secure an unusually successful girl). But once he is so 'hooked', basically it is the woman who controls the situation.

Then what does the ponce get out of it all? First, obviously, easy money, and lots of it: rising sometimes to a weekly (untaxed) income of several hundred pounds. Next, in a great many cases, profound satisfaction to his ego. Think of it! All those hundreds of mugs paying up, and I get it all—and get her for free! Then—'kicks'. For the ponce by temperament the life is exciting and, as with criminals in general, the inverted freedoms of illegality are an added inducement.

And what does the ponce 'do'? Apart from satisfying the woman, practically nothing: and least of all does he 'protect' her (as is so often supposed) in any physical way. She does this herself, if need be, very ably assisted, in most cases, by her 'maid' (often a retired female whore, sometimes a homosexual male): a formidable duo, who can handle any awkward client, even the most recalcitrant—except the (always feared) sex maniac. For only in certain set-ups will the ponce be seen anywhere within miles of his woman's place of business: the working and living premises are quite separate. Or if they are not, the ponce (except in squalid, semi-amateur joints) will be out and away during strictly business hours: partly to avoid obvious danger to himself, partly because the lurking presence of a rival male discourages clients, and partly because, so far as the physical (though not financial) part of her business is concerned, the ponce just doesn't 'want to know'.

So he does nothing: and yet, as I write that, I remember so many instances of the ponce's air of having a function, an occupation—one might even call it a job—which totally distinguishes him from the mere 'ligging' layabout. Those interminable phone calls, those eyes on the wrist-watch and sudden departures, those long sessions in the corner with this person or the other: for the conscientious ponce is constantly occupied in 'fixing' items of a financial, legal, social, sartorial, or emotional nature. It may be, of course, if his time-table seem to you quite unusually intricate, that he's one of those bold and vigorous spirits, the multiple ponce, with more than one woman 'on the game'. Each, or only one of the girls may know of this—for instance, an ageing 'girl' who'll pay this price so as still partly to hold her lover. But if the girls *don't* know, he must take special care the wires don't short-circuit, as the conventions of fidelity (of the ponce to the girl, and for the woman not to enjoy herself other than with the ponce) are naturally strict—though very often broken.

And what of the ponce's relations with 'the Law'? Somewhat naturally, his prime objective is not to have any at all. Apart from general astuteness and a loyal partner, the best means of assuring this has always been to work not with a street-walker, but with a call-girl. If the call-girl has never been convicted (and unlike the erstwhile street girls, a very great many of them have not), it is (short of a frame-up and perjured evidence which are of course unthinkable) by no means easy to pin an immoral earnings charge on a call-girl's ponce: since even if it can be proved he's taken her money, it has first to be proved that she's made that money by prostitution. The most usual tactic, in the case of call-girls, has been (and presumably now increasingly will be) to raid the premises, if known, with a warrant for suspected brothel-keeping and hope to sweep the ponce into the net as well. One consequence, incidentally, of the new laws on prostitution, is that a great many of the girls have now 'gone on the phone' and rented a 'straight place' at up to £10 a week (I was told of one who's moved into a council flat), instead of the former 'crooked place' (perhaps at £40) which they rented in street-walking days. It seems generally believed that as call-girl work is specialised, and more sophisticated than street-walking used to be, there has probably been a drop in the total number of prostitutes and, consequently, of ponces. ('Just as much sex, but fewer girls,' one of them said to me.) On the other hand, in the new 'straight gaff', the girl,

until detected by (if unbribable) caretakers or friendly neigh-
bours and thrown out, may hope to operate more cheaply and,
for her ponce (if the girl had been on the streets before), rather
more safely.

And what are they like, the ponces? If any lawyer reader will
forgive the comparison (since I choose his profession at random), I would reply that while lawyers are as varied as it's
possible to be in age, physical appearance, character and intelligence, they all have a certain legal 'thing' about them that
makes one almost always able, with experience, to identify them
when introduced. So it is with ponces. I have known ponces
who are old and ugly, young and extremely glamorous (even
teenagers), kind and generous, mean and crafty, homosexual ('in
business' with a male prostitute) and even female (likewise, with
Lesbian girls). Some dress like peacocks, some like civil servants. Some have a compulsive urge to spend, immediately,
everything they get, or gamble it away: either because their
trade encourages a spendthrift nature, or because of their fear
of having to account, suddenly, for the possession of wads of
fivers—or even sometimes, possibly, because of the feeling it's
'unlucky money'. But others (usually the elder or more experienced men) may be saving to become bookmakers, club
owners, or to open a garage. Any such saving *must* (if frightful
rows are to be avoided) be with the knowledge and approval of
the girl: just as any clandestine saving on *her* part is absolutely
taboo. But in general, these joint saving operations are unusual
since so many girls like their lovers to be public spenders because this heightens their own reputations as good earners and,
even more, binds the man closer to them, for when money's
spent, he'll have to return for more.

But what all ponces do have in common (as well as, presumably, high sexual potency) is a greater or less degree of amorality.
For obvious reasons, ponce society lives close to criminal
society in general. But even were poncing not illegal, ponces,
by nature, have certain marked anti-social tendencies, the
chief being the parasitic one: which, I may add, is also to be
found in many quite legal activities—in advertising, in tele-

vision, and in show-business management, to name but these. On the other hand—and it is this, even more than their propensity to buy you drinks, that makes their company in some ways so delightful—they are, I would say almost to a man, free from the favourite sins of the respectable—hypocrisy and spiritual pride. They are, moreover, sometimes capable of unexpectedly decent and humane behaviour. The sceptical reader may not believe the following instance, but I give it because of the universal belief that ponces are invariably monsters, and also because it is true.

The ponce decided (no doubt from very mixed motives) he wanted to leave 'the game', but not leave the girl. Accordingly one morning, without revealing his true reason, he told her they were to marry in a few weeks' time. The girl expressed mild surprise since she knew the man wasn't naïve enough to suppose this would make him any safer, or more sure of her, and they'd been quite happy and successful as they were. The wedding duly took place; and outside the registry office, the man told the girl she was no longer to be a prostitute, nor he a ponce. If he'd told her before, she'd have refused to marry; and now he'd given her the only proof of his sincerity he could, and taken a chance she might still return to her old trade. After some demur she agreed, and for years now they've stuck it out harmoniously on a weekly income considerably less than their previous daily one.

This case is, of course, untypical. In any ultimate sense a ponce *is* an unworthy person, and one should resist any inclination to romanticize him or, in any serious way, justify his conduct. After all, quite apart from anything else, and to put it at its simplest and crudest, there *is* something disgusting in going with a woman who's just been with dozens of men— however hygienic she may be (and most prostitutes are), and however much one may find disconcerting parallels in respectable society . . . and however little, be it added, an identical consideration will inhibit the multitudinous anonymous clients of the girl. (I once took the plunge, and asked a ponce if he ever thought of this. He answered slowly, 'That's a very nice question,' and changed the subject.)[1] Nevertheless: I think there's no doubt that the hatred of ponces by the virtuous is often motivated not, as they may imagine, by a high sense of civic rectitude, but by these three unadmitted factors. First, a—possibly unconscious—transference to the ponce of the client's own sense of guilt at his association with the prostitute; second, a resentment at having to pay for what the ponce is paid for; and third, by sexual jealousy of the ponce.

To return, then, to our triangle: which of the three parties is most 'to blame'? All one can say with certainty is this. The number of clients vastly exceeds—probably by hundreds of thousands—the number of ponces and of prostitutes in our land. And no one will ever sell anything, or profit by that sale, if there are not a great many people who are willing to buy it.

The Twentieth Century, February 1960

NOW WE plunge back, and for the last time, among teenage society, in another of those pieces that have inspired some reviewers to call me a 'documentary' writer.

Of a short essay such as this next one, about teenage clothing, I can accept the description: though it seems to me to leave out what I was chiefly aiming at in these pieces, which was to

[1]*Later:* In point of fact, he didn't; but I thought what he did answer might be more than readers of *The Twentieth Century* could take. The ponce (after the initial sentence I have quoted) said that yes, he did think of this, but that the sight of the money, the fact that he was usually 'high' by the time the girl came in and, most of all, that he just didn't want to think about how she'd earned it, made this slightly unpleasant physical fact acceptable. I think that this man, in his niceness of feeling, was probably quite exceptional among ponces: most just don't care at all; even as —unbelievable though it may seem to delicate natures—vast numbers of non-ponce males would not be troubled in the slightest by a previous, recent intimacy of the woman. Some, if of vicious disposition (certain clients of whores, especially), actually appear to relish this thought.

draw the social inferences from observation of some aspect of the current scene. But when the term 'documentary' is applied to books like *City of Spades* or *Absolute Beginners*, it seems to me to reveal a failure to grasp the writer's nature, processes and, I hope, achievement.

I suppose a 'documentary' novelist would be one who selects some social theme that genuinely preoccupies him and who, after a study of its outer forms and even inner meaning, clothes this factual survey in a fictional apparel. If that is a just description of his experience, it is not what has ever happened to me.

In my own case a theme, later to be evoked in fiction, has always 'moved in on' me and has become, without any deliberate intent, a part of my life almost before I was aware of it, and certainly long before I thought of writing of it. During this period of saturation such apprehension as I have is intuitive, then thoughtful; the factual 'documentation' always comes long afterwards—a check-up on outer shapes of essences with which I am familiar. I cannot conceive of writing anything about a theme that does not already interest me profoundly through direct experience; and the notion of going 'on location' to 'study' a subject is completely alien to my (in any case idle and impatient) temperament.

I would thus describe *City of Spades* or *Absolute Beginners*— no doubt flatteringly—as poetic evocations of a human situation, with undertones of social criticism of it: wildly romantic in mood, and as rigorously analytic as I can be, by implication.[1] To convey this to the reader I chose a language for 'coloured people', or for teenagers, that was almost entirely an invented one: though true, so far as I could make it, to the minds and spirits of the characters I was describing. Strict naturalism of language (about which there is no practical difficulty if one has 'an ear') would, in the case of social exotics such as these, result in a 'period dialect': pedestrian, and fixed for ever in the

---

[1]As was immediately recognized, alone among reviewers whom I know of, by Francis Wyndham writing in *The London Magazine*, and by Charles Hamblett in *Lilliput*.

time-stream. So I tried in each case to re-invent, from reality, a more 'real'—and therefore timeless—language, as Dickens did, I believe, with Samuel Weller's speech: which I am sure is not how Sam's many originals spoke at all, but which seems to us to be so now; and years after the event, sounds totally convincing.

★

To check on my observation of kids' clothes, I asked for the help of younger friends who dress much as they do (or who contrapuntally adapt some of their sartorial notions). Such minutiae it will be increasingly hard to notice, because teenagery has passed its spring. Their startling initial impact on their elders, and their own amazed discovery of themselves, had already waned by the end of the last decade; and had become on the kids' part rather craftily self-conscious, and by adult parasites, quickly exploited without sympathy or understanding.

I expect that the teenagers of the 1960s will be accepted as a familiar feature of the social landscape. It is about the ex-teenager that the new discoveries can be made: what sort of husbands and wives, and fathers and mothers, the boys and girls who first enjoyed this dazzling experience, will be.

SHARP SCHMUTTER

THIS IS the agressively elegant silhouette of any sharp English working-class boy today:

Hat. No hat: unless a rear-buckled cap, or very small-brimmed, circular, often furry, lid.

Hair. Sharp hair-dos are now all short (though not 'cropped'): e g, the 'College Boy', 'fashioned' to lie flat, with burned-in parting. The long, curled, brow-camouflaging 'styled' fashions of the early fifties are right out. So, completely, is the crew-cut (though any short hair style is still so described by the un-scholarly).

Jacket. Let's begin by describing schmutter a sharp kid wouldn't be seen dead in.

(a) *The tweedy thing*. Neither in the upper-class-casual form (though this is quite attractive in a Macmillany, 'I've had this thing thirty years,' sort of way); nor in the university student leather-elbowed, or the Jag-driving checked 'sports jacket' forms; nor, especially, in the horribly debased, mass-manu-factured, drooping, *déclassé* hacking-jacket form, with its innumerable grotesque vents and 'ticket pockets' (used for what? tickets, possibly?) stuck on, often at slanting angles, all over the place.

(b) *The 'men's wear' thing*. This was, is, and doubtless long will be, the staple style of the great self-confidently tasteless mass of reliable English petty-bourgeois males. Three-piece of solid materials; but dung-coloured 'lovat' shades, total lack of chic or imagination in the floppy, flappy, shapeless 'cut', the lines *following* (albeit vaguely) those of the body instead of enhancing or contrasting with them (e g, jacket *semi*-pinched-in at the waist)—and reaching its maximum formless horror in dressy Irish labourers (and, for that matter, prosperous visitors from beyond the Karl Marx line).

(c) *'American drape.'* This hit Charing Cross road in the late 1940s and constituted, with the Ted thing (see below), the first underground revolt against wartime uniforms and sackcloth, and the whole 'men's wear' conception of English male attire. Padded shoulders, straight, waistless coat hanging well below what tailors call the 'seat'. Material flannel or gaber-dine. Still seen occasionally in seaside Dreamlands, and small provincial car-parks.

(d) *The Ted thing*. In the 1940s, a Tory-romantic, W I-ish, 'Edwardian' style of brief duration, crossed the Thames, via Westminster bridge, to the Walworth road and Newington Butts, and re-appeared, transmuted into a proletarian caricature, as the 'Teddy boy' style. At this stage, the American drape

(sharp and 'respectable') and the Ted style (sharp and delinquent) were, in a sense, rival ideological uniforms.[1]

Though caricaturists (who really ought to start looking a
bit—even the best of them) still draw dated Ted stereotypes,
the style, in its authentic pure absurdity, is now only to be
found in outlying holes and corners (I last saw it in a caff at
Goring-on-Thames). Teds, of course, still exist—very much so:
but are increasingly indistinguishable, sartorially, from other
youngsters—though immediately recognizable by, among
other things, their grubbiness, awkward uncouth energy, and
general air of built-in self-dissatisfaction, like monstrous
ingrown toe-nails.

So what jacket *would* our sharp number be wearing? Certainly,
some variation of the *Italian* style—which, first appearing in
the early summer of 1958, has now swept the land. In brief,
this style revives the elegant, sexy line of the 1400s: that is,
very short hanging surcoat, and skin-tight leg wear that both
reveal and set off any natural physical graces that be available.[2]
It looks terrific on shortish, chunky (i e, Italian) bodies, and
dreadful on the very tall or short.

Well, now—that jacket. Single-breasted, 'button three,'
'natural' shoulders dropping straight down without shaped
waist to the pubic line. No flaps to pockets, maybe single two-
inch baby vent. Material: medium dark, dark, or striped:
nothing 'sporting' or checky.

Slacks (or trousers, as they used to be called). Off duty (or is

---

[1]No study that gets anywhere beneath the surface has yet been
written of the whole Ted thing, though many journalists have scalded
their fingers trying to skim the cream. For instance—and arising from
the above: was there anything 'anti-American', initially, in the dogmatically provincial-English styles of Teddy dress?

[2]Complete description of the Italian thing, kindly furnished by a
teenage tailor: 1. Sloping shoulders. 2. Flat, rounded-off sleeve heads.
3. Close notched lapels, worn narrow and straight on outer edge.
4. Jacket worn shorter, and cut on loose semi-slack lines tapering to
the hips. 5. Trousers worn close on thigh, tapering to 16 inches with
plain bottoms shaped over shoe. 6. Lining of jackets in contrasted
shades.

it *on* duty? anway, when working or loafing—not parading)—
jeans: the emblematic garment of the teenage jean-age. Initially,
of course, a US working garment, then a student campus casual
garment which first arrived here in its original washed-blue,
turned-up-base-of-legs form (when it was considered daring,
and worn by the bourgeoisie round the coffee bars). But now,
crossed, as it were, with the Italian style, an even closer-fitting
un-turned-up jean of almost any bright colour (as well as striped
and even khaki denim) has come into general use.

On duty, for parade, the accompanying slacks to the Italian
jacket: i e, cut low on hips (*not* hitched up under arm-pits, as in
'men's wear'), 'shaped to seat,' tapering to 16-inch base maximum, often no turn-ups and with 'raised' seams down the sides.
Zip fly, no braces (what *can* be happening to the button
industry?), possibly a slender, purely decorative, belt.

'*Wool shirt*' or '*jumper*'. This new and delightful garment, which
doesn't seem yet to have collected a stable name—it's a cross
between a shirt, a singlet and a light-weight sweater—is now
used universally for both casual and formal wear except in
those places where a collar and tie are still insisted on (except to
Mr Wolf Mankowitz[1]—they've given up). Of all shades and
materials, and chiefly of Franco-Italian origin. (There's another
useful hybrid—the semi-shirt, semi-jacket of light material
and without side pockets, for summer wear.)

Shirt. Probably white and, if so, drip-dry: a great and beneficient
revolution in male cleanliness and elegance. The papery,
contraceptive-like synthetic fabrics, so prized a decade ago, are
much less used. Separate collars, together with such oddities
as studs and cuff-links, are already in the sociological museums.
'Men's wear'-style tails, dangling ridiculously and unnecessarily to the boney knees, are now snipped straight and short.
For casual wear, vigorously striped shirts ('Italian' again).

[1]*Later:* To whom I am most grateful—though I'm not blaming
him for the consequences at all—for the encouragement he gave me
to write about teenagers.

Tie. None (see 'wool shirt' above), or slim (not 'string') with parallel edges, flat base, and probably horizontal stripes.

Socks. Either very light or very dark, and very short.

Shoes. 'Italian' once again: pointed, light-weight, almost always leather, and almost always 'casual' (i e, no laces). Science-fiction Teddy-style two-inch-sole monsters have disappeared. Suede, once gentlemanly, is now debased to 'men's wear', but sharp kiddos sometimes use it, very light, in pointed casuals.[1]

Miscellaneous. Underclothes: minimal, white, and easily washable (the 1940s-style decorated facetious-erotic are right out). *Overcoats and Macs:* light shades, very short (no lower than knees), and new light-weight materials—an enormous boon. *'Sleep wear':* much less pyjama-y: short pants, collarless jacket. *Waistcoat:* not worn (except for weddings) by any sharp number: only to be found in 'men's wear', in bourgeois 'fancy' velours, and in the (former) Teddy-Louis xxviii 'silk brocade' ranges.[2]

And what will this sharp cat's bird, or chick, have on? She is, if possible, even more elegant than he—and the pair of them, stepping it out to the jazz club, the Odeon, or to cha-cha at the palais, make a delightful spectacle. She's hatless, her hair is 'elfin' or 'puffed' and probably tinctured. Her face is pallid—'natural' make-up with a dash of mauve or creamy 'rose cameo' and, in either case, mascara round the eyes as if under artificial light at noon. Cotton *décolleté* blouse (with short blazer jacket if it's chilly, or she wants some pockets). Short, voluminous skirt with rattling paper-nylon petticoats (up to five or six of them)—or, if it's cooler, one of buttock-revealing tightness. Seamless stockings and pointed light-coloured shoes with 'stiletto' heels, both very flattering even to legs that are re-

[1] *Later:* The elongated 'winkle-picker', a mannerist development since late 1959, had not yet appeared.
[2] *Later:* In lieu of waistcoats, wool cardigans are used—Latin, Austro-Swiss, Scandinavian and Scottish designs rivalling one another annually in growing subtlety and splendour.

calcitrant. Light, hanging bag. General air (from the age of thirteen upwards) of formidable self-possession.

★

The economic basis of all this is, of course, the teenage revolution (it really is one) whereby this age group now has (according to *The Economist*, no less) several hundred millions every year to spend.[1] The social basis is the vigorous upsurge of the working-classes. Recently interviewed, on a visit to London, Miss Nancy Mitford[2] declared that working-class girls and boys are incomparably smarter than the others—and this *is* accurate, and no exaggeration. Compare the publics in Oxford street and Bond street of now and of however far your memory goes back, and the present superiority of Oxford street is startling. You will also observe there—as in any proletarian district of the capital—the lavish, colourful eruption of gay stores selling 'separates' to the girls, and sharp schmutter to the kids: shining, enticing shops like candy-floss. But the transformation of the working-class to power and relative affluence means that these styles (except, possibly, for the now archaic Ted style) are no longer 'working-class' in the old sense at all. The belted corduroy and choker, though still found in older men (and in Giles cartoons), or the seemly but hideous 'Sunday best' of blue serge and female flowered 'frocks' or 'coats and skirts', have now given way to a style which is really classless: 'informal-formal', and far too smart and elegant to be called proletarian in any of its pre-1950 meanings.

What are its sartorial origins? Essentially, one might say, an anglicised adaptation of Continental European (particularly French and Italian) and of American styles. To examine the

---

[1] *Later:* I do hope the reader is not wearied by this reiteration that the *money* element was so important in the whole teenage phenomenon. We realize it now, but at the outset so many didn't—or didn't want to because they 'disapproved' (rather as one might do of a tide, or wind, or waterfall).

[2] *Later:* I sent Miss Mitford a copy of this essay which she acknowledged most kindly, though ticking me off severely for my strictures (later in the piece) on 'English gentlemanly' attire.

US influence first (though I believe it to be the waning one), this was initially due, of course, to the presence of the ubiquitous GI, and to the prestige of American films which created youthful 'heroes' of the Brando, Dean and, latterly, Presley varieties. These 'heroes', however different, have in common a certain degree of anti-social (or, at any rate, anti-parental) frustration, expressed sartorially by a sort of casual, erotic elegance. Examples of this are, of course, jeans, 'Wild One' leather jackets, short hair cuts, 'moccasin' shoes—a general appearance, in fact, like that of an urban, motorised cowboy.[1] If this US influence has declined somewhat from its initial supremacy, this is partly, of course, because original (i e, not 'UK-styled') American clothes are much more difficult to buy here;[2] but also, I think, because the American 'hero' has been increasingly replaced by European models, largely of Continental origin. The explanations here may be cheaper travel, the increased prestige of Continental films—and, of course, the astute promotion, by the Shaftesbury avenue Svengalis, exploiting (or perhaps, to be fair, creating) the teenage market. But it may also go deeper, and hint at a certain degree not of 'anti-Americanism' so much as of growing indifference to America—to which may also bear witness the abrupt emergence, in the past few years in England, of native-born singing, motor-racing and athletic heroes and, in general, of a more aggressively confident 'European' spirit.

*

Getting back into my depth, I'd like to refer to several other subsidiary dress styles outside the mainstream of the Anglo-Italo-American staple style. The first (and I apologize for leaving it till now) is the Savile Row English gentlemanly style,

[1]Note how the 'fifteenth century' silhouette, described above in the 'Italian' style, is also to be found in these transatlantic combinations.

[2]*Later:* Much less so since restrictions on dollar imports were lifted after this piece appeared. It has yet to be seen whether US clothing exporters will attack the UK market as the Italians did in 1958; and if they do, if they succeed.

which still survives vigorously among those who can afford it and who can manfully support anything so uncomfortable and, as I think, unattractive. For although one may concede that, in a peculiar sort of way, a group of Guards officers off duty, or of City brokers on it, look rather striking in this attire, there is always something about their appearance which suggests a bevy of footman at their annual convention. Nor do I believe that its prestige stands, internationally, so high as we might like to think: these tales of American and Oriental potentates who have their standing order for a dozen suits with Messrs So-and-So may very well be true; but so far as I can discover most foreigners are delighted the English continue to wear this style (and our soldiers red coats, and our judges wigs) so long as they don't have to wear it themselves. Basically, the style doesn't seem greatly to have evolved—except perhaps in oddities like the brown clubland 'Robin Hood' hat[1] which contrives to hint that the contemporary Sheriff of Nottingham is a Socialist. Indeed, it doesn't seem that Savile row *creates* styles, strategically, as the Italian tailors do, but merely makes periodical forays into finnicky details like cuffs on coat sleeves, lapels on waistcoats, numbers of buttons and suchlike trivia.[2]

Then, there are the unpredictable vogues for particular garments. Thus, at one time, everyone in the Lounge Bar of provincial hotels wore blue double-breasted blazers with brass buttons if they were pseudo-gents, and suede jackets with zips and plaited leather cuff buttons if they were racy, frankly uninhibited cads. Pop male jewellery, once ornate, is now light-weight: heavy 'identity' wrist chains, for example, have gone out, while delicate silver neck chains sprout increasingly on hairy upper torsos. A vogue for camp, rather too pretty garments (not to be confused with the virile elegance of the Italian style) has also spread from shoplets in north-west Soho into the most unlikely places. And the pop drain-pipe line of

[1] *Later:* This—no longer brown exclusively—became sharp proletarian in Spring, 1960: cf the fall (or is it rise?) of 'Edwardian' style to Ted.

[2] Cf motor-car styling, for which British firms are now forced to sign on Italian designers.

Spitalfields is suddenly echoed, Chelsea-wards, by fawn 'cavalry' twill slacks you have to amputate both feet to get into (or out of) at all.[1]

Probing deep, one may also discover that even within a particular group in a particular area, there are remarkably contrasting sub-species. A visit, for example, to a 'modernist' jazz club will reveal boys and girls attired much as I have described them earlier on. But to mark their ideological hostility to the 'modernist', the 'Trad' (traditionalist) fans will be in dogmatically 'bohemian' attire.[2] If boys, they will have longish brushless hair, white (soiled) stiff-starched collars, striped shirt, tie all of one colour, short very ancient (this is vital) riding-jacket, tighter than skin-tight wide-striped slacks, *no* socks, and *boots*. If girls, long untidy hair with fringe, *male* shirt or floppy knee-length coloured sweater (often embellished by a twelve-foot scarf), possibly slacks, possibly woollen waist-high balletic tights, possibly even a skirt and single-coloured wool or nylon stockings, and flat, clanking, 'dash-about' wedge-heeled shoes.

*

As it's unseemly to write for an English periodical without striking a moral (or moralising) note, we must now ask . . . is all this a sign that young English males are becoming effete, and young English girls more frivolous than ever? Or (and perhaps this is the real question) is the society that produces them so becoming?

On the positive side, I cannot see that to feel it's wonderful to be young, energetic, and handsome or pretty is in any way reprehensible: rather does the dogmatic drabness of the 'men's wear' world seem to me profoundly unattractive and even

---

[1] *Later:* As has often been noticed by dress sociologists, 'top' and 'pop' clothing are usually closer in style (and influence each other more) than either is to the wide intermediate ranges of bourgeois and petty-bourgeois dress.

[2] There's a more than vestimentary reason for this. Trad fans, these days, are mostly students and middle class; modernists, working-class and already earning. So the Trad boys and girls, children of the new poor, simply haven't got the money for sharp clothing.

unworthy of the coldly honourable name of 'puritan'.[1] Another enormous virtue of the new styles is that they encourage cleanliness since they're bright and therefore have to be kept clean, and made of materials that are very easily washable. The older conception that clothes should be made to last, insanitarily, forever, and fashions change, if at all, only every decade or so, has disappeared.[2] Anyway—what was ever the point of this? Cheap clothes didn't last anyhow, and those who could afford the expensive could afford the new. At all events, the pattern now is quick cash and quick changes; and also cheaper and cheaper clothes of quality, as regular visits to, for instance, Marks & Spencer's, will bear witness.

On the negative side—since the nagging inner voice must state it—isn't there something fatuous in this formidable expertise, among English boys and girls, about the minutiae of dress? For I assure the reader that if this brief essay may seem knowledgeable, any sharp cat and his bird would regard it as elementary in the extreme. Isn't there something mildly revolting about the obsession with telly fashion programmes and window-shopping at the multiple teenage stores? With spending hours in male and female hairdressers, and buying millions of pounds worth of cosmetics, after-shave lotions, and bisexual remedies for body odours?

Well—yes: I suppose so—*if* this phenomenon is considered in isolation, and *if* this were the only preoccupation of the young. But is it? Isn't it rather a minor (and pleasant) part of an international upheaval which is changing, behind the lock-jawed deadlocks of the politically mighty, all forms of social intercourse, the world's boundaries, thought, art—everything, almost?

The Twentieth Century, August 1959

[1]*Later:* The original Puritans were in fact, in their chill prim way, quite dressy. The pressing of those funnelled hats! The laundering of chaste hose, and burnishing of buckled pumps! That vast starched collar!

[2]In English Music Hall songs there are frequent references to *inherited* garments: e g, in J C Heffron's *Where Did You Get That Hat?*

THE HEART OF A LEGEND

The Writings of Ada Leverson

IT IS an unjust fate for a great artist to become so much en-tangled in a legend that a personality is better known than an achievement. This has been the lot of Ada Leverson, whose name is so honourably remembered, and whose writing remains disproportionately unread. The legend is a particularly obstinate barrier to her art, because it is threefold: one part of it mis-leadingly surrounding her own self, the other two parts willed on her by fellow artists whom she loved and served.

To dispose first, if one can, of the most tenacious of these legendary reputations: the one arising from her friendship for Oscar Wilde. Now, of Oscar Wilde it is impossible, in most senses, to write with other than a total admiration. The human person—who, though known only to us by report, is instantly realized to be as splendid as extraordinary—and the writer of the one great play (but I think of nothing else) can never be praised enough, nor honoured. But as for the trials and their ensuing catastrophe, the time has surely come to say that they have become an appalling nuisance and, so far as Wilde the artist is concerned, essentially an irrelevance.

It must be said—though with entire commiseration for his suffering—that Oscar Wilde the 'homosexual martyr' was no martyr, and Oscar Wilde the 'artist hero' was no hero. That he did not say out loud and clear, in 1895, 'Very well, I am—now justify your law' is all too understandable; yet only by saying this would he have been heroic. That the social rules on homosexuality, however idiotic and inhuman, were perfectly well known, must mean that anyone who provoked their drastic application was no martyr. Wilde was not pursued and perse-cuted by authority: he invited it to ruin him. His provocation was no desperate device to discredit an evil law: he accepted the rules, and imagined he could twist them. And when the inevitable ensued, one cannot but feel—if alone from the evidence of his own previous writing—that the catastrophe was one he in some ways had always longed for. All this makes his fate pitiful, certainly; and furnishes no excuse to those who, from the passage of the bad law until his final condemnation, first baited and then sprung their snare. But it was not a tragic fate, despite his dignity and courage: it was one pathetic and self-chosen.

The deep, the morbid, the strangely excessive interest in Wilde's trials is due, I believe, chiefly to our own equally morbid, excessive, and grotesque obsession with the fact of homosexuality: of which we have contrived, with poisonous effect, to make a 'problem' altogether vaster than its real moral, personal and social problems are. This sick interest, it would also seem to me, is that of a people fundamentally indifferent and even hostile to art and artists, since the trials present, to such superficial minds, the triple advantage of demonstrating that one of our most gifted and attractive writers was a monster; more still, of satisfying a distortedly 'dramatic' conception of what 'the artist' is (a man of self-sought sorrows and not, as essentially, a creative worker); and mostly of relieving such persons from the necessity of reading anything Wilde wrote: since thanks to the trials (and to the infinity of books, and now films, that monotonously and inaccurately describe them), everyone 'knows all about him'.

As also is now well known, among the half dozen men and women in all Europe who, in his disaster, were true to their friendship for Wilde (and to all they had said to him, and about him, in his days of glory), the most outstanding—and most beautiful by the practical tact of what she did for him—was Ada Leverson. The best account of what took place remains her own[1]; and I should wish to add—as this is usually neglected —that it seems to me the conduct of her husband, Ernest Leverson, was also most noble: since—as we must always remind ourselves when giving its true weight to what she and he both did—'society', in 1895, could be irrevocably ruthless to those who offended it; and conduct deemed 'inappropriate'

[1]*Letters to the Sphinx from Oscar Wilde.* Duckworth, 1930.

in a husband might well have been judged even more severely than would his wife's. What Ada Leverson herself did is quite beyond praise: it all seems so obvious now, and yet a moment's honest reflection should persuade most of us that we would not ourselves have done it—perhaps not even thought of doing it. Nevertheless: anyone who thinks, as I most surely do, that Ada Leverson is in her own right and by her own achievement a very great artist indeed, may feel that from the point of view of her own literary reputation (which is, of course, a factor that her generous soul would not even have considered), the most fatal step she ever took was to behave, to Wilde, so well and so unselfishly. For Wilde, most unquestionably, is in the matter of his 'legend' a terrible vampire: like some strange, greedy planet, his name and repute have absorbed and flung into orbit round his memory so many human moons—and even, in the case of Ada Leverson, one rare star. It is surely high time that as an artist she be rescued from this association most honourable to herself; and that it be realized, as I hope to demonstrate, that save for *The Importance of Being Earnest*, Ada Leverson was certainly Wilde's equal and, I believe, ultimately a finer writer.

The next legend that must be unravelled, or set in its fit proportion, is that woven round Ada Leverson's name by Sir Osbert Sitwell in the fifth volume of his autobiographical *Left Hand, Right Hand!*; and called, it will be remembered, *Noble Essences, or Courteous Recollections*. Of the four prior volumes I would say that their author has created (if that is the word to apply to an actual person), in his study of Sir George Sitwell his father, one of the most extraordinary 'characters' of English literature. The vast halls and ante-rooms of the book which conduct us, finally and superbly, to the revelations of Sir George's private dwelling, resemble, by the encumbrance of accessory and often immensely tedious detail—and by the neo-baroque convolutions and ornate parodies of prose by which these are described—a sort of *Sagrada Familia* erected by a literary Gaudí; but all this cannot detract from the ultimate triumph of the portrait of Sir George; and does indeed serve, by the very contrast of the obsessive perambulations of the minor themes and of the polished peculiarities of language, to provide a complicated yet most effective décor in which the fine realism and deep imagination of the evocation of the writer's father are eventually, and most marvellously, presented.

But when we come to read the *Noble Essences*—which are, of course, in a sense a book apart—the impression is often, to be frank, unpleasant. It is but damning with faint praise to say that one is grateful for the information the author gives about these splendid men and women; and in the case of Ada Leverson herself, I must own it was not until I read this book that I knew she was a writer. But the great defect is this: it is precisely *not* as a writer that, in the book, Ada Leverson is portrayed. It is as a sort of adjunct, or satellite, or mascot even of the author: loved and admired, most certainly, and greatly esteemed, but condescended to; and not seemingly cherished for what ought to be the most important thing about her—that she was an artist also; and in her case, a great one. And although this was certainly not the intention of the volume—which clearly was to do high honour to the artists whom it celebrates—the unfortunate impression grows upon the reader that beyond all the noble essences therein described, there stands one nobler even than them all.

*

The third 'legend' shrouding Ada Leverson which one must also try to peel aside, is the one created unintentionally by herself. It is a regrettable reality of the 'literary world'—yet one of which any writer concerned with his ultimate 'reputation' must take some account—that writers, to a great extent, are valued in their day, and even by posterity, very much at the value which they seem to place upon themselves; or which they permit, by genuine indifference or neglect, their contemporaries to place upon them. Of course no reputation, be it nursed however ardently, can be sustained without the presence of a talent; and it is true that later re-assessments of neglected or self-neglected artists, sometimes do take place. Yet because it is hard to learn and easy to forget, 'the world', if not reminded, will prefer to leave a talent in oblivion.

As an artist, no one could have been more careless of her 'literary reputation' than was Ada Leverson (which is one of the many attractive things about her). Although in quantitative fact and, as I hope to show, by quality, she was in the most entire sense a professional writer, she never was, nor cared to be, a *femme de lettres*: the notion would have seemed to her preposterous, a bore. Throughout the 1890s, she printed innumerable occasional pieces in topical magazines—many of which are only now being disinterred; and between 1907 and 1916 she published six novels of outstanding merit. But all this was made to seem 'effortless' in two ways. The style itself, and the whole tone of these six volumes, convey—unless one is attentive—the impression that the thing is all too easy: as if it were set down, in random moments, by a beautiful and brilliant lover of life and art between outings on idle afternoons. So far as her own attitude to her work went, she was the kind of person—as wonderful as rare—whose sense of *chic* and inborn dislike of all pomposities (not least among 'creative' people) would forbid her to make claims for herself that others would not spontaneously make for her. Her chief delight was in the victorious achievement of her friends; for friendship was as dear to her as love, and she was in both an artist. Thus, one can imagine her joy if on the publication of a novel, a friend told her he admired it (the more so if he could tell her, very exactly, why). But to imagine her pressing a volume into a friend's hand, let alone undertaking that kind of artistic lobbying which helps to establish and preserve a literary 'name', is quite impossible. Of Edith Ottley, heroine in three of her novels, and whom one may with little doubt assume to be something of a self-portrait, Ada Leverson has this to say:

> Such vanity as she had was not in an uneasy condition; she cared very little for general admiration, and had no feeling for competition. She was without ambition to be superior to others.

★

It is thus that the notion has arisen—and has been sustained in many a preposterous study of 'the nineties' or of 'the Edwardian era'—that as well as being a literary acolyte (albeit one greatly cherished) Ada Leverson was a gifted, casual non-professional. To this absurd impertinence, her writings now may make reply.

The Twelfth Hour, her first novel, was published when she was already reaching her middle years.[1] The competence of plot and structure, the swift, sharp establishment of character, and the easy, laconic urbanity of style suggest—which was indeed the case—that although a 'first novel', this is the work of an experienced writer. Subsequently to be developed in depth and range, the essential Ada Leverson themes and tone are already apparent. Her two chief themes are: first, the relations of men and women bound by marriage or—put less convention-ally—the reconciliation of the eagerness for individual life and personal fulfilment, in each of the two partners, with the moral imperative of their promise to each other: for marriage, or love-in-marriage (rather than love before it, or outside it) is seen in terms of a bond of loyalty—the free promise—much more than of ties imposed by faith or law. And since she clearly approves of and delights in the life-loving individuality of the wife and husband, and yet as equally believes a promise *is* a pro-mise and that full personal self-realization can best be achieved through keeping this primal vow, the central conflict of her books is always the way in which their two protagonists, the married man and woman, will confront and resolve this situa-tion. Her secondary theme—though almost of equal weight—is friendship, to which it is clear she attached great human value. It is often believed that friendship is a masculine speciality. In the Ada Leverson world, at all events, it isn't: for though there are competent descriptions of friendships between men, the most sensitive and complex are those she creates between women and men (and these *are* real friendships, not failed or

[1]Ada Leverson was born in 1862 and died, aged seventy, in 1933. Her six novels, originally published by Grant Richards, and re-issued during 1950-1951 by Chapman & Hall, are: *The Twelfth Hour*, 1907; *Love's Shadow*, 1908; *The Limit*, 1911; *Tenterhooks*, 1912; *Bird of Paradise*, 1914; *Love at Second Sight*, 1916.

potential love affairs) and just as effectively—if surprisingly—friendships between women themselves. As for the Ada Leverson tone or mood, it is one of amused, affectionate, and occasionally ironic or contemptuous acceptance of her characters' behaviour: often presented in scenes of such deadpan absurdity that the reader must be alert indeed to catch, in so many throw-away lines, each double meaning. This is not to say that her attitude to her characters (and hence to life) is not critical: indeed it is, and the 'detached' urbanity of tone never entirely masks (unless the reader wishes to see no further) her underlying seriousness about life, and what matters most in it. But she never 'judges': never bullies her characters, or erects them to knock them down; and never forces her own views (while making them quite apparent) upon the reader, to whom she clearly feels her duty is to entertain and, if 'instruct', only to do so by providing all the clues by which the reader can do this for himself if he so wishes.

Ada Leverson belongs, in fact, to a category of writer rather unusual in England—and of which Congreve may be the great exemplar—the classic author of the comedy of manners. This sort of art reveals itself, in form, by a harmonious construction, parts deftly related to the whole, subsidiary themes neatly tucked away in echoing counterpoint; next, in language, by a studied but easy and relaxed precision, with flights of dialogue tossed to and fro like aery but well-directed shuttlecocks; and then in theme, by the perpetually underlying presence, amid all this apparent accident of episode, of an essential drama: sometimes hinted at with such obliqueness that the sudden glimpses of its dangerous deep turbulence can be, to the reader (if he does not miss them), quite alarming; and at last, after phrases and chapters have skimmed like butterflies or birds over a clear still pool, there is the abrupt, positive confrontation—often on the very brink of irredeemable disaster —with the conflict in its total, perilous reality. Once it is thus realized what the writer is about, the gay, flitting, entertaining and, apparently, 'inconsequential' chapters soon assume their other as yet unstated, but already fully present, dramatic dimension. The 'frivolity' becomes meaningful, the nonsense potentially sad. This is not farce, not 'witty writing', but true comedy: and of it, Ada Leverson is a master.

Though one mode of writing may not be more or less 'difficult' than another (to whoever may be good at either), it would seem the classic writer must be technically more assured. To appear not to be saying what in fact you are, to achieve, save in rare 'moments of truth', effects of feeling (those both of characters and writer) by implication, demands a tight-rope dexterity, since to hit the wrong note is to tumble at once into sentiment or farce; and to develop all the themes, major and minor, hold them in a firm yet delicate grip, and conduct them at the correct pace in each episode—and as if by the wish of nature—with a swift final sweep to their 'inevitable' resolution, requires enormous talent and self-discipline. It will escape no attentive reader of Ada Leverson's books that she has surely been much influenced—or helped—in achieving some of these effects by her love for and knowledge of the theatre: indeed, many of her scenes in which the dialogue develops entirely without 'author's interjections', seem almost borrowed from an unpublished play. More peculiar still (although admittedly the bioscope was well enough known by the turn of the century—but not yet the innovations of D W Griffith) is her frequent use of film scenario devices: 'cutting' briskly from scene to scene, or situation to situation, without any 'explanation' (of which indeed, so neatly is it done, there is no need); and even more strangely, 'editing in' scenes and themes apparently unrelated to the one that, in realistic terms, she is just then evoking.

A final but persistent error about her art (one held, I suppose, by those who have not read her or with one eye open only) must be assailed before her novels are examined in more detail: and this is that Ada Leverson is an 'Edwardian' or 'period' writer. Our custom, in thinking of the past (especially the recent English past), would seem to be to get into our heads some notion about an epoch (the 'nineties', the 'twenties', or whenever it may be), and then imperatively demand that any actual 'figure' of that period should conform to the stereotype of our imaginings; and also fail wilfully to remember (in our blindfold thirst for 'period atmosphere') that the past always was, at one time, its own present. The word 'Edwardian', for example, conjures up a host of clichés about which the chief point, so far as Ada Leverson is concerned, is that even were these all exact she could never have herself conformed to them, as a woman or a writer, because she was, in every page of everything she wrote, an acutely devastating critic of her own age. It is hopeless to look in her books for 'Edwardian raw material' which we of today may then digest and comment on: for she herself, anticipating us by a half century, has already performed this task. The key to 'situating' her in this respect is to grasp (as on reading her one so swiftly can) that she was not an 'Edwardian natural' at all, but a most sharp (albeit most indulgent) observer of all things Edwardian. As a writer, in consequence, she is in no sense 'period': no one, in fact, could be of their own day more 'modern': which is precisely what gives to her books— except for their inevitable account of the accessory paraphernalia of Edwardian life—their timeless actuality.[1]

As a corollary to this, she has also dourly been reproached with a culpable unawareness of social and material factors of her period. This seems to me an amazingly blind charge, since how things work, and what things cost, and how it feels to be rich or poor (she had, in her own life, experience of both)— often, indeed, precisely demonstrated with figures spelled out in pounds shillings and pence—are constantly recurring preoccupations. As for the social structure of her day, the variety of social groups her characters are drawn from, and

[1]Not only was she well 'abreast of' her times, but so often proves herself to have been well ahead of them. Among countless instances of this (always introduced with characteristic aplomb and indifference to effect) are a reference, in *Tenterhooks* (published in 1912 and presumably written in 1911), to Cubist paintings (the first Cubist picture was painted in 1906) and to 'primitive art': both surely little known at that time in England, even in *avant-garde* circles. In *Love at Second Sight* (1916) there is an extremely astute analysis of Futurism, which begins, 'Well, of course, they are already past. They always were . . .'

the fullness of her knowledge of them all, are equally apparent. (As one would expect, when the 1914 war comes, it also comes organically into her picture of the new Georgian society.) In short, although a classicist in form, she is most certainly a realist in content. Edwardian 'society' evidently interested (and diverted) her, and she knew very much about it; but it is the social relations of human persons, and not 'society' itself, that is her chief and most cherished raw material.

★

In *The Twelfth Hour*, then, the central situation is that the young marriage between Felicity and her husband Chetwode is imperilled not because of dangers from without, but because he (who loves horses and antique furniture second only to herself) is taking her fidelity outrageously for granted, and she is too proud—or respects herself too much—to tell him so. The sub-plots are the love of Felicity's younger sister, Sylvia, for Woodville, who is 'eligible' in every way except for the essential financial; and of the divided love of Felicity's younger brother Savile (who is sixteen) for Dolly (fourteen) and, at the same fatal time, for the celebrated *diva* Mme Adelina Patti. Subsidiary characters are the brother and sisters' devotedly bullying Aunt William (so called because her late husband, Uncle Mary, seemed to them less a man than she); Sir James Crofton, their father, a pompous, self-contradictory, good-hearted parliamentarian; Mr Ridokanaki, the Greek financier, initially (and vainly) in love with Sylvia, and ultimately to be the *deus ex machina*; the 'artistic' ('in a continual state of vague enthusiasm') Vera Ogilvie; and such fleeting figures as Agatha, Mrs Wilkinson, so named by the family because, although a commoner, her mien is decidedly aristocratic.

Let us first observe the swift economy with which Ada Leverson presents some of her characters:

'No hurry, no hurry,' said Sir James, with that air of self-denial that conveys the urgent necessity of intense speed.

He pondered a few moments about nothing whatever . . . (*Sir James again.*)

Sylvia had that curious gift, abstract beauty, the sort of beauty that recalls vaguely some ideal or antique memory.

And she would receive excuses from servants with a smile so sweet yet so incredulous that it disarmed deceit and made incompetence hide its head (or give notice). (*Sylvia once more.*)

Before he left, Aunt William pressed a sovereign into his hand guiltily, as if it were conscience money. He, on his side, took it as though it were a doctor's fee, and both ignored the transaction. (*Aunt William tipping her nephew Savile.*)

He had a triangular face, the details of which were vague though the outline was clear, like a negative that has been left too long in the sun. (*Mr Ridokanaki.*)

Ridokanaki looked at the clock. It immediately struck ten, tactfully, in a clear subdued tone.

Woodville met unflinchingly that terrible gaze of the inquisitional innocent woman, before which men, guilty or guiltless equally, assume the same self-conscious air of shame. (*Woodville at odds with Sylvia.*)

One really rare possession she certainly had—a husband who, notwithstanding that he felt a mild dislike for her merely, bullied her and interfered with her quite as much as if he were wildly in love. (*Mr and Mrs Ogilvie.*)

He pressed her hand with a look that he hoped conveyed the highest respect, the tenderest sympathy, a deep, though carefully suppressed passion, and a longing to administer some refined and courteous consolation, and went away. (*Bertie Wilton, Felicity's ineffective—and unsuccessful—admirer.*)

'I didn't hear,' he answered. 'I was listening to your voice.' (*Chetwode to his wife Felicity, after their final reconciliation.*)

Sir James was extremely annoyed with the weather. (*Opening sentence of the final chapter.*)

Let us also see how she establishes décor—always integral to the situation she is describing.

Sir James sat down slowly on a depressed leather uneasy chair, and said . . .

A palm, on its last legs, draped in shabby green silk, was dying by the window.

Comparatively early, and quite suddenly, the rooms were

crowded on the usual principle that no one will arrive till everyone is there. They were filled with that inaudible yet loud chatter and the uncomfortable throng which is the one certain sign that a party is a success. (*Reception at Sir James's.*)

The party met fairly punctually in the hideous hall, furnished with draughts and red velvet. The gloom was intensified by the sound of an emaciated orchestra playing 'She was a Miller's Daughter', with a thin reckless airiness that was almost ghostly. (*Visit to Mme Tussaud's.*)

It was the end of a warm April day; they passed quickly, in the jingling cab, through the stale London streets, breathing the spring air that paradoxically suggested country walks, tender vows, sentiment and romance . . .

Two short quotations that define the potential 'drama' between Felicity and her loving, but too casual husband, Chetwode.

Men who indulge in inexpensive cynicism say that women are complex and difficult to understand. This may be true of an ambitious and hard woman, but nothing can be more simple and direct than a woman in love.

And he ought not always to be satisfied to leave her safe as the gem of the collection—and just come and look at it sometimes.

But to illustrate the development of her main themes, and particularly the harrowing skill which with the tragedy, as yet undeclared, can be suddenly and dangerously seen (although in fact, in this book, it is to be prevented at 'the twelfth hour' by the husband and wife's moment of self-realization), only extended quotation would be effective. (Readers may be referred for the chief instance of this to Chapter 24—*The Explanation.*) Such moments of peril are made all the more telling by the counterpoint of comedy—particularly evident in the juxta-positions of the five final chapters. I cannot leave this book without pointing out two notable minor felicities: the art and understanding by which Ada Leverson makes so apparent that the sisters and brother, Felicity, Sylvia and Savile, although so different, are most manifestly consanguinious; and the

adorable portrait of young Savile himself—who by his immense
assurance and his immense gaps of ignorance, seems a prototype
for the contemporary teenager. Savile, in fact, almost steals the
book, and captures its final sentence. The writer is describing,
at the 'happy ending' (happy, that is, once the tragedy of its
two chief characters has been laid bare and avoided), the
marriage of the sub-heroine, Sylvia, to Woodville.

> Of course it was to be a long engagement and a quiet wedding;
> but entirely through the eager impetuosity of Sir James, they were
> married in six weeks, and every one said that in general splendour
> and gorgeousness it surpassed even the wedding of Sir James's
> elder daughter. Savile's attitude as best man was of such extra-
> ordinary correctness that it was the feature of the ceremony, and
> even distracted public attention from the bride and bridegroom.

★

I omit for the moment the next book (*Love's Shadow*) since it is
the first of three that have the same heroine, Edith Ottley, and
which I would therefore like to discuss together. The third book,
then, *The Limit*, has essentially the same theme as *The Twelfth
Hour* but with developments in depth and even harshness:
since in this case the husband and wife, Romer and Valentia,
are not such amiable persons as were Chetwode and Felicity;
and the potential lover, Harry de Freyne, in addition to being
an unworthy 'charmer', is clearly a more real danger to the
marriage than was, in *The Twelfth Hour*, the vacuously agreeable
Bertie Wilton. Thus, of Romer the husband his creator says,
'Apparently cool and matter of fact, he was in reality a reticent
fanatic.' And as for Valentia his wife, she is the nearest thing
in Ada Leverson's books to an 'immoral'—at any rate an
unprincipled—woman: playing with two fires at once, and
knowing it. This situation between the trio reaches danger
points that are dramatic—almost melodramatic; and only at
'the limit' (beyond, even, the 'twelfth hour') is the marriage
saved from wreckage by three factors: that Romer, the
husband, behaves though with violence, with nobility; that

Harry the lover is revealed at last to Valentia as a creature lacking all profundity; and that Valentia herself, once her all too silent husband's devotion is splendidly disclosed, has still sufficient love in her, and honour, to react passionately in his favour.

Decidedly, this book is more imperfect than some others: the 'plot' creaks at times, with 'coincidences' rather nonchalantly contrived; there is even, most unusually for Ada Leverson, some padding; and the final resolution, though effective and credible psychologically, seems hurried and 'theatrical' (the last words of the book, one feels, should be not 'The End' but 'Curtain'). Nor are the secondary characters so assured: there are a 'funny' American and a 'funny' Belgian who are not so very; though Mrs Wyburn, Romer's mother, is a splendidly drawn monster ('Eagerness, impatience, love of teasing and sharp wit were visible in her face to one who could read between the lines'). What is happening in this book, one feels, is that the writer is stepping boldly outside her usual range (almost like her heroine, Valentia) to see just what will happen: thus attaining, as an artist, to her own 'limit' of naturally manageable theme. So that though one may 'fault' *The Limit*, there is little doubt that writing it enabled Ada Leverson, in the next books, to profit by the wider experience it gave her and develop, within her natural artistic boundaries, situations and characters of greater complexity and depth.

Yet it is only by the standards of other books that *The Limit* can be judged a failure. For I have left un-praised those scores, literally, of minor joys of commentary and description by which Ada Leverson constantly delights us. From among these I select two aphorisms, to illustrate in what way they rarely are, with her, mere paradoxes (mere inversions of the commonsensical obvious) as is so often, with writers considered 'wittier', most tediously the case:

> It is an infallible sign of the second-rate in nature and intellect to make use of everything and everyone.

> The marvellous instinct with which women are usually credited seems too often to desert them on the only occasions when it would

be of any real use. One would say it was there for trivialities only, since in a crisis they are usually dense, fatally doing the wrong thing. It is hardly too much to say that most domestic tragedies are caused by the feminine intuition of men and the want of it in women.

★

I only pause to recall the fifth book, *Bird of Paradise*, whose chief and terrible theme is the consequence of 'marrying for money'. I do so largely for reasons of space, and partly because the writer is marking time, so to speak, in this last novel but one, as she gathers strength before her final triumph; and I come now to the three Edith Ottley books, for which the writing of the others, each in turn, may seem in retrospect to be a preparation. These Edith Ottley novels (numbers two, four, and six in sequence) are *Love's Shadow*, *Tenterhooks*, and *Love at Second Sight*; and by their understanding and perfection they are the chief demonstration of the writer's art and vision.

To consider how much Edith really is (as I have suggested) a self-portrait of the writer, or a portrait of the kind of woman that she most admired. As to the second, this is certain; both because of Edith Ottley's central position in the canon, and because as a character she is more firmly and fully defined than any other. As to the first, we may safely assume that in describing Edith and her husband Bruce and their two children, Ada Leverson is drawing on experience that was closest and most personal to her. Though I should make clear that while Edith emerges finally as a woman the reader cannot but admire, she is presented as being fallible, however much endearing; nor is there any note whatever of that kind of auto-projection by which inferior writers manifestly seek, in their creation of a 'heroine', to justify themselves in fancy to themselves in fact.

To understand the 'problem' of Edith's marriage, and to assess the rightness of the way by which, in the last book of the three, she ultimately 'solves' it, we must first understand her husband Bruce and their two children, Archie and Dilly. We have all met Bruce (though nowhere so accurately pinned

down as in these volumes): he is the utterly selfish, utterly
irresponsible, self-pitying and self-admiring bore who nevertheless does have the quality of attracting friends, and even
the fidelity of his closest relatives, because of a bland, blind,
total unawareness of how terrible he is. He is a 'natural', an adult
infant and—as everyone except himself observes—potentially
a victim. The Bruces of this world may summon to their persons,
as does sharp pins a magnet, emotions of exasperation and
contempt: but they also effortlessly contrive to win affection,
devotion, protection, even pity. (Bruce was also—as such men
often are—a beau.) As for the two children, it is clear from the
outset that Edith undemandingly adores them; and that their
young existence is a chief cement of a marriage otherwise
bereft of love—not for the conventional reason that 'having
children' must mean 'settling down', but because of the constant
thought in Edith's watchful brain of what might be the consequence to them if her marriage were allowed to become
publicly the failure it already is in fact. The force of this
sentiment the writer in part makes manifest by the rare feat of
creating, in the infant son and daughter—first as babies then
as growing children—characters in their own right (not merely
foils to their parents) that are entirely convincing and most
lovable: a rare feat because to see children much as they see
themselves—and even to describe babies as they may be supposed to do so too—is one, in adult writing, that is as frequently
attempted as it is most uncommonly achieved without embar-
rassment.

In *Love's Shadow* the tone is light. The Bruce-Edith dialogues
(delicious in print, but oh how dreadful they would be in fact!)
are purest fun. Edith, a young wife as yet, is still at the stage
of putting up with much too much and letting Bruce pontificate
and get (apparently) his 'way'. These two key personages are
also introduced most subtly to this first book in which the
reader meets them, as subsidiary characters—the main 'intrigue'
being elsewhere: they are still so far—as everyone in the novel
calls them—'the little Ottleys': at present acting as a comic foil
to the major, but much more conventional 'drama', of the

apparent heroine Hyacinth Verney, of her adoringly jealous friend Anne Yeo, of her vapid lover Cecil Reeve, and of the (not unamiable) *femme fatale* of Cecil's vacillating predilection, Mrs Eugenia Raymond (whose presence is, in Cecil's fresh love for Hyacinth, 'love's shadow'—though we may come to feel it is over Edith that the darker shadow really looms). And since the courtship of Hyacinth by Cecil takes up much more of the book than does the brief description of their ensuing marriage, there is contrasted to the mere drama of marrying, the much more important drama (always, to Ada Leverson), in Edith and Bruce's case, of being married.

Of Bruce absurd, we have such episodes as his convenient proclivity, in moments of tiresome stress, for falling self-sorrowingly ill, and of his running the remarkable temperature —so he declares—of 119° Fahrenheit. We also hear much of Bruce's never-written (nor even begun) play, whose triumph will restore his fortunes (and buttress his immense self-satisfaction). Bruce, who works (or rather, doesn't) at the Foreign Office, has of course no notion of what 'writing a play' means; and this enables Ada Leverson to mount a pointed satire on the attitude to art of the non-artist dilettante. There are adequate hints, too, that Bruce's rich fund of egotism will eventually—as indeed it later does—become monstrously destructive, even wicked. A prescient sentence (though in fact referring to Hyacinth and Cecil) may herald the deep injury that Bruce, in later books, will do to Edith:

> As a rule the person found out in a betrayal of love holds, all the same, the superior position of the two. It is the betrayed one who is humiliated.[1]

★

[1] I must not leave this book without quotation of yet another instance of Ada Leverson's prophetically critical acumen: this time of a figure whom, one might suppose, a 'cultivated Edwardian' would unreservedly admire. As will be seen, her estimate in fact is of the 1960s (*avant-garde*): 'Then he remembered that it was an exhibition of Max Beerbohm's caricatures, and that people's spirits were naturally raised at the sight of cruel distortions, ridiculous situations, and fantastic misrepresentations of their friends and acquaintances on the walls.'

In *Tenterhooks*, the second Edith Ottley book (and the reader will no longer need an explanation of the novels' titles), the drama is laid bare, though only provisionally resolved. It opens with a ludicrous—and faintly macabre—episode (that I long to see one day filmed) in which Bruce is conducting Edith to a dinner party give by a Foreign Office colleague, and gets the address wrong; taking her, in increasingly outraged frustration, and with mounting anxiety and hysteria (all Londoners will sympathise with Bruce a little), to 168 Hamilton Place, Park Lane (which turns out to be Lord Rosenberg's, with a butler and 'four powdered footmen'), to 168 Hamilton Gardens (a deserted tenement in Marylebone), and to 168 Hamilton Terrace, St John's Wood—where they arrive at a quarter to ten to find the party was the evening before. This comic first chapter shows three significant things, though: Edith is both more resigned, and yet more brusque, with Bruce; she still respects marriage, but no longer her husband simply because he is her partner in it; and that the Ottleys are this time presented, from the outset, with the authority of chief characters.

Vincy (in full, Vincy Wenham Vincy) is next introduced as Edith's confidant and friend: and the clear definition that he is no more than this (and that neither he nor she wishes it to be otherwise) prepares us for the introduction of the third (apart from the children) essential character in Edith's life—Aylmer Ross, who soon loves her and awakes her love. Aylmer enters the book—and Edith's existence—so decisively and powerfully that the reader is at once certain this is no Bertie, Harry, or Cecil, as before, but the essential man who will combine the qualities that Edith (and her creator) seek in their ideal figure of the husband-lover; and since Edith's devotion to her marriage is known to be so absolute, the question at once assails the reader's mind (as it was no doubt intended to) as to whether and how the writer will contrive, within her own now well-defined concept of what marriage is, and what its obligations, to unite Edith with Aylmer, or whether the conflict of love and honour (rather than 'duty') will perhaps destroy her.

In this book, at last, the central theme (because the protagonists are now worthy of it) is confronted boldly. And although for quite logical reasons of the characters' psychology no 'affair' outside marriage does actually take place, the sexual dilemma of the heroine is now brought frankly into the open. It is not that the writer loses any of the reticence about this that is natural to her and which was, in earlier books, appropriate to their lighter or more superficial tone and characters: the fact of sex is not, I mean, unnecessarily projected—used merely to heighten 'drama'. But it is present now, and stated: both by what the characters are made to say, and by the injection of an element of physical violence that is directly related to the revealed realities of the chief characters' desires. Thus, for the first time in the novels, we have scenes of physical assault (though not reaching their 'culmination') when Aylmer embraces Edith, and even Bruce 'uses force'. Edith herself is also driven by her feelings into coquetry, at moments 'provoking' Aylmer almost as if she were an inferior person like Valentia of *The Limit*; and in her rejoinders to her husband, speaking with undisguised tartness that barely veils (from the reader, if not from obtuse Bruce) a threat of infidelity. All three of them are now 'on the brink': wife, lover and even husband: for Bruce, who of course supposes that any intrigue by a 'devoted married man' (such as himself) is not one, and who, like so many 'good sorts', is an inveterate flirt, involves himself first with his children's governess (which Edith, as much by style as by a consciousness of her own faithlessness of heart if not yet of fact, forgives), and then decisively deserts her in favour of one Mavis Argles. To Aylmer Ross the lover, this desertion seems (as it might well, initially, to the reader) the perfectly honourable (and socially acceptable) pretext for Edith to leave her husband, sue for divorce and marry him: for realizing that Edith's love can only be fully given within a totally embracing vow, and being himself a man of such quality as despises, in the case of anyone he values and respects, a mere 'affair', Aylmer longs now to marry her. But it was Bruce's all unconscious master stroke to elope with somebody like Mavis Argles, and do so to, of all places, Australia. For Edith knows better than he does that the adventure will be a failure (Mavis in fact 'gets off' with someone else while still on the high seas), that he will return, and that if she abandons him he will not just be the failure that he is, but shrink into a ruin. So she rejects her freedom—and her love.

Love's agony, and jealousy, and pain in joy are present in *Tenterhooks* to such effect that those who, being in love, may read it, had better not, and those who have been, but are not now, will sharply be reminded of what they may think they have forgotten. The temperature of emotion rises steadily in the book until it stands unbearably (somewhat like Bruce's) at its fever heat. To convey this accumulated tension by quotation is of course impossible: here, nevertheless, are two brief extracts that may induce a painful twinge of recollection:

> Then there was an extraordinary pause, in which neither of them seemed able to think of anything to say. There was a curious sort of vibration in the air.
>
> You don't know a woman until you have had a letter from her.

With the final book, *Love at Second Sight*, it is clear that the writer has committed herself to re-shaping Edith's life in terms satisfactory to Edith herself, to the writer's clearly enunciated code, and to the reader's heightened expectations. How, short of some sudden death or dire fatality—neither of which, the reader may rightly feel, would be appropriate—is she to accomplish this? The answer will be that with entire credibility and consummate art, she will transform Aylmer, the lover, into the 'husband' whom, to win Edith, he must first become: not, I mean, 'husband' merely in fact, but in psychological reality.

To achieve this we see, first of all, how the two earlier Edith Ottley books (and more tangentially, the three others) will serve their purpose. Edith is now thirty-five, Aylmer forty-two, so it is 'now or never'. They have been entirely separated, since Edith's earlier rejection of him, by three years of time during which their feeling has not waned but deepened. Bruce has learned nothing, is more dreadfully himself than ever—so much so that to anyone who had not read of his earlier behaviour to her, it would seem from his attitude to Edith that she has nothing to forgive him. The children are older, and are beginning to see through their father. The 1914 war (as I hinted earlier) is also pressed organically into service: for while Bruce has not joined the New Army (he suffers from a 'neurotic heart'), Aylmer, disguising his age, has gone to the Front and—doubly subtle touch—his son by a first marriage, Teddy, also disguising his (he is underage to fight), is in khaki too; and the social tensions of the war will favour any drastic personal readjustment:

> When a woman knows that the man she loves has risked his life, and is only too anxious to risk it again—well, it's natural that she should feel she is also willing to risk something.

And yet:

> She had a curious sense of responsibility towards Bruce, which came in the way.

The means to the final union of Edith and Aylmer (though not the essential reason), and the catalyst of the whole situation, is one of Ada Leverson's most original, appalling and hilarious creations, Mme Eglantine Frabelle. Mme Frabelle (English, but the relict of a French wine merchant) is a woman who gets everything wrong, never stops saying so, but who is so affably and predictably mistaken, and so unfeignedly interested in whoever, at that moment, is her interlocutor, that everybody (except, significantly, Aylmer and Edith's boy Archie) likes her.

> People were not charmed with Eglantine because she herself was charming, but because she was charmed.

She has descended on the Ottleys with a letter of introduction from a friend who, it later transpires, knows nothing whatever about her—and indeed, once Mme Frabelle has settled like a benevolent cuckoo in the Ottleys' house, this friend asks *them* to tell her who this woman she introduced into their midst, may be. Bruce, flattered by her attention (despite her being older than he, and far from beautiful—or perhaps even because of this), is quite enchanted with her indefatigable solicitude. And so, in a different way, is Edith: for when in doubt—as she is often, now—a conversation with her guest will serve to resolve perplexities because of Edith's faith in Eglantine's sure instinct for giving to any question an answer unfailingly and reliably incorrect. For example:

'Oh, men are all alike!' exclaimed Madame Frabelle cynically.

'Only some men,' said Edith. 'Besides, to a woman—I mean, a nice woman—there is no such thing as men. There is a man; and either she is so fond of him that she can talk of nothing else, however unfavourably, or so much in love with him that she never mentions his name.'

'Men often say women are all alike,' said Madame Frabelle.

'When a man says that, he means there is only one woman in the world, and he's in love with her, and she is not in love with him.'

'Men are not so faithful as women,' remarked Madame Frabelle, with the air of a discovery.

So Mme Frabelle provides, initially, the atmosphere of almost crazy unreality in which reality can best declare itself. Meanwhile, Edith's visits to Aylmer, who is wounded and on leave in London, become increasingly tense and desperate. The word love, and the fact of it, are now openly declared between them. And so are even—though in conversations not with Aylmer, but with one of Edith's confidants, Sir Tito Landi the composer —the possible facts of infidelity, of divorce, of second marriage. Two sharp hints of what will happen are when Archie, Edith's son, says to her, 'Mother, I wish Aylmer was my father.' And obliquely, when Edith is leaving London on a visit, her husband bids her his farewell with

'Perhaps we shall never meet again,' said Bruce pleasantly, as Edith, Dilly and the nurse were starting; 'either the Zeppelins may come while you're away, or they may set your hotel at Eastcliff on fire. Just the place for them.'

The visit to Eastcliff is of course (and of course with Bruce's indifferent agreement) to see Aylmer, who is convalescing there;

and during it, Edith at last commits herself. Aylmer is soon to return to the war in France; and Edith tells him she will leave Bruce—who, they both accurately assess, will not want to keep the children (too much bother)—and henceforth they are, in their own eyes and hearts, 'engaged'. In this almost final scene, the writer establishes two essential things: that Edith, sure of his love and hers, and sure as she can be of the children's future, is prepared to 'desert' her husband and accept 'social disgrace'; and that in spite of the urgencies of their feeling for each other, and of the overhanging war, neither he nor she wish for physical union until they can be pledged entirely to each other.

And now Mme Frabelle plays from afar (in fact, from Liverpool) the unexpected and unhoped for final card that will give Edith not only the whole game, but game with honours. For Mme Frabelle is waiting to cross the Atlantic, and Bruce is going to cross it with her: this time, we know, in a grasp far more irrevocable than Mavis Argles'. On his earlier flight with Mavis, Bruce had announced it to his wife by letter; but now her lingering doubt will not be satisfied with less than an avowal from her husband. This—as necessary psychologically to both Bruce and Edith as artistically to the writer—Bruce provides her with: and tells her face to face why it is 'I can't endure married life any longer'. The last link breaks finally when Edith, accepting this (not on this occasion as we know, without relief) asks Bruce if he would wish to see their child Dilly before he goes. He doesn't want to; and she no longer wants him in any way at all.

In this book, the chief themes of all her art are finally united and resolved: friendship, love and honour become one. Technically, it is her most perfect: even the decorative chapter headings of the earlier five books have vanished in the assured pace with which she sets down her final testament. Two decades of Ada Leverson's life remained to her, but she never wrote another novel; and one may conjecture this was most because the meaning that life held for her had now been given, in her art, entire expression.

★

On the evidence of these books, we now see clearly defined what
Ada Leverson most admired in men and women, and most
disliked; and can so deduce, from the consistency with which
she reveals these attitudes through her characters' sayings and
behaviour, what is the nature of the essentially moral instinct
on which her whole outlook as an artist was ultimately based.
One may say first of all, on the positive side, that she loved
those who loved life, who were spirited yet considerate and kind,
and that she liked good manners (while caring nothing whatever
for conventional 'status'). She adored the young (including the
special category of children), and she admired poised old age.
She liked women as well as men (whom she liked even more),
and to both she could give friendship, of which she well knew
the boundaries, as well as she could give love (of which she knew
all the rareness and the peril and the need for nourishing it
with absolute devotion). She liked people who did things, but
didn't mind when they did nothing if they did it with style.
She respected most of all men and women who, involving
themselves in a human situation, take their due share of responsibility, and try to preserve it and enrich it.

She disliked the mean, the self-important, the tale-bearers
and those lacking candour when to withhold it can do damage:
though she disliked equally the indiscreet, and the superfluously
'outspoken'. She despised duplicity, but did not mind artifice.
Most of all, I think—and this is perhaps the only cardinal sin
in Ada Leverson's indulgent and forgiving code—she detested
cruelty, especially when wanton and aware. Yet almost all
these blemishes she was ready to pardon, or to make allowances
for, if the culprit—as culprits often are—was really unconscious
of his fault.

In its simplest essence, one may say of her vision that it is—
though this is an odd word to use—a healthy one: where life
glowed, there her heart was, and her active sympathy. Although,
as a writer, she is 'worldly' (in the sense of knowing precisely
what the rules are), she emerges from her pages as an artist who,
however knowledgeable and difficult to deceive, is innocent
and pure. To her readers—even to her characters . . . and even

to the most dreadful among these—she is like a fairy godmother: eager to bestow gifts; courteous and considerate to her public, and too good-natured, often, even to hurt her own creations when they most deserve it. Really to know life and to accept it—while always wishing it were better and striving, in one's own human relations, to make it so—and once knowing it, to grow to love it more and more in spite of its conditions, is the indication in any human person of maturity and wisdom. Such a person Ada Leverson was, and of this kind of being all her writing is a celebration.

In *The Twelfth Hour*, Felicity, during a moment of doubt about her marriage and herself, consults a female Celtic sooth-sayer (called Madame Zero) who thus reveals Felicity's own character to her:

> You have a curious temperament. You are easily impressed by the personality of other people. You are impulsive and emotional, and yet you have a remarkable amount of calm judgement, so that you can analyse, and watch your own feelings and those of the other persons as well as if it were a matter of indifference to you. Your strong affections never blind you to the faults and weaknesses of their object, and those faults do not make you care for them less, but in some cases attach you even more strongly. You are fond of gaiety; your moods vary easily, because you vibrate to music, bright surroundings, and sympathy. But you have depth, and in an emergency I should say you would be capable even of heroism.

Edith Ottley, three times a heroine, may best seem, as we now know, to personify—insofar as any character does, or can, its own creator— the woman Ada Leverson felt herself to be. Yet may not this short description—a fragment from the picture of the first heroine she invented and admired—be also her earliest self-portrait? Certainly, it evokes a woman who, after one has read her books and learned what she loved and didn't, one may grow to believe was very like her indeed.

Encounter, May 1961

JOSHUA REBORN

DAVID LLOYD GEORGE, who didn't admire generals, found one exception among the sorry legion of failed leaders of 1914–18:

> . . . the only soldier thrown up by the war on the British side who possessed the necessary qualifications . . . He was a civilian soldier when the war broke out.

Captain Liddell Hart, no great enthusiast either for the top brass of World War I, made an even wider claim for the same man:

> He probably had the greatest capacity for command in modern war among all those who held command.

The general officer they both wrote of, may provide this post-script to the events that made him chief commander of his nation:

> From the far off days of 1914 . . . until the last shot was fired, every day was filled with loathing, horror, and distress.

General Sir John Monash was born in Melbourne, Victoria, in 1865. He went to Scotch College (the oldest—and largest—academy in his state) and, at the University of Melbourne, he graduated in Engineering, Law and Arts—all three—while studying, in his spare time, medicine, history and archaeology. He was a competent artist and musician, well read in old and modern literature, and he could speak French and German. Professionally, he became a civil engineer, and his chief outside interest was in the Australian Citizen Forces, in which he was commissioned as a lieutenant in 1887, and had become a colonel, at the age of 48, by 1913.

He was also, by race and practising faith, a Jew. At this point in his career we may pause to notice, first, that before 1914 it was deemed highly eccentric for a serious professional man of any racial origin to be even a part-time soldier: for the well-known pugnacity of the Australians is matched by their equally intense dislike of all authority—particularly of any dressed in uniform; and this was even more so before the chastening experience of two world wars. In addition to this, many Australians must have then believed—as highly-placed and well-informed Gentiles did in all lands of European stock—that a Jew might be many things, but not a soldier: still less, the military leader of a people. Everyone—it may be, in these Christian countries—had read in their Old Testament of Jewish warriors as well as of the great prophets; but while sages and prophets had recognizably remained to guide the Jewish people, for centuries the warriors had vanished from the world communities of Jews.

For one month after August 1914, Monash was made chief censor of the Commonwealth—no doubt because, for six years before its outbreak, he had been transferred from artillery commands to military intelligence. Soon after this false start, he was appointed commander of the 4th Infantry Brigade and he soon set sail, with his hastily-trained legions of recalcitrant volunteers, for the conquest of Gallipoli. This forlorn and glorious adventure—in which the entire Anzac force hung desperately on to an area about the size of Regents Park—has, for Australians (and has even today after so many subsequent feats of arms), the quality of a tragic epic, and is the substance of a national myth. For the first time in their brief history, young Australians—like the young Greeks who fought as hopelessly and valiantly at nearby Troy—had left their distant homes to win an instant and lasting reputation from their enemies and friends. It was at Gallipoli that Australia, as a nation, really first began. Monash was among the earliest troops to land—in what was to become 'Monash Valley'—and among the last to go. He was three times mentioned in despatches.

But it was in France, on the dreadful, stagnant Western Front, that the qualities which Lloyd George and Liddell Hart have later recognized, became apparent. The technical key to Monash's success in a field where so many gilded and resounding names had floundered in mud and wire is that he was a civilian soldier, and a skilled and practical engineer. It occurred to him —as it seems not to have done for years to anyone else—that the hundred-mile frontiers of trenches could be pierced only by tactics involving the positive co-ordination of the infantry with the 'independent' tanks, artillery and planes. A master of organisation, he rejected the frivolous, haphazard use of these auxiliary arms and, first smashing through prejudice and punctilio, he shook and shaped these weapons into one and then used them all to smash through and beyond the Hindenburg Line. His human 'secret'—also a very 'simple' one—was to ask (which he did constantly and inexorably from everyone), to think, and then to explain: he detested, and would not permit in himself or any officer, ambiguity. From his staff he expected, and gave, total loyalty:

> I don't care a damn for your loyal service when you think I am right; when I really want it most is when you think I am *wrong*.

As for the notoriously 'undisciplined' Australian soldiers he commanded, he wrote this:

> Psychologically, he was easy to lead but difficult to drive. His imagination was readily fired . . .

So Monash, using his own imagination, fired and led the diggers. By early 1916, he was Major-General in command of the 3rd Australian Division; by May 1918, Lieutenant-General commanding the Australian Army Corps. When the war ended, he was leading eight divisions of the most obstinate and xenophobic soldiers in the world.

Readers of D H Lawrence's *Kangaroo* may have wondered why Kangaroo himself, the proto-fascist leader of an incipient movement of discontented ex-servicemen, should have been pictured as a Jew. The reason may be that Lawrence (who, in those short weeks on the continent, certainly discovered so much, and so piercingly), knowing about Monash, perceived—or thought he did—some possibility of this kind. But so far as reality goes, Monash, when the war was over, after first staying on in Europe until his troops had all been repatriated, came home to private life and, as he said, 'went back to concrete', taking no active part in politics whatever. No doubt this was, in part, because he didn't want to do anything else, and in part because he knew that the best service he could give to Australia, as well as to his own community, was to remain what he had now become: the undisputed first citizen of the nation. Accordingly, he was active in national engineering projects and in private industry, a leading figure in scientific and scholastic circles, and, as a private person, an active patron and participant in the country's cultural life. He died in 1931, still in his mature prime at 66; 300,000 Australians followed his coffin at a state funeral; and he is remembered today by public monuments, by the new Monash University and, most of all, as one of his country's finest and most admirable sons.

Because of the lucky chances that I went to his old school, and that my parents knew him, I met Monash several times as a boy. In physique, he was short yet powerful: his face, with two dark, resounding eyes, was calm and very determined. He listened, asked questions, and spoke softly with unforced authority. My last sight of him was when, at the age of 16, I was just about to leave Australia for England. A friend who had a later appointment with 'the General' had asked me to lunch, and took me on afterwards to say good-bye to Monash. Their place of rendezvous was on a street in central Melbourne; and looking across, I saw him standing waiting, shoulders a bit hunched, gazing into the future with the crowds hurrying by. An instinct—prompted, I believe, by some good sense as well as by adolescent timidity—told me that to confront Monash as a young man was no longer the same thing as to address him, as I had done earlier, with that natural right which boys have to approach the mighty without danger to themselves. So I said good-bye to my friend only, and watched their meeting from the far side of the road.

A key event in European history, and a critical one in the centuries of warfare between Jews and Gentiles, was the ghetto uprising in Warsaw: here, for the first time since the days of the Old Testament, the Jewish warriors erupted, though their names remain unknown to us, from their centuries of pain and silence. Since then, Israeli commanders have given ample proof that the warrior Jew has permanently re-appeared. I know that before Monash's day, as well as in the armies of the 1914 war (including even the German), there were many Jews who fought and who commanded. Yet I do not believe that until the events which followed after 1939 there is any other example of a Jewish soldier who commanded a whole people—and that one of the most intractable and violent—until Colonel John Monash began, after 1914, his swift rise to a high command that was undisputed by Australians, by his enemies, and even by his allies.

What influence this extraordinary achievement may have had on later Jewish leaders who had heard of him, I do not know. But what is certain is that, for more than a decade until his death, Monash, by the simple fact of his presence and prestige, made anti-Semitism, as a 'respectable' attitude, impossible in Australia. Throughout this period racialism, elsewhere in Europe and in America, was a poisonously growing force; and in Australia itself, there was no lack of the usual snide whisperings. Often, as a boy, I have sat in on gatherings of old soldiers fighting at Gallipoli and in France again, around the attendant demijohn of whisky. These men, tough, cruel and valiant, might throw up their hands, certainly, and cry, 'What! More Jews in Parliament?' But when they spoke of Monash, they spoke with reverence: really the only word that fits, and an attitude uncommon in the extreme among Australians to anyone—or anything. And worshipping him as they did (and through him, their own youth and courage), they could never publicly deny the hero they themselves had freely followed: nor could they deny his people. Monash, alone, stood guardian over his community and his nation's conscience.

When he was asked, by the 'house' at Scotch College that had been named after him, to provide them with a motto, the one Monash chose (expressed in Gaelic about which, characteristically, he knew quite a lot) was, in translation, *Make Certain:* which is just what he himself, as a soldier, always tried to do and, so far as any one man ever can, he did. I have a photograph I cherish of him in France, captioned 'General Sir

John Monash presents a VC in the Field.' The VC, a private, and as smartened-up as much—or as little—as any commander may hope a digger ever to be, is standing—but not too much so —at attention. Somewhat to the rear, elegantly poised, is a sashed and nonchalant staff officer with the appropriate air of courteously bored attentiveness. Between these two men, relaxed yet alert, and a head shorter than either—but an infinity as big and broad—is Monash, holding the medal before pinning it on the bold and untidy breast. He is gazing straight at the soldier, and speaking to him: saying, we can be certain, something fine and simple on this occasion when to hit the right note is quite impossible unless the commander feels it, and is one in a position worthily to utter it: and his whole mien and posture so much conveying, to anyone who looks now at this snapshot taken unawares two generations ago, the impression that what he may be telling this young hero is something that will give him a belief in greatness.

A lot of generals, after the victory and the laurels, have spoken of their sorrow at the carnage and destruction: which, though we may accept their words, we do not much believe, because ruin and slaughter are, after all, a general's chief business. But Monash being what he was—essentially a civilian, professionally a builder, and one of the first soldiers to learn and understand what modern warfare is—we may give credit to his epitaph on the huge struggle:

> I deplored all the time the loss of precious life and the waste of human effort. Nothing could have been more repugnant to me than the realization of the dreadful inefficiency and the misspent energy of war.[1]

Saltire Review, November 1960

[1] Later I owe to David Sylvester the thought of writing about Monash—as I do many ideas which his generous and creative mind has helped me to discover in my own.

THE PIECE that comes now on Sidney Nolan is the first I wrote about Australia since *June in her Spring* was published in 1952.[1] This short sad lyric about adolescent girl and boyhood in 'the Bush', the best thing I've yet written, was commercially and by the meagre notice it aroused, a total failure.

Though possibly salutary, this kind of experience is most disheartening to a writer. One is assailed by doubts whether what one wants to say has value, and even if one can communicate at all. With more courage and self-confidence I would have defied this defeat by writing another original work at once: as it was, I waited four years to do so.

The invitation that came from Bryan Robertson, in the spring of 1957, to write again about Australia in a catalogue introduction to Sidney Nolan's retrospective exhibition at the Whitechapel Art Gallery, was therefore a most welcome one. It revived my wounded interest in the Australian theme, and enabled me to say some of my admiration for Nolan as a man and artist. Bryan, with the sure impresario touch that is one of his many talents, asked me to write as freely and fully as I could about Australia, as well as about the paintings of its splendid son.

SIDNEY NOLAN: THE SEARCH FOR AN AUSTRALIAN MYTH

AUSTRALIA IS an Asiatic island that Europeans inhabited by accident. For centuries, they had tried hard not do to so: the miscellaneous navigators approached, peered tentatively at the monster continent, and sheered off northwards to the Spice Islands in dismay. The first Englishman to set eyes on Australia (characteristically, he was a pirate) said, 'If it were not for that sort of pleasure which results from the discovery even of the barrenest spot on the globe, this coast would not have charmed me much.'

[1] Republished in 1960 by Ace Books.

Everything about Australia is bizarre. Even on the map it looks peculiar, with Cape York poking its defensive immigration officer's finger up at Asia, and Tasmania falling off Victoria into the Antarctic—a huge isolated land mass surrounded by myriads of islands in vast oceans, like satellites in space of an indifferent planet. The three million square miles, one third of them desert, are all ancient: the Alpine Storm that created the picturesque landscapes of the 'old world' ignored Australia; there are no great mountains and, except in the Fertile Crescent of the south-eastern coasts, few rivers, or rivers that rise fitfully, then disappear.

On this dry, hot land, grows a strange vegetation. There are 10,000 species of Australian flora, far more than in Europe, but only three indigenous edible fruits. Near the fertile coast are some eccentric patches of hot, wet jungle, with monster tree-ferns, crawling vines and creepers, and flame-trees like those of the Illawarra Mountains whose red glare is visible far out to sea. Inland, the olive grey-green eucalyptuses are sometimes giants, rising to close on 500 feet; and 300 varieties of acacia (Australian, 'wattle'; English, 'mimosa') fill the valleys with a sticky scent of gold. In Empty Australia the plants have names like mallee, scrub and mulga that betray their nature; and matching the conflagrations that from time to time engulf great areas of 'the Bush', the fire-tree of the West consumes itself in an orange blaze of flower.

The eccentricity of the animals is better known. Only the opossum of America represents, outside Australia, the extraordinary family of marsupials that hop, leap, scuttle and even fly about the continent. Of the platypus—a link, apparently, between the furry mammals and the prehistoric dinosaurs—the less said the better: he is a creature so improbable that even when one sees him (as I once did, swimming peacefully parallel, his bill elevated like a questing periscope), one may believe more easily in the existence of Australia's mythological beast, the Bunyip, than in him. The kangaroo, although he's made his reputation as a boxer, looks more like any senior member of any Austrialan cricket team—what other country could *he* possibly belong to? The koala bear reeks of eucalyptus (he digests an epicure's selection of the 320 varieties in an eight foot appendix), probably has nits, and is utterly delightful. The elusive wombat, a nocturnal bear, lives by day in a burrow of his own creation. Only the yellow dingo seems vaguely European—but mistakenly, for he is an Asiatic wolf.

That Australia should produce *black* swans is symptomatic of her attitude to birds: only the unusual will do. Consider the emu: a heraldic beast less appropriate, surely, even than the unicorn. The kookaburra, whose raucous voice is the most insulting and degrading in creation. The lyre-bird: a name that seems a pun, since the bird is a phenomenal mimic of its fellows. That connoisseur of bric-a-brac, the bower-bird, who decorates its nest in the manner of an old curiosity shop. The cumbersomely balletic brolga. The fruit-salad flutterings of parrots, and the formation flights against a hot, blue sky of white or black cockatoos. And must one not include, among the birds, the flying-foxes who, when they cascade among the trees in vertiginous parabolas, make one momentarily believe the laws of gravity are suspended?

Reptiles: the crocodile and alligator must yield their odious claim as the most revolting creatures on the globe to Australia's goanna: a six-foot dragon of repellent aspect, who drags his disgusting weight up trees. The blue-tongued lizard sits and spits. There is a plentiful abundance of snakes, both biters and constrictors. In the sea, beside the docile dugong, are sharks, six to eighteen feet . . . but more of these monsters later.

And what of the human inhabitants of the continent? They came there in three waves. At the end of the Ice Age, the Tasmanian aborigines: so called because, when the sea swept back into the Bass Strait, they survived only on this island— naked, woolly-haired, and eating shell-fish, possibly the most ancient human species in the world until the arrival of the Europeans, who eliminated them.

A little later, the Australian aborigines, who probably came initially from India, descended from New Guinea across what is now Torres Strait (bringing with them the dingo), and spread across the continent. Unrelated, apparently, either to the original Tasmanians or to any contemporary Papuan, Malay or Maori people, they are coffee-skinned, straight-haired, and when left in their natural state, which they rarely have been, live in the conditions of a stone-age culture for which their skills and intelligence are as admirably adapted as they are hopelessly inadequate to confront the culture imported by Europeans. Recognizing this deficiency, the Europeans shot them like kangaroos or, more subtly, gave them arsenic-filled food. Less than 50,000 pure-bred Australian aborigines survive, and most white Australians have never seen one.

The first European settlers were 1,200 convicts and guards who arrived in eleven ships at Port Jackson (now Sydney) in 1788. (It is important, I think, to remember this date, and how fantastically recent the European settlement of Australia is.) Among the prisoners in subsequent convoys were women, most of whom became, if they were not already, prostitutes. Quoting Mr Ian Grey, in *The Sunburnt Country*, published by the Society of Australian Writers in 1953:

> Between 130,000 and 160,000 convicts were deported and, despite the low proportion of women convicts, their descendants must be numerous. Of the crimes that earned the sentence of deportation, forgery . . . and robbery with violence were far more typical than poaching.

I quote this because I think it vital for the understanding of Australia (and of some of the mythology of Sidney Nolan's art) to establish that criminal elements *did* play a large part in the foundation of the country, and that these criminals *were* criminals. Speaking personally, I would much prefer to be descended from an Irish robber (as Ned Kelly was, of whom more later) than from a Pilgrim Father; but many Australians seem, quite understandably, to feel otherwise, and have tried to forget that, for a third of its history, Australia was exclusively a penal colony. I think this is a mistake: for the obvious reason that a criminal tendency is by no means necessarily transmissible to later generations and, even more, because it is the

criminal past that explains certain marked Australian characteristics—the violence, the cruelty, the detestation of authority,
the laconic, sardonic realism, the hard determination to
survive.

*

It would seem I have been describing an alarming, uninviting
country: I have, Australia is; and yet no one who has been
there has failed to be obsessed by the spirit, the atmosphere, of
the continent—by its haunting, unpredictable oddity. Australia
is, in the most literal sense, unforgettable. It has also some
rare and highly attractive qualities, of which I would mention
these.

The climate: throughout the continent, it ranges from the
Nigerian to the Spanish. The 'Nigerian' sector of Empty
Australia is inhabited either by nobody, or by 1 per cent of the
population. The 'Spanish' sector, in the Fertile Crescent, is
mostly hot and dry—the ideal climate for man, if not always for
stock and crops. This means that Australians live out of doors:
at home, on the ubiquitous verandah; if near the sea—where
all the State capitals are sited, and more than 60 per cent of the
population lives—then on the beach or in the ocean. The sun
and sea have rinsed and baked the Australians into their present
mould.

'The Bush'. The urban population lived, at any rate till
recently, 'off the sheep's back'—and off the bullock's too. It is
the sheep and cattle stations, and the wild Bush beyond them,
that everyone feels to be the 'real' Australia—the repository of
the virtues of an older way of life, and still the fountain of
prosperity. A sheep or cattle station is a self-contained community where work is play, and man is nature: a place where
what has to be done, and what is necessary, and what is agreeable, are all identical. As for the Bush itself, those who know
only the new, man-manufactured landscapes of the 'old world'
can scarcely conceive of the sense of awe and mystery with which
the prospect of the vast, untidy, ancient inland country of
Australia strikes the soul of the beholder.

The people—the 'Aussies'. They have terrible defects: they are cruel, censorious, incurious, flinty-hearted, and vain as Lucifer at being all these things. But their virtues! Phenomenally brave, open-handed, shrewd, humorous, adventurous, fanatically independent and, most blessed of all, contemptuous of fuss. There is indubitably a greatness about the Australian people: a bigness, a wideness, an inborn capacity for the large, the heroic gesture. If peoples are born serfs or princes—as they are—the Aussies are a kingly race.

Let us consider three key characteristics—their courage, their individuality, and their profound national instinct. Except for the incidents of the Eureka Stockade (1854), the 'Kelly War' (1878–1880), and the odd bomb dropped on Darwin by the Japanese, there have never been battles in Australia; but it suffices to read Alan Moorehead's *Gallipoli*, or Russell Braddon's *The Naked Island*, to catch the spirit of that Spartan contempt for death and danger which is peculiarly Australian. In the Dardanelles, they fought like the Greeks there in the Trojan wars before them, with a total disdain of the impossible. In Malaya, like the Spartans at Thermopylae, they tried to hold the swarming Japanese, though their native realism told them, long before anyone else, that they could not conceivably do so. The Australian is not just a fighter: he is a warrior, dedicated to battle.

Yet how reluctantly he dons his uniform, and how casually he wears it! Can there ever have been such appalling soldiers behind the combat areas? The defiance of all authority is the basic dogma, the very claim to his individuality, of the Australian. Small wonder that this is the country of Labour power, of equality legislation, and of a fiercely democratic instinct quite unknown in England, for example, where equality is thought of as economic, not personal and social. In Australia, no one would think of saying, 'Jack's as good as his master': it is 'Jack's as good as Jack.' Nationally, these qualities express themselves in a xenophobia that exceeds even that of the South Africans. These two peoples have one great point of resemblance—each is a minute European minority trying to survive amid the resurgent African, and Asian, millions that surround them. But between the Afrikaners and Australians, there is one essential difference. The Australians are the only people of European stock in the entire world who, living in a torrid climate, have resolutely refused to batten on coolie labour. To realize this is to see the 'White Australia' policy, so shocking to liberal inclination, in an entirely different light. To bar the way to Asians was to reject the pleasures of a parasite existence, and to decide that all the manual labour in Australia would be performed by Australian hands.

It is when the positive, aggressive instinct of the Australians serves some end that is instinctively, deeply desired, that their achievement is richest and most remarkable. To take a seemingly small instance, which may symbolise others that could be greater, I would name the life-savers. As everyone knows, the Australians love bathing and surfing: what is perhaps less well known is that every year some bathers and surfers get eaten, because most Australian seas are infested with sharks: tigers, grey nurses and hammerheads, who cruise eagerly off-shore at sixty miles an hour. To indulge their favourite passions, the Australians gamble recklessly with their lives (I have seen men with shot-guns firing into the sea at sharks where half an hour ago everyone was bathing.)

The public guardians against sharks—and against the more normal dangers of being engulfed in the huge 'dumpers'—are the life-savers. These are picked bodies of men, all volunteers, of quite incredible physical prowess, valour and self-discipline who, on the least provocation, will lash out to sea among the grey nurses and hammerheads, carrying rescuing lines to succour those in danger (they will even succour you when in no danger at all, if they feel like it, and drag you through the waves to unwanted safety, and a restorative pummelling on the beach). To see these men at work is an impressive sight: apart from their prodigious efficiency, there seems something so un-Australian about their more-than-military bearing, though something very Australian about the initiative and ferocity of their behaviour. Here, it dawns on you, are the

Australian warriors at play: the Spartans practising, of their own free will, a perilous military manœuvre in time of peace.

★

What place has art in this philistine, extraverted country? Surprisingly, a big one. The chief reason is that being unencumbered by tradition (which, if not constantly re-created, can be as much a mill-stone as a mill-wheel), Australians have not been surprised by the notion of men writing, painting, singing. In literature, the early Australian masters like Gordon, Paterson and splendid Henry Lawson, all wrote in terms that were generally comprehensible, on themes of immediate appeal. In music, the example of Nellie Melba had an effect that can scarcely be exaggerated for she was, and possibly still is, the only Australian internationally renowned, and the fact that an artist won this kind of fame impressed itself on the otherwise indifferent populace. As for painters, ever since the days of the 'Heidelberg school' in the 1890s they have been concerned not, like the Europeans, with introspection, but with the pictorial discovery of a continent which, having never been painted before, could be vividly portrayed free from the inhibiting example of a hundred old masters whose shades, here in Europe, gaze censoriously over the shoulders of contemporary painters.

Into this climate Sidney Nolan was born in April, 1917, at Carlton, Melbourne, of an Irish working family with no artistic traditions of any kind. This date—1917—is important, because anyone who, even as a boy, knew Australia up till the 1930s could have spoken with men who clearly remembered the pioneering era of the 'wild colonial boys' of which vestiges lingered on until the war of the 1940s, when the umbilical cord that still tied Australia to England was finally and for ever severed. Nolan drew when still a lad, frequented the National Gallery of Melbourne (one of the richest in the Commonwealth), and worked at odd jobs until his first marriage in 1938 when he became a full-time painter. (When I asked the artist about these preliminary jobs he said, 'Picking asparagus, designing in a hat factory, hamburger cook, mining gold up bush . . .').

I cannot, myself, detect any evident 'influences' in the paintings of Sidney Nolan that I have seen—for the work of the artist's first ten years, that is up till about 1947, has not been shown in England, and is not included in this exhibition. These early pictures are, apparently, essays in various School of Paris styles—for Nolan is an artist who has evolved from the conceptual to the figurative rather than, as is more usual, the other way about; though one must add that in his figurative pictures, though the subject is always quite identifiable in naturalistic terms, there is in fact a high degree of abstraction in the forms and colours.

We have, then, to consider the pictures of the last decade when the artist's styles were already quite mature; and as these works divide themselves conveniently into a number of chosen themes that have preoccupied him—some Australian, some European—I shall introduce them to the reader in this fashion.

The Kelly paintings

Of these there are two groups, one painted in 1945–47 in Melbourne, the other in 1954–55 in Europe.

Briefly, the story of Edward ('Ned') Kelly is this. He was born in 1855, the son of an Irish convict, and for two years until his execution at the age of 25, he and three other men, all younger than himself, fought a private war against the entire police force and army of the colony of Victoria. What makes Kelly unlike any of the bushrangers of the fifties and sixties is that he robbed only banks, never individuals; that he was remarkably eloquent and thoughtful—his 'Jerilderie Letter', which explains and justifies his motives, is a key document in early Australian literature; and that he enjoyed enormous popular support among the dispossessed. He was, in fact, a failed revolutionary leader, like the consecrated heroes of the revolts in his native Ireland.

Modern Australians have a thoroughly ambivalent attitude towards Ned. Intensely proud of him in private, they always try to play his reputation down in public, no doubt because of their sensitivity about the country's criminal origins. Thus, though he is a figure of myth, the only one Australia has yet produced, the myth is a secret one, privately cherished and guarded suspiciously against the outward tribute even of a native Australian son.

In these paintings, Nolan has set out to redeem the Kelly myth and restore to it, in the face even of his fellow countrymen, the full glory of an Australian saga. For think what one will of bushrangers, banks and hangmen, Kelly was not only a remarkable figure in himself, but even the prototype (however much they may deny him) of the Australian's own idea about himself: a noble tough, a violent champion, whose example has potently helped to mould the national character.

The 30 paintings of the first series are in a 'folk art' style appropriate to a hero of folk-lore; and since no folk art tradition existed in Australia (other than the aboriginal), Nolan invented his own, the ingredients being (I quote the artist) 'Kelly's own words, and Rousseau, and sunlight'. The effect of these images may sometimes seem—in the case of an artist so accomplished —to be rather deliberately naïve; yet they do undoubtedly convey the atmosphere of this young man's life of plunder, revolt and tragedy, his deep instinct of protest, and his thoroughly Australian feeling for the Bush, which enabled him to elude his pursuers on countless critical occasions.

The European series (still uncompleted) are, pictorially, incomparably finer. The 'naïve' style has gone, and the invented shapes are intellectually more coherent, and plastically more ingenious. The presentation of the Kelly myth has gained a new magic and imaginative power; and all the loss and sorrow of this rare young life thrown on to the scrap-heap are dignified, ennobled, and redeemed.

The Desert paintings

There are 47 of these, painted in 1949–50, when Nolan flew all over the continent, and specially over the central desert—the second largest, after the Sahara, in the world. In the artist's youth, the historic flights of Cobham, Amy Johnson and Kingsford-Smith impressed themselves on every mind because they plucked Australia, for the first time in history, out of its enormous isolation. The later inland explorations by air which, by the time of the 1940 war, had become a commonplace, revealed the heart of the country to Australians—of which very few, travelling on camels like the explorers of antiquity, had hitherto the faintest conception. Flight has given Australians a sense of the scale of their continent, and in these landscapes, mostly seen from overhead, the pink and purple panoramas seem like the country of a dream.

The Explorer paintings

If the English reader will recall the effect on his own mind of tales like those of Scott and Shackleton, of Livingstone and Mungo Park, and then imagine that these men discovered not other countries but his own, and that almost within living memory—he will understand the power over Australian imaginations of names like Wentworth, Lawson and Blaxland, who first crossed the Blue Mountains from infant Sydney; of solitary Eyre, who mapped the immense south coast with his aboriginal companion, Wylie; or of tragic Burke and Wills who crossed the continent from south to north, and lost their lives on their return to immortality. Such intrepid men traversed and unfolded Australia with what seems now an almost foolhardy enterprise, and of all their stories that of the Irishmen Burke and Wills is, both by the magnitude of the exploit and the totality of the sacrifice, the most impressive. This theme of their short fruitful lives preoccupied the artist throughout the year 1952.

The Drought paintings

Australia is a country of fire, flood and drought. The rainfall is eccentric, and periodically great Belsens and Auchwitzes of tens of thousands of carcasses of cattle lie scattered over vast areas, like corpses on enormous animal battlefields. The sun preserves the cadavers like Egyptian mummies, or like the creatures disinterred from the ashes of Pompeii. The paintings the artist did of this phenomenon, in 1952, have an almost human agony, and however fantastic the mute twisted figures in this great cemetery may appear, the photographs that have been published of these macabre disasters reveal them to be almost naturalistic.

The 'Outback' paintings

For a year in 1947 the artist wandered about Queensland, and recorded the colonial architecture of the 'outback' townships whose utter remoteness and self-sufficiency have been so vividly described in the tales of Henry Lawson's *While the Billy Boils*. The inhabitants are the same forgotten men of Chaplin's *Gold Rush*—save that sand is the enemy element, and not the snow. The native birds and beasts often play leading roles in these melancholy, laconic evocations: sometimes the birds fly, perversely, upside-down—which, so the artist assures me, when the winds howl in the wastes, they often find they have to.

This is the Australian yesterday that still survives in the 'back blocks', whose imagery the artist also uses in the pictures of historic themes in other series.

The Eureka paintings

In 1854, 10,000 Victorian gold-diggers, protesting against the Government licence fees, fought a body of police outside the Eureka Hotel. This 'battle' of the Eureka Stockade was fundamentally political in its motives—a republican protest by the dispossessed against the 'squattocracy' (big landowners) and against alien English rule. The affray, so small in its dimensions—as if the Tolpuddle Martyrs had fought at Peterloo —was vital in its effects, for self-government was soon 'granted' to the colony, and the 'Flag of Stars' of the Eureka rebels was embodied in the national flag.

There are 66 pictures of this episode, painted in 1949 on glass.

The Convict paintings

Of these, the most remarkable are the 'Mrs Fraser' series, painted in 1947–48. Mrs Fraser (so runs the legend) was a

Scottish lady who was shipwrecked on what is now Fraser Island, off the Queensland coast. She lived for six months among the aborigines, rapidly losing her clothes, until she was discovered by one Bracefell, a deserting convict who himself had hidden for ten years among the primitive Australians. The lady asked the criminal to restore her to civilization, which he agreed to do if she would promise to intercede for his free pardon from the Governor. The bargain was sealed, and the couple set off inland. At the first sight of European settlement, Mrs Fraser rounded on her benefactor and threatened to deliver him up to justice if he did not immediately decamp. Bracefell returned, disillusioned, to the hospitable Bush, and Mrs Fraser's adventures aroused such admiring interest that, on her return to Europe, she was able to exhibit herself at 6d a showing in Hyde Park.

This 'betrayal' theme—in which the traitress is portrayed naked in grotesque postures, and the stripes of her saviour's convict dress in skeletonic bars—is evidently one that pre-occupies the artist, since he has returned to it in the present year (1957). Whether this is an allegory of some personal treachery or, as is possible, of some conception of a betrayal by the well-born alien European of the stalwart founding Australian, I do not know, and only the paintings can reveal.

The Italian paintings

Since the 1950s, Nolan, though he has also travelled in Asia, the Americas and Australia, has mostly worked in Europe, and in 1954–55 he lived in Italy. In Australia, the artist is constantly aware of the battle of mankind with his environment; in Europe, of the marriage that both have consummated throughout the centuries. The paintings of the Italian period, which reveal principally a study of Etruscan and Pompeiian art, and of the murals of Mantegna and Masaccio, may be described as a series of 'faces on frescoes': that is, of humanised beings—not wracked, like the Australian figures, by the birth pangs of consciousness—set in backgrounds that have the feeling of antiquity of the fresco paintings. They are not pastiches of the murals, but re-inter-pretations of them by eyes from a new world like that which these murals once portrayed.

The Greek paintings

In 1955–56, Nolan lived on Hydra Island in the Aegean, read Robert Graves on the pre-Hellenic myths, looked out of the window at the men and landscape, and found the precursor of Australia.

To a people like the English, nurtured in the worship of classical Greece (and feeling an almost proprietary instinct towards it), the notion that ancient Greece and modern Australia resemble each other in any respect whatever will appear, I am sure, sacrilegious if not idiotic. However:

It is the archaic, Homeric Greeks we are considering. These were a sun-drenched, wine-drinking, agricultural people, European in stock, but closely in contact with the Orient. They were violent, noble, crafty and quarrelsome, possessed by a passion for athletics, political intrigue, and war. All this might equally be said of the Australians.

It is not, of course, as if any actual parallel exists. It is that in Greece as it is and was, Nolan has found a familiar country, rich in myths, which, pictorially, he is now trying to understand in order to create myths for his own people. The feeling of these Greek pictures is pre-classical, but the forms are those that he, like all European artists, has inherited from classical Greece: it is the mood of the one civilization, expressed in the forms of the other.

Sometimes in these pictures, one may see Homeric warriors performing their rites in the shape and appearance of the shark-defying life-savers. The wrestlers in the ring may be the champions on the centre court. The archaic shield a tribesman holds may seem part Greek, part aboriginal, and the masks of the pre-Hellenic priests like those of the witch-doctors. Icarus and Daedalus fly into the unknown and to disaster, as did Burke and Wills. The Minotaur has the same sad menace of the Bunyip. The Boy King, wearing the masks of both an old and a young man, may be Australia; and blinded Orpheus, the artist who reveals her to herself.

★

Why should it matter to Australia that an Australian painter should try to give his country mythical emblems? Because without myths—without the symbols that enshrine its own highest conception of itself—no people can begin to exist at all. I have said that Australia, since the war of the 1940s, has now emerged, politically, as a nation; and that this island, a part of Asia but inhabited by Europeans, stands alone without, in the last resort, any succour but its own will to survive. Can one doubt that the test of the heroic quality of the Australians—no longer as individuals, but as a people—will come one day within the context of this situation?

To achieve his ambitious purpose, Sidney Nolan is equipped with a poetic imagination, a critical intelligence, and with pictorial gifts that admirably serve their ends. Saturated in the history, the atmosphere, the ideology of his own country, his spirit is equally at ease among the stories and the artistic inheritance of Europe, which are also his. Slow to reflect and ponder, he has an enviable ease of execution once the image has already formed itself within his mind. Fascinated by the past, he is even more obsessed by the living history of the present: which gives to his pictures an actuality, an immediacy, a thoroughly contemporary spirit. His rich pictorial language, fed on all sights —on paintings, on colour photography and, most of all, on those of life—expresses his ideas in fluent shapes and vivid colours that make pictures as memorable as their themes.

Catalogue introduction to the retrospective exhibition of paintings by Sidney Nolan, Whitechapel Art Gallery, June 1957

THE NINETEEN FIFTIES were an astonishing decade: during which England, under the twin shadows of the *Bomb* and its own sharp imperial decline, has altered more radically than it did in the silly twenties, the dreadful thirties, or in the certainly heroic but, in essence, static nineteen forties. Some of the changes in our social climate have been negative, frivolous and mean; but others have brought life and hope and what, since the nineteenth century, was unknown in England—a realization that tradition, by which we set such store, must, to have meaning, be constantly re-made.

Of this startling decade,[1] science and commerce have been most aware, and politics and social organisms least of all. Literature has missed golden opportunities. For instance: thousands of Cypriots emigrate to England, and thousands of English soldiers serve in Cyprus; and each court and sometimes marry, against both tribes' strongest opposition, the others' girls; for between the two countries there has broken out what was, though we refuse to call it so, a war. Here was the perfect Romeo and Juliet situation to evoke individual stress, as well as the deeper conflict between the groups from which each lover came. About this rich drama that touched us all intimately and painfully, what plays and novels have been written?

The chief and most uexpected artistic break-through has been in the theatre: in which the example of John Osborne has been capital, since by crashing his own way to glory he has left broken gates wide open for so many who came swiftly after. For this he has been rewarded both by fortune, and by the suspicious rancour of creatures who camp-follow any social or artistic 'movement'. In England today, any creative upsurge that strives to adapt the social life of our dear battered land to the chief hard imperatives of imperial contraction, and of educational and industrial expansion, is matched by the limpet persistence of the ponce groups: the social bodies powerful

[1] Of which the only literary-social account I know, so far, is Kenneth Allsop's *The Angry Decade:* a book written hectically, but packed with observation.

by the force of their own decay, that batten parasitically on those who hold the hope of our survival.

A TASTE OF REALITY

SHELAGH DELANEY'S *A Taste of Honey* is the first English play I've seen in which a coloured man, and a queer boy, are presented as natural characters, factually, without a nudge or shudder. It is also the first play I can remember about working-class people that entirely escapes being a 'working-class play': no patronage, no dogma, just the thing as it is, taken straight. In general hilarious and sardonic, the play has authentic lyrical moments arising naturally from the very situations that created the hilarity; and however tart and ludicrous, it gives a final overwhelming impression of good health—of a feeling for life that is positive, sensible, and generous.

With a small chosen range of five persons, remarkable variations are played. The mother and daughter are firmly fixed and held as absolutely central figures: their drama is the eternal struggle of the generations, and what binds them together (in spite of the irrelevancies of the three men) is their instinct for continuing life, whatever its conditions. With the men, the choice of the mother's lounge-bar lover, and of the coloured and queer boys referred to, enables the author to introduce the subsidiary themes of faded commercial love, of compulsive young animal love, and of tender but sterile love, all with assurance, tact, and skill. And because the relationships between all the five characters have been completely worked out (in so far as they appear on the stage together), we even have such sub-sub themes as the reaction of the 'normal' mother to the queer boy, and of the daughter's attraction-repulsion to her mother's H-certificate Lothario.

It is, of course, wonderful that a woman of nineteen has written this play, but I must make it clear I think no note of condescension is permissible on account of Shelagh Delaney's age. The play lives in its own right entirely. It is true it is so very good one feels that the author could, at certain moments, have gone even deeper—but perhaps not without upsetting the structure, which as present exactly holds the weight of the dramatic situations. Greater depth, if necessary, will doubtless come with the next play, and the next. The only defects I could see were that the girl's mental-spiritual-physical age seemed to fluctuate a bit disturbingly (especially between Scenes 1 and 2), and that the mother's solo piece on the wonder of first love verged (for an agonised moment) on the purple aria.

The play gives a great thirst for more authentic portraits of the mid twentieth-century English world. As one skips through contemporary novels, or scans the acreage of fish-and-chip dailies and the very square footage of the very predictable weeklies, as one blinks unbelievingly at 'British' films and stares boss-eyed at the frantic race against time that constitutes the telly, it is amazing—it really is—how very little one can learn about life in England here and now. Consider only some themes suggested in *A Taste of Honey:* what have we learned, elsewhere, about working-class child-mothers, ageing semi-professional whores, the authentic agonies of homosexual love, and the new race of English-born coloured boys? Or, to consider other contemporary themes, what really revealing things have we had about the millions of teenagers, about the Teds, or about the multitudinous Commonwealth minorities in our midst— the Cypriots, the Maltese, and the many thousand Pakistanis? What do we know about the new men of the 1950s—the advertising intermediaries, the television witch-doctors, and the show-business buccaneers? Has there been anything good about emblematic figures like the house-property dealers, the upstart travel agents, and the men behind the chain stores that sell separates to the girls and Italian suitings to the boys? And most of all—most, most of all—what do we know about 'uneducated' people, their daily lives, and their vast pop culture? The answer is nothing much. This last decade will be remembered as the one in which the biggest social changes happened and the very least was discovered about them by 'the arts'.

I think there are two causes for this, for the rareness of Delaneys. The first is that divine curiosity seems to have deserted our writers altogether. The second and deeper reason (it probably determines the first) is that the 'educated' public— the chief absorbers of 'culture' above the pop level—are themselves prodigiously self-insulated against experience. In the popular phrase, they just 'don't want to know'. Around them seethes a great flux of bizarre new social groupings through which they proceed, like tourists traversing the casbah, unseeing and unaware. Economic conditions are still such that it is possible for the 'educated' to lead worthy and quite well-remunerated lives without having the remotest notion of what is really happening in England—let alone outside it, in its name. And the instinct not to want to know is powerfully reinforced by that blind universal faith so many educated English men and women have today—that if you don't look closely at what the world, near and far, is growing to be like, it somehow won't be like that at all.

'The arts' thus become not a mirror held to nature, but a mirror that reflects simply these 'arts' themselves. We have novels about books, newspapers about the press, plays about actors, films about the cinema (no, about nothing), and telly programmes that disclose only the internal confusions of the corporations and companies that project them. Then down from Salford comes this splendid young prophetess who, with typical good sense, calls at the right address among the conspirators in Stratford E 15, who then carry her voice into 'the Heart of Theatreland'. At Wyndham's, we have been looking back with that Boy Friend for years, and the question now is whether we can see that the 1950s are so much more peculiar and disturbing than the 1920s ever weren't. As Helen and Josephine walk on to John Bury's bleak, poetic set, one glances round the stalls and holds one's breath. Are they slumming, or are they listening at last?

Encounter, April 1959

FAREWELL, FOR CHARLES CAUSLEY

I FIRST MET Charles Causley when we were both imprisoned by warfare—he an unreluctant mariner, I an unarmed warrior —on the 3 by ¾ mile rock of Gibraltar: an experience by which none who endured it have been left unmarked; for the paradox of sunlight, no black-out by night, and shops groaning with propaganda goods in the only remaining allied foothold on the European mainland, accompanied an exclusively male society (except for eighteen, I think, Wrens), the tantalising daily spectacle of forbidden Spain, and for most of us locked up there, a two-year stint to do.

When we met again in England, Charles had already become what, from birth, he always must have been, a poet; and one for whose verses I felt then and have done increasingly (were that possible), as his great gifts have matured, a total admiration. Some have been deceived by the 'simplicity' of Causley's forms, and by his obsession with many timeless themes—especially those of the sea, of death, of enduring love and of quickly passing youth—into supposing he was a 'regional natural': not at once perceiving that these eternally recurring human situations had been given new life in terms of our own times; and that the 'ballad style' had always been manipulated by a consummate and extremely contemporary technician. Yet for all their art and skill, what is most compelling and endearing about Charles Causley's poetry is that heavenly gift which he possesses of effusion: of singing like a bard from the mind, heart and soul, certainly, and also with a perpetual siren voice that first sang somewhere in Greece, in Egypt, and in Eden.

This splendid poet, Cornish by intuition, Devonian by sagacity, has honoured me with his friendship and by a con-. stantly solicitous vigilance of criticism and encouragement that enables anyone who dreams into words to feel that one ear, at least, is listening, even when he may think there are no others. Which is why I have asked him most kindly to accept the dedication of this group of pieces.

THE HOGARTH PRESS

This is a paperback list for today's readers – but it holds to a tradition of adventurous and original publishing set by Leonard and Virginia Woolf when they founded The Hogarth Press in 1917 and started their first paperback series in 1924.

Some of the books are light-hearted, some serious, and include Fiction, Lives and Letters, Travel, Critics, Poetry, History and Hogarth Crime and Gaslight Crime.

A list of our books already published, together with some of our forthcoming titles, follows. If you would like more information about Hogarth Press books, write to us for a catalogue:

40 William IV Street, London WC2N 4DF

Please send a large stamped addressed envelope

HOGARTH FICTION

HOGARTH LIVES AND LETTERS

The Smith of Smiths by Hesketh Pearson
New Introduction by Richard Ingrams

Flannelled Fool by T.C. Worsley
New Introduction by Alan Ross

HOGARTH CRITICS

Tradition and Dream: The English and American Novel from the Twenties to Our Time by Walter Allen
New Afterword by the Author

The Condemned Playground: Essays 1927-1944 by Cyril Connolly
New Introduction by Philip Larkin

Seven Types of Ambiguity by William Empson
Some Versions of Pastoral by William Empson
The Structure of Complex Words by William Empson

Music Ho!: A Study of Music in Decline by Constant Lambert
New Introduction by Angus Morrison

The Common Pursuit by F.R. Leavis

England, Half English by Colin MacInnes
New Foreword by Paul Weller

By Way of Sainte-Beuve by Marcel Proust
Translated by Sylvia Townsend Warner
New Introduction by Terence Kilmartin

The Country and the City by Raymond Williams
The English Novel from Dickens to Lawrence by Raymond Williams

The Common Reader 1 by Virginia Woolf
The Common Reader 2 by Virginia Woolf
Edited and Introduced by Andrew McNeillie
Three Guineas by Virginia Woolf
New Introduction by Hermione Lee

Colin MacInnes
All Day Saturday

New Introduction by Tony Gould

Everybody loves Mrs Helen Bailey – everybody, that is, except her husband Walter, who sits alone in the Australian sun, polishing his guns. For Helen, a faded *femme fatale*, destiny seems to hold only embittered passion, infertility and a lifetime of tea parties. But one Saturday a young stranger arrives – and the lives and loves on the Baileys' sheep station are altered forever.

A novel which may surprise those who know Colin MacInnes through *Absolute Beginners*, *All Day Saturday* is, at once, a telling portrait of a troubled marriage, a comic evocation of life in the Bush, and a classical drama – where the fates of many are decreed in a day.

Graham McInnes
The Road to Gundagai

New Introduction by Robertson Davies

Lauded by John Betjeman, birthplace of Germaine Greer, home of Dame Edna Everage and source of Foster's lager, the city of Melbourne is regarded as one of the most gracious in the world. But not by the novelist Angela Thirkell – uprooted from England in 1919 with her two sons, Graham and Colin McInnes – who viewed all Australians as being both down and under. The boys, however, took to Australia with gusto, and this is the memoir, wonderfully, wittily told, of their adventures in that strange, compelling land. *The Road to Gundagai* shows us 'boyhood in essence' (Angus Wilson), but it is, too, a portrait of a beautiful city, an astonishing country, a devastating mother – 'a work of literary art' (*Times Literary Supplement*).